SAILORS
SETTLERS
& SINNERS

SAILORS SETTLERS & SINNERS

The Hall family
in Hull and New Zealand,
1795-1907

MOIRA TAYLOR

DEDICATION

To my parents, Tom (T. R.) and Helen Hall, and my
siblings, Jan, John, Bob, Alan and Ali.

CONTENTS

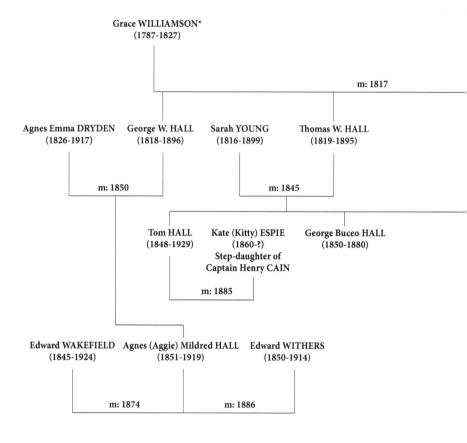

Grace WILLIAMSON*
(1787-1827)

m: 1817

Agnes Emma DRYDEN
(1826-1917)

George W. HALL
(1818-1896)

Sarah YOUNG
(1816-1899)

Thomas W. HALL
(1819-1895)

m: 1850

m: 1845

Tom HALL
(1848-1929)

Kate (Kitty) ESPIE
(1860-?)
Step-daughter of
Captain Henry CAIN

George Buceo HALL
(1850-1880)

m: 1885

Edward WAKEFIELD
(1845-1924)

Agnes (Aggie) Mildred HALL
(1851-1919)

Edward WITHERS
(1850-1914)

m: 1874

m: 1886

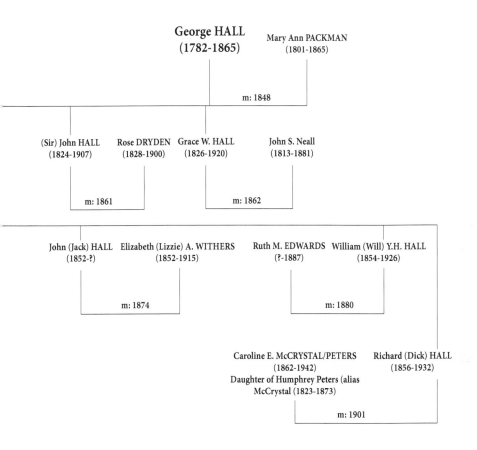

GEORGE HALL FAMILY TREE

* Grace died in 1827, leaving four children. Her sister Mildred cared for
the youngest, Grace, and possibly her siblings, until she married
William B. Fowler in 1832.

AUTHOR NOTE

Moira Taylor (née Hall) was born in New Zealand and now lives in London. She graduated with a BA and post-graduate Diploma in Journalism from the University of Canterbury. She was a reporter on the Christchurch *Star* newspaper before going to England as the Robert Bell Travelling Scholar in Journalism, where she worked for the New Zealand Press Association, based in London. In addition to book reviews for Radio New Zealand and articles for *The New Zealand Listener*, she wrote and recorded a radio documentary, *Her Bright Image: Impressions of Katherine Mansfield*, recently rebroadcast as part of New Zealand's *KM 130* commemoration of the New Zealand-born writer. In 1995 she was appointed the first Textbook Development Editor for the UK academic publisher Routledge and remained a Senior Development Editor until 2011. Her chapter, 'A View from Inside', was published in *Instead of Fullstops* (ed. Susan Sellers), Women's Press (1996). From 2013-2016 she was Secretary of the New Zealand Studies Network in London. She has contributed articles to the international Katherine Mansfield Society's newsletter, to its online critical journal *Tinakori* and to the forthcoming *Collected Letters of Katherine Mansfield* from Edinburgh University Press (eds Claire Davison and Gerri Kimber). She is married to Brent Taylor (Emeritus Professor at University College London) and has two children and five grandchildren.

INTRODUCTION

My father told me virtually nothing about his parents or grandparents so it was a surprise to find that his antecedents included a notorious poisoner, a fraudster surgeon and a prime minister, or 'premier' as he was then called in colonial New Zealand. The first inkling of this rich family history came to me in 1974, in my early twenties in London, when I was researching the New Zealand short story writer and poet, Katherine Mansfield. I had left my job as a newspaper reporter to have a baby. In the New Zealand House library on Haymarket I was reaching for the Antony Alpers biography of Mansfield when I noticed a book sitting next to it with an ancient brown cotton binding. It was *Cheerful Yesterdays* by another Alpers, the father of my author. Alpers senior turned out to be a judge reviewing his legal career in New Zealand and on impulse I took both books home.

Sitting on the living-room floor in our tiny flat in Millman Street, London WC1, with my baby son crawling beside me, I opened *Cheerful Yesterdays*, presumably intended as an ironic title, because the grim chapter that fell open as the most fingered was about a nineteenth-century poisoner. He happened to have the same name as my father, whose father (my grandfather) was the poisoner's younger brother. I began to understand why my father had protected his six children from this unpleasant story of their ancestral past. Reading *Cheerful Yesterdays* had a galvanising effect. I had to know more about the man who Alpers senior, echoing the presiding judge in his case, described as one of the most despicable criminals of the nineteenth century. I later discovered he was a desperate bankrupt, taking morphine for pain relief. His victim, who survived, continued to think enough of him to pay him an allowance for life and petition for his release from gaol.

My early research was done in a rather dilatory fashion, like a cat who sleeps with one eye open, because I had other preoccupations like full-time work, a husband and bringing up children. The task of exploring my ancestral past in greater depth only became possible when I retired in 2011 from a career in publishing in London and had time to indulge in the research required.

As I began to accumulate information I realised that my family's early recorded maritime history and emigration to New Zealand in the mid-nineteenth century reflected the transformation of Britain in an increasingly global world. Growing up in New Zealand in a large family of six children, and going to university there at a time when New Zealand Studies was in its infancy, my earlier knowledge of colonial history was limited to a patchwork of famous figures who did massively important things – the coloniser, Edward Gibbon Wakefield, the brilliant explorer Captain James Cook – or detail about things we children should know – the technique of making a Māori oven. I lived in Palmerston North, a city close to Dannevirke, the town founded by Scandinavian settlers whose primary purpose was to supply totara-wood sleepers for the railway linking the port of Napier to Wellington in the North Island. None of my teachers had thought it might be useful to explain the significance of the town's name or that European migrants had helped in the building of a North Island transport network. As a child at primary school, I recall our collective classroom treating another group of migrants, the 'transit camp kids', who resided in temporary accommodation outside Palmerston North, with suspicion. They were different, but we were never told exactly why or even who they were. Some were children rescued from a Stalinist labour camp in Siberia after the Second World War.[1]

As I write, some members of the British government, on the verge of exiting the European Union, are realising the importance of its history of empire now that the UK seeks to re-establish links with its former colonies as trading partners. This neglected part of its history might come to be taught in schools from a contemporary, more inclusive, more nuanced perspective, largely as a result of pressure from special interest groups – the descendants of those from former colonies – wanting cultural validation.

The John Hall Papers in the Alexander Turnbull Library in Wellington and those at his former home, the Terrace Station Archive in Hororata, Canterbury, contained family letters that would add detail and colour to my history. If some of the facts turned out to be more sensational than I expected, I could not help that; I was too far in to pull back. It was immensely exciting. One of the joys of the research was that it took me into the maritime world of the late eighteenth and early nineteenth centuries when thousands of sailing ships criss-crossed the world on the high seas, much as planes traverse the skies above us today. It gave me an excuse to revisit the novels of Joseph Conrad, and read the journals of contemporaries of my great-grandfather and great-great-grandfather who had sailed to the same places with similar hazards, hopes and horrors to endure. It allowed me to explore hitherto unknown-to-me cities like Hull and Scarborough on the Yorkshire coast, with their fascinating maritime memorabilia, and to visit other maritime museums around the English coastline, such as Portsmouth and Falmouth. The research required three returns to New Zealand to uncover more letters from the family, to soak up the atmosphere of the tussockland of the Mackenzie Country in the South Island with its vast starry night skies, and to stay at the Canterbury homestead of my Great-Great-Uncle John, with its gigantic woolshed and dilapidated wooden outhouses. Facts I had assumed to be correct were overturned by new evidence and new fascinating facts found; it was an endless task.

Because the majority of letters are written to Sir John Hall (1824–1907), a former premier of New Zealand and younger brother of my great-grandfather Thomas W. Hall (1819–1895), John proved to be a central figure in the story as paterfamilias and the man the family relied on for advice and to pull strings. I hope also to have revealed his connection to his brothers, sisters-in-law, nephews and niece as a more complex one than may have been realised, particularly in the case of the fallen young Tom Hall. While John Hall was the most prominent of public figures, who has his own biography by Dr Jean Garner, I have broadened the role of his two older brothers, George and Thomas, in advising him on the New Zealand emigration project in its early stages and revealed their rich maritime backgrounds. I've also provided more detail on John Hall's early life, derived from his father's letters to his sons before emigration to New Zealand.

At the end of his life, Sir John employed a secretary to type his private diaries, which were then bound. In an entry for 16 April 1906, the year before his death, he wrote 'Am very anxious to get these diaries transcribed and got into intelligible order for those I leave behind me'. This was my clarion call. His papers and diaries had been explored by his biographer and various members of his family, but no one had attempted to extract the family letters over a lifetime and connect the pre-emigration, predominantly maritime story of his father and brothers, to the post-emigration, predominantly pastoral and political story.

The most fascinating part of the exercise was to read the letters of my ancestors to each other, to experience their excitement, humour, despair, anger, love and tenderness, and to understand their difficulties in starting life in a new colony at the beginning of its social and political formation. The three brothers who emigrated to New Zealand were strong-minded, practical and ethical; two of them, George and Thomas, far from being as one Ashburton historian described, 'of negligible importance', were interesting to me as men who had gone to sea as boys on some of the most dangerous passages in the world and were highly literate and compassionate people. Their children – Tom, George Buceo, Jack, Aggie and Richard Hall – all came to grief, perhaps in part from such lofty reputations and standards to live up to, but also as the beneficiaries of the rewards of their father's endeavours. The immediacy of the letters and the problems encountered in them are as fresh as they were at the time of writing. Were it not for the linguistic expressions which sometimes date them, the political and social problems they reveal could be our own.

I belong to a truly lucky generation who benefitted from the liberal democracy constructed in a small country by enterprising men and women looking for adventure and escape from an increasingly competitive world in England and Europe. My generation were spared the horrors of the First and Second World Wars and the deprivations of the Great Depression of the 1930s. Many of the people who lived through those experiences were too traumatised to tell their stories. My father, for his entire life, sat on a family history that was explosive. Thomas Richard Hall, named after his grandfather, Thomas Williamson Hall, and his father Richard, always signed himself T. R. Hall to avoid being confused with his uncle. He kept his silence and died before I began this book, but I know he would have been fascinated to learn of the history of his Hall forebears and to read the family letters which in his lifetime were inaccessible to him.

In *The Paris Review Interviews* Norman Mailer discusses the relationship between fact and fiction as well as his writing experience in conceiving *The Executioner's Tale*, his novel about Lee Harvey Oswald and other projects:

> There exists a funny reciprocal relation between fact and fiction. I had this feeling that I can't really justify or explain, that the closer this book stayed to the given statements the more fictional it would be. When you have a collection of bare facts, the trouble is that most of the facts are not – what's the word I'm looking for – refined. They are warped. They're scabby. They're distorted. Very often they're false facts. And there's a tendency when you don't have to live with these facts to lump them all together, and so the story very often ends, despite good and serious efforts, with a betrayal of the reality [...] The history that gets built entirely upon fact is going to be full of error and will be misleading. It's the human mind that is able to synthesize what the reality might have been. Now, that reality doesn't have to be the one that took place, it has to be a reality that people can live with in their narrow minds, as the likelihood of how something took place. And that's the key difference. If you read a book and say, Yes this is how it could have taken place, your mind has been enriched.[2]

While I am not an academic, nor an authority, I have tried to supply an historical and social context in which these family letters can be read and to synthesise the scabby facts I found into something resembling a coherent whole. I recognise that the views of my nineteenth-century ancestors are far removed from their descendants today. They were living at the zenith of Britain's power, viewing the world through the lens of a major hegemon bringing civilisation to less developed parts of the world.

Far from feeling guilty about my colonial forebears, I am amazed at the enterprise and effort they made to construct a new society thousands of miles away from Britain. That some of their children came to grief in the process was partly a result of changing beliefs and fast-moving events over which they appeared to have little control.

At the time of writing this introduction, students at Oxford University have denounced a professor for arguing in a *Times* column that guilt around British colonialism may have gone too far. He was responding to the outcry over an article by political scientist, Bruce Gilley, who argued it was time to question the orthodox view that western colonialism has a bad name. The article had exposed a rising tide of intolerance on university campuses and within the academic profession to colonial history, one campaign calling for the 'decolonization' of the curriculum at Oxford. Over 80 academics globally have published a letter to *The Times* newspaper, defending the right of an academic journal to publish any work, however controversial, provided it merits exposure and debate. The history of empire is complex. While I recognise the needs of students of identity politics to feel validated and to have equal dignity to any other student on the campus, I also recognise that if we are to pass through this period of reassessment without violence, we need to find a framework to discuss issues of colonisation without being bullied by demands to 'decolonise your bookshelf' or the tendency of some activists to devalue people whose ideas do not square with their own world view.

References

1. Krystine Tomaszyk, *Essence*, New Zealand: Dunmore Press, 2004.
2. *The Paris Review Interviews*, vol. 111, Picador, 2008.

ACKNOWLEDGEMENTS

My thanks go to all who helped and stimulated this project. First, to Kate Foster, the great-granddaughter of Sir John Hall. She was generous in sharing the letters of Agnes, Sarah and Rose Hall in proof form which became the book *Letters to Grace*. She granted me access to the extraordinary Terrace Station archive and maintained a lively interest in the project, offering hospitality with her husband Richard and a thoughtful reading of early draft chapters of a much longer book. Others who provided invaluable information along the way are Dr Jean Garner, Russell Tuffery, Tim Rix, Sylvia Booth, Raymond Matthews and his son Stephen, Jill Grenfell, Tui Lundi-Robertson, Dr Paul Johnston, Peter Shaw, John and Bob Hall, and Len Barnett.

My grateful thanks to all those who supported the project by reading draft chapters – Professor Janet Wilson, Dr Gerri Kimber, Dr Robb Robinson, Roger Steele, Peter Sowden, Richard Johnson, Dr Kate Stringaris, John Hall, Lani Morris and, most of all, my husband, Professor Brent Taylor, who also compiled maps and gave invaluable moral support.

The staff in the wonderful Alexander Turnbull Library in Wellington were helpful during an intense month in January 2013.

They rescued my camera left behind after dream-like immersion in ancestral letters and were considerate in leaving me to my own devices. I am also grateful to my sister-in-law, Bron, who provided accommodation during this time. I thank also the staff of London Trinity House and Hull Trinity House who allowed me into their inner sanctums and to the staff of the Hull History Centre and the Guildhall Library, London.

As I went about my research, I was aware that I was starting a long way back with my great-great-grandfather's story and circling closer and closer to the mystery of my own father's life story as a child, which was virtually unknown to me. Invercargill and Ohakune were the places of his early history and his father's downward trajectory as a solicitor. As Alex de Tocqueville said in a note in his family archive, 'It is because I am the grandson of M. de Malesherbes that I have written these things.'[1] Likewise, it is because I am the daughter of T. R. Hall (Thomas Richard Hall) that I have written these things. Tocqueville's great-grandfather had been beheaded in 1794 after watching his daughter and granddaughter go to the scaffold in France. My father was forced to watch his father descend from solicitor to sawmill hand; to know that his uncle had attempted to poison his wife; to see one half-brother leave home and die; to see his epileptic half-brother charged with a murder he vowed he had not committed (that story is not here); to know that his mother had been arraigned before the court of public opinion in the 1890s, and certainly in the 1920s when to mount a defence for her son Reginald Matthews she had to reveal a history of her first husband's family instability which was exaggerated and exploited in the courtroom and in the press, in a society influenced by theories of eugenics. My father must have wondered about the society he was living in, the good luck and bad luck in life, the terror of poverty and the long vindictive memories of people. He put his head down, worked hard and kept silent. If I had not, by chance, found *Cheerful Yesterdays* in a library, I would never have questioned that silence.

T. S. Eliot's lines from the *Four Quartets* remind me of the sensation felt when uncovering parts of a family history never known before:

> Time present and time past
> Are both present in time future,
> And time future contained in time past. [...]
>
> There they were, dignified, invisible,
> Moving without pressure, over the dead leaves,
> In the autumn heat, through the vibrant air,
> And the bird called, in response to
> The unheard music hidden in the shrubbery,
> And the unseen eyebeam crossed, for the roses
> Had the look of flowers that are looked at.
> There they were as our guests, accepted and accepting.
> So we moved, and they, in formal pattern,
> Along the empty alley, into the box circle,
> To look down into the drained pool.
> Dry the pool, dry concrete, brown edged,
> And the pool was filled with water out of sunlight,
> And the lotos rose, quietly, quietly,
> The surface glittered out of heart of light,
> And they were behind us, reflected in the pool. [...][2]

References

1. Lucien Jaume, Arthur Goldhammer, *Tocqueville: The Aristocratic Sources of Liberty*, Princeton University Press, 2013, p. 298.
2. T.S. Eliot, extract from 'Burnt Norton', in *Four Quartets*, I, The Folio Society, London, 1968.

Illustrations

L.G.D. Acland, *The Early Canterbury Runs*, 4th edn, 1975, 6.5; Table 6.1.

Alexander Turnbull Library, Wellington, New Zealand, 7.3; 9.5 (The Press) Christchurch Collection ref. G-8713-1/1; 9.6 L.S. Nichol Collection ref. 5 (a) 2622-1/2; E2 ref. John Hall Papers, MS-Group-0033

Sylvia Booth, 11.4.

Roger Boutet de Monvel, *Eminent English Men and Women in Paris*, 1912, 1.5 (sketch by Richard Langton)

Canterbury Museum, 2.7 (a) ref. ARV Morton Collection 1877.361.20; 3.6 ref. 19XX.2.5003; 6.2 ref. 1977.361.9 ARV Morton Collection; 6.3 ref.2-500; 7.1 ref. 1977.361.21 ARV Morton Collection; 8.5 ref 19XX.2.5000; 9.1 ref. 1977.361.13; 9.2 ref. 19XX.2.4996; Walter Armiger Bowring lithograph, 10.6 ref. 19XX.2-5006; E3 ref. 1923.53.673.

Alexander Gardner, *Rays of Sunlight from South America*, 4.7

Sir George Grey Special Collections, Auckland Libraries, 6.6 ref. 406804; E1 ref. 7-A1 4496.

Joy Hall, 11.3.

Sir James Hight and C.R. Straubel, Gen. Eds, *A History of Canterbury*, Vol. 1, 6.1, engraving from painting by W. Fox.

Hull History Centre, 1.9 ref. DSTR.39, p. 238; 1.13 *Grace*, ref. vol.43, entry 438 DSTR 41.

Hull Trinity House, 1.12 (a) and (b); A. Storey, *Trinity House of Kingston upon Hull*, 1967, 2.8.

Illustrated London News Ltd/Mary Evans, 5.5.

P.B. Maling, 7.2

National Maritime Museum, Greenwich, UK, 3.1; 6.3 ref. 2-5000.

NPM, Tyree Studio Collection, Nelson, NZ, 9.4 ref. 67925/3.

Robert Pinney, *Early South Canterbury Runs*, 1971, source of Tables 6.1 and 6.2.

Public Record Office, National Archive, Kew, UK, 3.5 ref. PRO/ 5771; 3.8 ref. PRO/ BT 98/671; 4.2 ref. TNA:BT98/308; 4.4 ref. BT 98/375.

Gillian Rix, 10.2 (a) and (b).

South Africa Military Association, 7.4.

Professor Brent Taylor, all maps drawn.

Moira Taylor, 1.3, 1.4, 1.7-1.8, 1.14, 3.3, 5.1, 6.8 (a), 7.6, 9.8, 10.1, 10.4 (a) and (b), 11.1-11.2 (a) and (b), 11.5; Tables 1.1 and 2.1; E4.

Terrace Station Archive, Hororata, New Zealand: 1.1, 1.2, 1.6 (a) and (b), 1.10, 1.11, 2.1-2.7 (a) and (b), 3.2, 3.6-3.7, 3.10, 9.7, 10.1, 10.3, 10.4 (a) and (b), 10.5 (b).

W.Vance, *High Endeavour*, 2nd edn, 1965, ref. endpaper map.

Edward Wakefield, *New Zealand After Fifty Years*, 1889, 10.5 (a)

Poetry credit:

T. S. Eliot, extract from 'Burnt Norton', in *Four Quartets*, I, The Folio Society, London, 1968, and courtesy of Faber & Faber.

SOURCES AND EDITORIAL NOTES

Sources

The Hall family letters included in *Sailors, Settlers and Sinners* come primarily from a collection held in the John Hall Papers, Alexander Turnbull Library (ATL; MS-Group-0033), the national library of New Zealand. Others are from the John Hall Papers and photo collection held at the Terrace Station Archive (TSA), Hororata, Canterbury, New Zealand. Some excerpts used in the book are my selections from John Hall's diaries which he had typed by a personal secretary and bound before he died. Only the 1887 diary is in the ATL, the typed and original diaries are all at the TSA. He sometimes made some deliberate editorial omissions in this process. Where a subject is controversial I refer to the original.

The family letters in the John Hall Papers held in the ATL were on microfiche as handwritten originals. They appear randomly among the John Hall Papers in chronological order interspersed with letters from local and national political figures, his farm manager, suffragists eager for him to support and guide their cause, and others seeking his patronage. They were organised and individually marked by his secretary with the author's name in pencil. In order to transcribe the family letters from handwritten originals, I had to look at all the letters, political or otherwise, to identify them satisfactorily. I soon became familiar with the handwriting of different family members, none of whom could suppose their letters would end up in a national archive. These are predominantly letters *to* John Hall. He was much more circumspect about keeping his letters in reply and in one letterbook I found 12 pages torn out, though the fact that he left this much correspondence to the National Library means he was self-consciously aware that his life story was likely to be of some historical interest.

Early letters from George Hall to his children are written before emigration when the three brothers, George, Thomas and John were at school, or from George and Thomas when at sea, or when John was working away from their home town of Hull in London and elsewhere. Other letters were written after the brothers abandoned their combined working arrangement on Rakaia Terrace Station in 1852 and dispersed to other towns, or when they corresponded from Timaru, Christchurch or Invercargill during John Hall's ten visits back to England from New Zealand. Sometimes letters were cross-written to save paper, such as Thomas W. Hall's recounting of the family's shipwreck en route to New Zealand. Many of George Williamson Hall's letters were written after he and Agnes left New Zealand for England after the turbulent events of 1886. When the next generation of Halls, mainly Thomas's sons, Tom, Will and Richard ('Dick') began work in New Zealand, their letters to John Hall provided another rich resource.

Kate Foster, John's great-granddaughter, kindly permitted me to type out the George W. Hall letters in 2010 from handwritten originals kept in the Terrace Station Archive, Hororata, John Hall's former homestead. Tim Rix (1934–2012), the great-grandson of Grace Neall, younger sister of George W., Thomas W. and John Hall, also proved a useful repository of letters. When Tim and I first met in London in 2010, he was enjoying retirement, but had been an earlier chairman of Longman educational publishing company, a former board member of the British Library and the British Council and from 1982–1984, president of the Publishers' Association in Britain. He had given to the Archive the original manuscript of George Hall's

Journal of My Two Escapes, the letter to his sister Grace from G. W. Hall, 'Journey up to the City of Copiapo', and the long letter written to her on board the *Mary Miller*, dated 21 April 1846. Tim gave the letters of Agnes, Sarah and Rose Hall to Grace Neall (née Hall) during the years 1862–1877, helpful for the chapters on life after emigration in the early years of settlement in New Zealand, now published as *Letters to Grace*, edited by Dr Jean Garner and Kate Foster, with an introduction by Garner. Tim also gifted to the Archive the 1814 and 1827 remnants of diaries kept by our great-great-grandmother Grace Hall (née Williamson) and the almanacs of her mariner husband George Hall. All these items helped significantly in researching the Hull and Yorkshire background to the lives of the Hall brothers and their wives.

Tim and I met for the first time to discuss our common ancestors in a pub in central London and were amazed to find we had spent most of our working lives in academic/educational publishing companies, he as CEO of Longman, me as a development editor in textbooks for Routledge at the time of its merger with Taylor & Francis and thereafter until I retired. At that meeting he gave me the painting of George Hall's ship *Grace* to take back to the Terrace Station Archive and later also sent a portrait of John Hall and Grace as children with their family dog.

My maritime research into the voyages of George Hall senior began with his 1829 to 1839 almanacs which I had to transcribe with the use of a magnifying glass and a good reading light. The Muster Rolls, formerly kept by Hull Trinity House, now in the Hull Maritime Research Centre, and the records of the maritime insurers, Lloyd's, verified many of the voyages mentioned and these were also supported by shipping intelligence reports in the British newspaper archives. Once ship's names were discovered, I employed a maritime researcher, Len Barnett, to identify the maritime adventures of

George W. and Thomas W. Hall on crew agreements still stored in the National Archive at Kew.

The digitised New Zealand newspaper archive, Papers Past, was very helpful in providing colourful information and reportage on key moments in the New Zealand-based colonial stories, especially the reports on the Tom Hall trials and the case of Richard and Caroline Hall. I was also dependent on books about the early Canterbury runs and provincial life in Canterbury during this period written by L. G. D. Acland, William Vance, Robert Pinney and Oliver A. Gillespie. *Hansard*, the New Zealand parliamentary record, provided a full transcript of the long and fascinating resignation speech of J. G. Ward after his bankruptcy. I found Jean Garner's biography of John Hall, *By His Own Merits*, very helpful, though her focus and therefore bias, was mainly John Hall, difficult to avoid when surviving correspondence in the Hall Papers is mostly addressed to him. She was instrumental in pushing the modest Hall far further forward in the pantheon of eminent New Zealanders.

In the Hall family during the nineteenth century it was customary for men to write to men about worldly affairs and women to write to women about domestic and private affairs, although occasionally some critical private matters do intrude into the men-to-men letters. My focus on the men is primarily because that is where the evidence lay.

Distances between Invercargill, Christchurch and Timaru were significant and the telegram was used frequently in moments of crisis. Sometimes telegrams brought news of a death, or a critical illness. During the two trials of young Tom Hall they were more intense as the brothers discussed important developments and the fallout from what turned out to be fraudulent financial transactions, some of which affected his father as presumably guarantor of some of his loans.

John Hall was aware that his brothers' lives in New Zealand had been more complicated and less fortunate than his. Because of the painful legacy of their lives and the likelihood that they would not leave a record he was perhaps keener to ensure the family story told in his personal diaries was preserved 'for those I leave behind me'. He employed a genealogist to track down birth and death dates of his forebears on various trips to England, in order to compile a family tree. This was reproduced on a velum scroll in colour when he was knighted and was very helpful in my research.

The illustrations in *Sailors, Settlers and Sinners* come mainly from the Terrace Station Archive or from relatives. The archive contains many early daguerreotypes of members of the family as well as later photos from John Hall's photo album. My father left no trace of his ancestors except his sibling's birth certificates. I was given the photos of his grandparents, father and mother by his sister Tui, and his niece Sylvia. The artist behind the pencil drawing by 'J. E.' of 'Buenos Ayres', dated 1833 is a mystery though likely to have been a crew member or friend on voyages by George Hall. Other images come mainly from the Canterbury Museum or ATL collections. Young Tom Hall was a keen early photographer and I imagine took the photos of his parents at Elloughton Grange in Timaru.

The timelines are mine, constructed to help navigate my way through a massive amount of material and people. Writing a group biography is not an easy matter. The errors I hope are few. There are bound to be many interpretations of the facts I've unearthed. I welcome any further details or family stories from any reader who may know more.

Editorial notes

I have used ellipses [...] to indicate omissions within letters or where a word or phrase was simply indecipherable or did not add to the narrative. Where correspondents have underlined for emphasis I have substituted italics and where I have imposed italics for emphasis myself in reproducing a letter, I use '[my italics]'.

I have kept the variable early spelling used in family letters but used contemporary versions of words in my narrative. For instance, 'Buenos Ayres' within letters but otherwise 'Buenos Aires'; 'Leghorn', the rather clumsy English rendition of the Italian 'Livorno', in letters but otherwise Livorno. I have retained the nineteenth-century use of capital letters for nouns in correspondence.

A list of abbreviations at the end of the book assist in naming letter correspondents in the references. The forenames George, Thomas and John pass through three generations so are distinguished by middle name initials in the references [GH father; GWH son] and qualified in the narrative if two generations are present in the same sentence or paragraph. Where some have the same initials as someone in an earlier generation, I spell the name in full in the references if there is any doubt. Thomas W. Hall was addressed as 'Tom' by his brothers and wife in their letters but I have called him Thomas throughout to distinguish him from his son Tom. Richard Hall was known in letters as 'Dick' but I have called him Richard throughout since that is how he was known publicly. Young John was known as Jack to his family but is occasionally called 'John' within letters. I have supplied a family tree to assist understanding of generations.

Official comparison sites trying to equate nineteenth-century money with late twentieth-century money stopped operating in the early 1980s as they were thought to be providing a false index. There is no easy conversion factor because financial systems have changed considerably over the last 200 years with marked variation in fiscal policies (taxation and government spending) and in monetary policies (money supply and interest rates) which make direct comparisons difficult. I have therefore left sterling amounts in the book as they are without contemporary equivalents. One guide is that £400 sterling in 1840 is roughly equivalent to £33,150 in 2019 in terms of comparative standards of living. A good website for understanding these difficulties is www.measuringworth.com.

Moira Taylor, 2019

I

ESCAPING NAPOLEON: THE STORY OF GEORGE HALL (1782–1865)

Captain Christie: 'George will you stop with me, I like you.'
George Hall, cabin boy: 'But my friends know not where I am, and
I have a father and a mother.'[1]

George Hall took some time to answer Captain Christie's question, put to him in 1795 when he was a cabin boy of only 13, away from home in French waters at the height of the French Revolution. Should he remain on this American merchant ship or return to the port of his birth, Hull? His previous vessel, the *Windsor Castle*, had been captured by a French privateer. Terrified, he had been marched off between two soldiers with bayonets fixed to Rochefort. Here his French captors took pity on him and put him on *The Friends of New York* at La Rochelle under Captain Charles Christie's command. Fortunately, George decided to return to his parents in Hull, as otherwise this story would have been a very different one and I would not be telling it. His words come from a memoir of his life at sea as a boy, published at the end of the first edition of his *Journal of Two Escapes from French Prisons during the War with Napoleon* (1838), written for his family and friends as an introduction to that work.

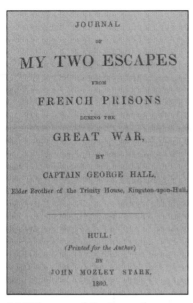

JOURNAL

OF

MY TWO ESCAPES

FROM

FRENCH PRISONS

DURING THE

GREAT WAR,

BY

CAPTAIN GEORGE HALL,

Elder Brother of the Trinity House, Kingston-upon-Hull.

————

HULL:
(*Printed for the Author*)
BY
JOHN MOZLEY STARK,
1860.

1.1 Title page of the *Journal*.

George was my great-great-grandfather, born during the reign of George III on 4 January 1782. He had a career at sea during the Napoleonic Wars, was imprisoned in France for six years and was one of a handful of the 22,000 prisoners held there who staged a successful escape back to England. He was the only male child to survive beyond the age of 21 in a family of 12 children born to John and Eleanor Hall of Hull.

Kingston upon Hull, to give the place its full name, was acquired by King Edward I and granted a royal charter in 1299. It is on the east coast of England, separated from its neighbours Norway, Denmark and, more distantly, Sweden and the Baltic States, by the turbulent and dangerous North Sea. George, his older brother John who died aged 20, and his two sisters Elizabeth and Eleanor, grew up in this bustling town at a time when it was becoming the largest British port involved in Arctic whaling. The Hull whaling fleet, if it could avoid being trapped in ice or wrecked in storms, or being pressed into service by the navy, would sail to Baffin Bay, between Baffin Island and the south-west coast of Greenland, to the Davis Strait and to Spitzbergen, the large island in northern Norway, and bring back cargoes of whale blubber to be boiled into lamp and machine oil. The fleet usually sailed in February and returned in October, in time for the famous Hull fair.

George's father John Hall (1742–1816) lived during the reigns of George II, George III and the Prince Regent, George

IV. He had served his own apprenticeship at sea with the master mariner William Hill[2] and was, according to his tombstone in St Peters, Drypool, Hull, 'many years master and owner in the Italian trade out of the Port'.[3] He became one of the younger brethren of Hull Trinity House and then one of the elder brethren on 26 July 1779. He was a good upper middle-class citizen. Trinity House and its guild members or brethren

1.2 Captain John Hall, George's father.

played a key role in the city's life, controlling the passage of shipping on the Humber River, placing buoys and lighting the waterways and near coastline of England. Elder brethren had powers to act as nautical assessors in the high court of Admiralty, to hear charges of piracy and decide issues of discipline or decide on questions relating to prizes acquired during war. It had other more charitable concerns, including the education of young mariners and the care of sick seamen. John Hall had his pilot's licence from Trinity House to conduct British and allied ships up the Humber into the safety of Hull Dock. He could also command ships on foreign-going voyages.

On 18 November 1768, in the magnificent medieval Holy Trinity Church, Hull, John Hall married Eleanor Dutchman (1750–1826), the daughter of a tailor.[4] The church, dating from the thirteenth century, still stands in the Old Town area of Hull and was central to the lives of the family and its descendants. It was here that George, the family's second son, was baptised on 6 February 1782. He was

|742

to lose eight of his 12 siblings during his mother's child-bearing years, four dying in infancy. John, the eldest son, died at Morant Bay, Jamaica, while captain of the vessel *Kingston*, in 1799. The brutal mortality rate in children demonstrated by George's family was not unusual at the time. In the 1750s, approximately two-thirds of children under the age of five died. Those who survived childhood generally did well. It is sad to later see George lose the company of three of his four children, all his sons in their maturity, when they decided to emigrate to New Zealand in the early 1850s.

1.3 Hull Trinity House on Trinity House Lane, showing a reclining Britannia and Neptune on its pediment.

When George was growing up, the centre of the eighteenth-century Italian trade in which his father was involved was the port of Livorno, then known by the British as Leghorn. Britain had traded with the city since the late sixteenth century and a British factory or agency had been there since the seventeenth century, enjoying special privileges over other foreign residents because of its importance to trade. Britain shipped cotton, woollen and linen manufactured goods, iron, steel and hardware, brass and copper manufactures, glass, lead and shot. Other goods came from Britain's colonies, such as coffee, rum, raw sugar and indigo, and were then distributed throughout the Mediterranean via the British Factory. Ships returning to Britain were loaded at Livorno with silk, olive oil, fruit and marble,[5] some of it used to cover the floors of Hull's increasingly rich merchant class. Maister House, one of Hull's remaining grand merchant houses, has floors of marble, checker-patterned in black and white, and Hull Trinity House has floors of gold marble with black veining, both sourced from Livorno.

Another early Hull merchant dwelling, now used as the Maritime Studies Department at Hull University, is Blaydes House, built in the late 1730s with its broad timber struts in the attic and large black and white diamond-shaped marble floor tiles. The Blaydes family owned two shipyards, providing ships for the navy and for the merchant marine. They would have hosted many dinners for people like George and his wife Grace, and before them John and his wife Eleanor, as they chatted with other ships' captains and their wives about plans for the next spring expedition to Russia and Riga, or Gothenburg, Bordeaux and Livorno.

The Livorno trade flourished in the eighteenth century. Elena Lazzarini has been able to identify this thriving trade through the meticulous health inspection records of ships docking at Livorno and cites a multitude of English and Scottish ports trading there at the time; these were, first London, then Liverpool, Bristol, Hull, Newcastle, Sunderland, Yarmouth, Greenock, Leith, Aberdeen and Dundee, followed by the Irish ports of Cork, Dublin, Limerick, Belfast and Waterford. Trade which was so stymied by France's blockade during the Napoleonic Wars (though a certain amount of unofficial trading went on despite war), was officially resumed after Napoleon's defeat at the Battle of Waterloo in June 1815 and for Hull merchants, continued into another generation. The port features in George Hall's almanac of 1839. On 2 August of that year he notes 'Wrote to Tom at Leghorn'.[6] On 5 September he wrote, 'Daniel Wheeler sailed from Leghorn'.[7] His son Thomas had served on this Hull ship as second mate, sailing from Leghorn to Malta and the Black Sea.

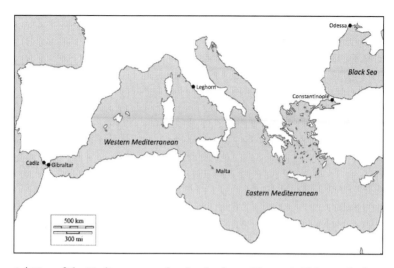

1.4 Map of the Mediterranean showing Leghorn (Livorno), Malta, and other ports visited by George Hall and his sons in their maritime careers.

George went to school in the village of Sproatley, about six miles north-east of Hull which at the time had a population of 30 families. By the age of 13 he was beginning his apprenticeship at sea and thereafter was self-educated.

George Hall's early maritime career

Boys going to sea were usually recruited from seafaring families and learnt the basics of navigation and shipping during an apprenticeship under the supervision of a first or second mate or seaman. They left their mothers as young as ten or 12, sometimes as servants on board ship, sometimes as top boys in the rigging. The chances of never returning were quite high, particularly if they were learning the ropes in rigging high above a wooden deck.

In his *Autobiography of a Little Sailor Boy*, originally published in 1838 as part of the first edition of his *Journal*, George Hall left his descendants an account of his experiences as a cabin boy at sea during the French Revolution. It gives us insight into the mind of a boy having to fend for himself, away from his family in dangerous circumstances. Much that happened to him was due to good luck, his good sense, his likeable disposition and the responsible advice given to him by a ship's master who may have known of his father by reputation.

George began his apprenticeship at sea two years after France had declared war on Britain. He was employed to wait on the captain and officers of the transport ship *Neptune* which set sail in January 1795. It left from a shipbuilding yard in Deptford on the River Thames, London, to take troops to Quiberon Bay, western France. On board were some soldiers, including artillery men, under the command of a Captain Wilson 'who spoke French well, and was a daring man, as well as being possessed of much good judgement and sound sense'.[8] France was in uproar as a result of the Revolution. The British troops were intended to protect French émigrés or counter-revolutionary troops who had been landed at Quiberon Bay to foster a counter-revolutionary movement in western France and restore the French monarchy. They were routed six months later in July 1795 by the 'sans-culotte' revolutionary army led by General Louis Lazare Hoche, so called because they wore long trousers not culottes like the bourgeoisie, and were for the most part lower-class urban labourers. George described the scene and his part in it:

> Our vessel arrived, along with the others, at Quiberon Bay, and our first roadstead [where the ship anchored near the port] was a very wild one, open to the sea; the fleet of which our transport formed part, was led by the Commodore's ship the *Melpomene*. We had a full view of the French army, which was a very large one, under General Hoche. […] I often went in the cutter to take

Captain Wilson, when he was required to attend councils of war, etc.[9]

The *Neptune*, controlled by the Transport Board, was ordered home only to be later instructed to go to Gibraltar, to meet Admiral Sir John Jervis's fleet which was guarding the Strait of Gibraltar, watching the Spanish fleet in Cadiz. Although George does not elaborate, the background to this expedition is that Spain, under French pressure, had declared war on Britain in October 1796. Four months later Sir John Jervis had defeated a Spanish fleet of 27 with his own fleet of 15 ships at the Battle of Cape St Vincent, Portugal. This victory had been won largely by the actions of Commodore Horatio Nelson who had left his position, sailed into the main body of the retreating Spanish ships, engaging three and capturing two Spanish first-rates. At Gibraltar, and before the battle, George is very close to Jervis's flagship, *Victory*:

One day, when near Europa Point, a large frigate came round the point. There had been a strong gale from the east south-east, and the frigate came through our fleet, close past the *Victory*, alongside of which our vessel was lying. When about half-way across the bay, up went a large Spanish ensign! I think I saw Sir John Jervis giving the signal to "Cut, and after him!" Very speedily a frigate was after him, the eyes of every man in the fleet being upon them. But as the Spanish vessel was over towards Algeciras, our frigate had to weather Cabbarita Point, which she did, going through the sea at a furious rate. Then came on a gale, that night being one never to be forgotten. The *Gibraltar*, the *Excellent*, and the *Corrague* – the three outermost ships – parted from their anchors.

The *Gibraltar* and the *Excellent* ran through the Gulf; but the *Corrague* was lost, and out of seven hundred men forming her crew, only about one hundred and fifty were saved, by clinging to the broken timbers, which were washed on to the African coast. These survivors were detained by the Moors as slaves, until they were released and restored, in consequence of the interposition of the English Consul at Algiers. Peace was afterwards concluded with Spain.[10]

slaves

George's ship was captured by a French privateer, near Lisbon, in the episode recounted at the beginning of this chapter when he found himself eventually on *The Friends of New York*, under the charge of Captain Charles Christie: 'If ever a boy was doubly diligent, I may say it was myself – with good wages, fearing no one, with my American protection, stating that I was a free citizen of the States!'[11]

Captain Christie and George were bound for the port of Havre le Grace. It is there, he says, a stranger asked for passage to America and was invited into the Captain's cabin for a meal. He was Thomas Paine (1737–1809), the English/American radical and libertarian pamphleteer, who began writing his *Rights of Man* while in a French prison. He had fled from England to France three years before to escape arrest for treason and was now seeking a passage to America under an American flag. His great work, *The Age of Reason* (1794–1795) was also started while in France. Paine advocated republicanism and complete independence for the American colonies which they *had* achieved in 1783. George, though only a boy, waited on Paine, whose anti-royalist pamphlet *Commonsense* (1776), widely read, provided the foundation document for the American Revolution and independence from Britain. He would become father to the man who, a century later, was the political strategist and parliamentarian guiding legislation to ensure women's suffrage in New Zealand, the first country in the world to grant this.

Captain Christie eventually recommended George to the master of an American brig going to Altona and advised him to seek out the proprietor of the American Hotel in Hamburg before leaving him. In this city, George found a vessel owned by William Field who had served an apprenticeship with his father, and thus found a passage back to Hull. George reflected in his account on 'this dreadful time':

> The French Revolution was at its height but there were few who were not insensible to human sympathy, or devoid of human feelings. I had, although very young, an opportunity of judging of some of the horrors of the revolution. The best reference I can make to it will be to say that it fell on the people as a thunderbolt from Heaven, fanned into a flame by songs and martial music, which excited the wild spirits of the age. Their Marseillaise Hymn contained words, for strength of meaning never equalled, which were sung in the streets. Religion was trodden underfoot and the brevet of a General was often but the stepping-stone to the scaffold; the national cockade had to be worn, in the army as well as among the civilians. It was the reign of terror; and it stamped a feeling on my mind which will never be forgotten.[12]

Hull in the late eighteenth and early nineteenth centuries

When George was serving his apprenticeship and rising through the ranks in the mercantile marine to become a master mariner, Hull was pre-eminent in its thriving trade with the Baltic States and Russia. Merchants and shipowners were wealthy people and his father, John, had considerable status in the town. The town was lively, according to William Wilberforce, the great anti-slavery advocate and a native of the city. He spent his childhood there, in the decade from 1759 to 1768 and wrote:

Tom 1792 ?

see p 31

> It was then as gay a place as could be found out of London. The theatre, balls, great suppers, and card-parties were the delight of the principal families in the town. [...] As grandson to one of the principal inhabitants, I was every where invited and caressed: my voice and love of music made me still more acceptable.[13]

In June 1798, once war with France was underway, the Trinity House brethren had been called on by the Admiralty to arm the House yacht, which reconnoitred the Humber monitoring buoyage, and had furnished her with 'carriage guns, small arms powder shot and other ordnance'[14] to defend the port of Hull from the enemy if called upon. It was manned by Younger Brethren. By 1801, three years before George Hall was captured as a young captain on the man-of-war *Enterprize*, the Admiralty was planning its attack on Copenhagen and the Danish fleet which was blockading Copenhagen Harbour and asked Hull Trinity House how many North Sea pilots it could supply. The brethren replied that 'many are at sea as masters and mates of merchant ships and several are detained in Russia, not more than twelve are in Hull at present.'[15] By March 1801, 12 North Sea pilots were sent to Admiral Sir Hyde Parker at Yarmouth and a further six, four days later. He was commander of the fleet in the Battle of Copenhagen on 2 April with Vice-Admiral Horatio Nelson as his second-in-command. The brethren also asked the Admiralty for more floating defence for the mouth of the Humber since 150 to 200 sailing ships in bad weather often resorted to shelter there and with no defence 'many could be captured or destroyed by an enemy before protection could be given by men of war lying in Grimsby Roads'. Also, enemy ships might get up the river and damage shipping and trade.[16] The navy responded by arming six small pilot cutters plus the Trinity House yacht to defend the Humber and Hull. Similar schemes were adopted around the coasts of Britain.

The details of George's career as a seaman and mate before he obtained his first command is presently unknown, but took place against the background of war with Napoleon at a time when William Pitt the Younger was prime minister (he had assumed the role in 1784 at the breathtakingly young age of 24) and George III was on the throne. Merchant ships were forced to sail in convoy escorted by Royal Navy frigates to protect them from French privateers who were mainly attacking smaller trading ships such as the one George Hall would command, often lurking in waters hidden by headlands. The inevitable happened and his ship was intercepted.

Capture and imprisonment in France 1804–1810
The greatest story of George Hall's life was his escape from a six-year-long imprisonment in France during the Napoleonic Wars. He was just 22 at the time of his capture and had already reached the rank of captain, an achievement attained four years younger than his two mariner sons. The *Enterprize*, a ship of 130 tons and a man-of-war, according to Admiralty papers[17] was captured at sea by a French privateer while on a homeward-bound journey from the Baltic port of Kœnigsburg to Hull.[18] George was landed at Dunkirk on 1 December 1804 and from there was marched (or perhaps offered wheeled transport as a member of the officer class) first to Valenciennes, then Verdun, the fortified town on the left bank of the River Meuse where military and naval officers were held on parole; that is, on their word of honour not to attempt escape. In the last year of his captivity he was moved to Auxonne, near Dijon. His incarceration as a young

man is recorded in *Journal of My Two Escapes from French Prisons During the War With Napoleon,*[19] published for his family and friends. It is an extraordinarily rare report since very few men escaped from France during that period.

George's conclusion in the published journal describes his captivity as being of six years and one month's duration, so his initial capture from the *Enterprize* must have dated from approximately November 1804, a month before Napoleon Bonaparte was crowned Emperor of the French in Notre Dame, Paris, on 2 December 1804. Another detainee, the diarist Revd J. B. Maude, has recorded that 430 merchant captains and mates were held in the citadel or were living on parole in the town of Verdun. Of these, the first 50 were marched out under strong guard on 14 November 1809, dates that match with George's account of his arrival at Auxonne in the last year of his captivity.

1.5 Convoy of English prisoners, sketch by Richard Langton from *Eminent English Men and Women in Paris*.

George gives no description of his longer captivity in Verdun and perhaps discretion was the better part of valour in his case.

He was young and unmarried. After the almost fantastical life of Englishmen in Verdun, evident in other accounts published in England, a fuller account may not have pleased the burghers of Hull. Following his first escape from Auxonne and his subsequent recapture, he mentions writing to friends in Verdun to update them on events, so perhaps some of his crew remained in the town.

Napoleon began his methodical, bloody and astonishing conquest of Europe in 1796. There was a brief interlude of peace between Britain and France sanctioned by the signing of the Treaty of Amiens (27 March 1802–18 May 1803), which established free movement between France and England, but the agreement was breached by the English who fired on French privateers. In May 1803, Napoleon immediately declared a state of war between the two countries and announced that any Englishman in France at the time connected with the military service or liable to serve in the militia from the ages of 18 to 60 would be arrested and treated as a prisoner of war. Thereafter, officers and crews of British merchant ships captured by French privateers – George Hall among them – were included in this roundup. About 7,000 men had to report for detention and were posted off to fortified towns for internment. These towns included Auxonne, Verdun, Sarrelouis, Sedan, Bitche, Cambrai, Dijon, Arras, Langres and Briançon. Verdun was the central depot.

The men were deprived of their passports and had their letters censored; they had orders to report to the governor at 10 a.m. every morning and to be back at their houses of internment at 9 p.m. on the peal of church bells. They comprised midshipmen, sailors, masters of merchantmen like George Hall, and military prisoners brought back from Frances's war with Spain. They were permitted three *sous* a day and half a pound of bread. Relief committees were started by the prisoners themselves. Those with means could bribe better terms out of these rules, such as attending only one roll call and permission to pass through the town gates providing they returned at a certain time. Some more fortunate prisoners were released through the interventions of powerful friends, but most were not released till 1814 when Napoleon was exiled to Elba after his initial abdication. There was no access to English newspapers, but prisoners were permitted to use whatever money they had to entertain themselves. The rich among them caused some spectacular transformations in the cities of captivity. In Verdun, for instance, the prosperous prisoners had a Jockey Club, hosted masked balls to which they invited city dignitaries, held horse races and went hunting. The availability of money stimulated commercial developments in their towns of captivity.

The extracts below are taken from *Eminent English Men and Women in Paris* written by Roger Boutet de Monvel and translated for publication in London in 1912. Several Englishmen left accounts of their internment in France during the Napoleonic Wars – James Forbes, Richard Langton, J. H. Lawrence and Lord Blayney, for instance, all of whom de Monvel quotes. Only Langton was at Auxonne, and escaped after George, but these other accounts serve to flesh out the attitudes of the French to the British and the difference that money could make in ensuring that imprisonment was endurable. Though written by captive men of a different class from George, they give a vivid description of what Verdun was like at the time.

Blayney reports:

Not only did the town wake up in an unforeseen manner, but it immediately assumed a thriving and prosperous appearance that altered its aspect altogether. For [...] there were not merely poor and destitute people among the prisoners; many of them were possessed of considerable fortunes. They had come to France with their horses, their carriages, and their lackeys, and although prisoners they continued to live in style. Except for a few nobles who had been deprived of their estates under the Republic, the [native] population of Verdun consisted entirely of small bourgeois, morose and mean, to a degree. The arrival of the prisoners changed everything; the silence and stagnation gave place to excitement and extravagance, and a perpetual round of banquets and gaieties. Very soon it was only the English people at Verdun who counted at all. They were to be seen everywhere, and nothing was heard or talked about but their clubs, their balls, and their sports. The cost of living doubled and trebled, and so many foreigners gathered together at once in this quiet corner [...] So much luxury in the midst of its customary simplicity, gave the old town an indescribably cosmopolitan air, similar to a fashionable seaside resort, or a watering place during the summer.

[...] Most of the English ladies who happened to be in France at the time that war was declared remained with their husbands, while others who had stayed in England did not hesitate to come and share their exile with them. [...] They quickly organised themselves, and the first care of the prisoners was to help one another [...][20]

But while the wealthy could live it up, the soldiers and sailors were enduring a far less elevated existence and George Hall, as a sea captain, would have been in this category unless he was able to receive help from his parents and family in Hull. In Verdun, where he spent five out of his six years of internment, according to Blayney, 'every midshipman became a professional jockey, and every able-bodied seaman an expert groom, while the foremost thought in everyone's mind was how he could best parade his knowledge of equine matters.' A market for women became the norm in Verdun:

> The bait of lucre made more than one mother sell her daughter's virtue to the highest bidder, while she raised or lowered her demands according to the impatience or indifference of the amateurs; and as the greatest connoisseurs can be deceived in this commerce, the same article was frequently sold to different purchasers. The young midshipmen, just released from parental supervision, were the first to look favourably on this state of things, and they indulged freely.[21]

Some women actively consorted and helped prisoners to obtain passports and means of escape. While the police offered rewards for recapture, the prisoners themselves offered local people rewards for assisting escape. One escape attempt was rewarded by Napoleon himself. Prisoner Mogg, whom Blayney refers to, had escaped from Arras, hidden in a wood near the coast, and made himself a boat capable of taking him across the English Channel. The story of his near escape 'reached the Emperor's ears, and he sent for Mogg and, as a reward for his ingenuity, gave him his liberty, not omitting to provide him with a certain sum of money'.[22]

Richard Langton, who escaped successfully in 1804 and had been in captivity since 1800, describes the Grande Rue de Verdun at 3 a.m. in the afternoon:

> To a stranger [it] presented a curious scene. Here were carriages of various descriptions belonging to

Englishmen; others on horseback attended by grooms; it did not seem as if we were in captivity. There were shops kept by the English, eating-houses, club-houses, livery stables, news-rooms, and an English church; the sight of the congregation issuing thence was singular. Our countrymen [...] when attending worship, almost inspired the English spectator with the idea that he was once more at home.[23]

J. H. Lawrence's account says there were five English clubs in Verdun, of which the Charon with 125 members was the most influential, with a library and games of whist played. Another club held social meetings for women and men, weekly balls, dinners at Christmas, lotteries and theatricals, and had gambling. Jews in the town, says Lawrence, loaned money at 100 per cent interest.

A published account of a midshipman Maurice Hewson, from County Kerry, records that he was captured near Brest in 1803 and, like George Hall, imprisoned in Verdun. For Hewson, imprisonment was a welcome relief from life as a midshipman at the time Britain was blockading French ports. Like George he learnt French in his free time. There is no mention in George's account of his longer imprisonment in Verdun, of working for money or 'going into service', a step out of his class. His internment is likely to have resembled the account below, except that George probably lived off his own savings:

The Liberty of going about the Town and walking in the country at certain hours by a permit which Captain Brenton obtained [Captains undertook to look after their own crews in the town], made Verdun a paradise for me – it was such a contrast to what I had been lately enduring.

[…] As soon as I could walk without assistance, the variety of the country, and fishing, afforded me great amusement – and when at home my hours were occupied in the study of French.

[…] We had our dinner sent to us from a Traiteur, under covers, for the small sum of fifteen sous each, and lived very comfortably. We had a French master to attend us, and learning French was the order of the day. In these economical habits of life I found I could support myself with respect for Thirty Pounds a year with the addition of twenty eight livres allowed us by the French Government. Through the kindness of the Revd Mr L. Lee I was enabled to procure money at no great trouble for my Bills. The class most to be commiserated with were the Masters of Merchantmen who having but the same subsistence were obliged to have recourse to their small savings in England – when that was exhausted they were necessitated to go into service; and their families […] driven to the heartrending necessity of claiming relief from their parishes.[24]

Prior to the collapse of the Peace of Amiens between France and Britain which lasted a year from March 1802 to 1803, it was customary for officers after capture by the French to be officially exchanged for French POWs captured by the British. They gave their word of honour, or *parole d'honneur*, not to serve in their country's navy or army until the conflict was over and, while in captivity, their word of honour not to escape. At the time of George's capture, this exchange of prisoners had been abandoned, since Napoleon believed the prisoners once released would be eligible for active service. The prisoners therefore faced imprisonment until peace came in 1814. George taught himself French and plotted his escape.

Auxonne and two escapes

George Hall's *Journal* opens with the statement, 'It was always my intention from my first leaving Verdun to try how fortune would favour me in endeavouring to gain my liberty by escape.' Immediately after, he writes, 'I arrived at Auxonne on the 10th of December, 1809, and during the winter was laying plans how it might be the most easily effected, and with the least danger.'[25]

George's first escape from Auxonne on 1 March 1810 was

brilliantly engineered. Armed with a passport procured from a friend, George met a Hungarian officer in charge of 210 Austrian prisoners who had arrived in Auxonne. From him he bought an Austrian uniform and permission to answer as one of the deserted prisoners on the officer's list. He and his friend, Captain John Anderson, also from Hull, then marched homeward with the Austrians undetected, each using the name of one of the deserting soldiers to get rations of food and lodging for the night in homesteads along the way. They averaged about 16 miles a day:

1.6 (a) George Hall as a young sea captain; (b) His warrant or pilot's licence, 1812, from Hull Trinity House.

It was always our custom in passing any large town to buy meat sufficient for supper, as in a small village seldom any was to be had; and as yet we had found that our meat was by people with whom we lodged boiled in water sufficient to serve them and us also; but this day [5 March 1810] we began to cook for ourselves, which rather offended our landlord and family. At night he gave us but a small litter of straw for both and a cold room, but by laying close we kept each other warm till next morning.[26]

George and Captain Anderson were apprehended by the police on 12 March near Strasbourg and returned to Auxonne, but by November George escaped again, this time alone.

Auxonne today is still a walled town with four gates, one the Porte Comte, the eastern gate, built in 1503 with its small footbridge. Inside are the remains of a prison and a round tower, which have been converted to a museum to honour Napoleon. Around all is a forbidding stone wall with the town and a forest beyond. Outside this walled enclosure, the rest of the town looks like any smallish provincial French town towered over by the immense Burgundian Church of our Lady. In the market square is a statue of Napoleon, who had studied at the Auxonne artillery academy as a young man. George was billeted with the farming fraternity of Auxonne during his year-long sojourn there and built up such a friendship with the local townspeople that on his capture and return after his first escape he was again able to secure good lodgings for himself.

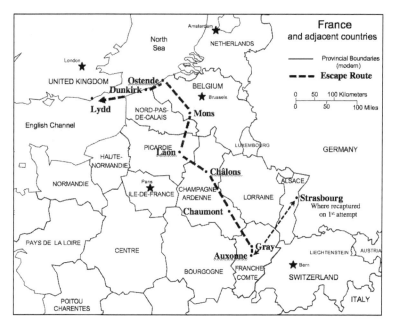

1.7 Map of France showing key towns in George Hall's imprisonment and his two escapes.

On his arrest and during his return to Auxonne, following his first escape attempt, George and his fellow prisoner had witnessed villagers festooning their towns with bunting and flowers to celebrate Napoleon's forthcoming marriage to Marie Louise. This raised their hopes, since it was often the case that national occasions were times for the release of prisoners. Depressed and mortified by the failure of his first escape, George was determined to try again, particularly on learning that the British representative in France, the English commissioner at Morlaix, Colonel McKinsey, was leaving France in disgust having made no progress in securing an exchange of prisoners with the French government. George was keen to remind his readers of the impossible difficulties of succeeding. William Titmore had got as far as Holland before being sent back to Auxonne; three others from Plymouth had traversed Switzerland but were taken in Baden by the French police; two Scotsmen were apprehended on the borders of Switzerland; four men from Sunderland escaped by boat and river, getting as far as the coast of France, but were detained on landing.[27]

Despite the winter weather, George was ready to go on 20 November 1810. He escaped through the gates of the town, concealed beside a cart's wheels, with his meagre provisions and some money. But he discovered with horror, after getting as far as Gray and Pontailler, that he had left much of his money behind. He therefore returned to Auxonne, but was unable to get through the town gate and had to turn back. He now began the immense 400-mile walk northwards to Ostend and along the coast to Dunkirk, avoiding city guards and police, speaking French like a local and evading detection. He washed in rivers and streams and scraped mud off his clothing before entering a town, found food where he could, and slept where he could find shelter. His sheer will to triumph over adversity and survive enabled him to achieve what seemed impossible. At every town were police and soldiers both within and outside the town gates. The country was at war and all escapees from prison or detention were soon known. As George noted:

> Invariably when any person deserts a description of his person is sent by circular letter to every prefect in the French Empire, and he is also requested to make the same known in like manner to the mayors and police officers in his department. By this means, within the week, there is not a police officer in the whole of the French Empire but who is on the lookout.[28]

His false passport depicted him as a stocking weaver from Lyons. He admitted the document was only good for showing to the proprietors of inns or other helpmates along the way and would have aroused suspicion with police or military personnel. He took the precaution of blacking his hair with gunpowder mixed with water and continued to 'make use of this stratagem all the way to the coast'.[29] His route on this second escape was in a north-west direction from Gray, near Dijon, via Chaumont, Châlons, Laon, Mons (in Belgium), Tournai to the port of Ostend from where he walked along the coastal road to Dunkirk. The last lap was cruelly hampered by bleeding feet and swollen lower legs, but his ingenuity in evading the police at each town, befriending trustworthy strangers, and hitching rides on carts or carriages got him to Ostend at last. Towards the end, his fatigue and failing health gave him desperate courage and permitted him to openly and boldly confront soldiers and police, helped by his excellent colloquial French.

Arriving in Ostend, he went to friends of his mother's and met Madame Bellroch. She had a mutual friend in Hull whose son had been a prisoner in Dunkirk six years before these events. A sticky moment ensued when Madame Bellroch professed still not to recognise George until he was able to tell an anecdote remembered about her from his mother. She immediately found him a sailor acquaintance who directed him to Dunkirk with an escort where he met the captain of a privateer who had escaped from an English prison, P. N. DeLille, who was glad to repay goodness shown him by the English. He gave George several days' lodging while arranging a safe passage back to England with sailors who would ferry him across the Channel once the moon had set, in order not to be intercepted by British cruisers or French privateers. His relief was immense:

> It is not possible to enumerate all the kindness of this family; everything I could wish for, either in meat or drink, was procured for me, clean linen was given me, in short when I left their house I was quite a different person.

There were a few of the captain's particular friends who used often to come and hearten me up, for the length of time I had been in the house made me apprehend some evil might arise by delay, but this they put off and told me to leave it all to them, and they would get me across, even if it were longer first. Now I cannot particularize the manner in which I got across the English Channel without exposing some very respectable families in Dunkirk, whose kindness it will never be in my power to reply; discretion was the only thing pointed out to me to ensure the safety of their families. [...][30]

George was set down on the Kent coast about a mile west of Dungeness lighthouse at about 1.15 in the morning on the first day of 1811:

I cannot describe my feelings at this moment. I stopped a short time just where I landed and looked around me to see if any one was near me. It appeared like a dream that I was in my own country and had no one to be afraid of. Six years and one month had that despotic Tyrant of Europe had me in his power, but now restored to liberty, with a fervent heart I thanked the All Wise Providence who had protected me in all the dangers I had escaped. As I had never been ashore here before I walked up the bank leading along the beach, and seeing a light at a small house not far off I made up to it and knocked at the door. The man who came to up to open it had on a flannel waistcoat and blue trousers. At first sight of him I shrank back, reason for fear was still too recent, but he asked who I was, and told me to come in, which I did, telling him and his wife who I was. What their business was to be up that time of the morning did not concern me. The wife I found sitting over the fireside with the Bible before her. Telling her my situation she made me a glass of hot rum and water, gave me also something to eat, and would willingly have had me to stop, but I wished to be further inland, as I had nothing to protect me from the pressgang, and I knew our small cruisers often had their boats ashore at Dungeness. As I had no English money I could but thank them for their kindness, and by directions given me made the best of my way to a village of the name of Lydd, where I arrived between three and four o'clock in the morning. At the first house I met with that had a sign I knocked until the door was opened. I told the young man who let me in who I was, and desired him to give me something warm, which he did, showed me to a good bed, and as all my clothes were wet in coming across, and in jumping out of the boat, I had torn my trousers, I gave him them all to get dry and mended, and myself to rest with that peace of mind which I had not for so long been in possession of. I took a by-coach from Lydd to New Romney, and from there to Hythe, leaving Lydd about ten in the morning, and in the evening taking the running coach to London.[31]

On both sides of the Channel, George had found people willing to cooperate in his escape. He, in gratitude, promised to assist in the release of a nephew of the family who helped him escape, a man called 'Edward Torris' [likely originally to have been Edouard Torres], who was still imprisoned in the notorious Mill Prison near Plymouth.

The traffic of prisoners back and forth across the Channel was frequent, but secrecy was paramount in protecting the agents of an escape for the penalty to those involved in assisting was transportation for life.[32]

On his return to Hull, George enlisted the help of a local MP, John Staniforth, who went on George's behalf to the Admiralty with his request for the release of Edward Torris. Staniforth's father was a Hull merchant, his two uncles were Hull shipowners and another uncle, Joseph Green, was based at Kœnigsberg,[33] where George's ship had traded before capture in 1804. It is possible he was doing business with the Staniforth family in the Baltic at the time. Staniforth was successful, his request granted, and he instructed George to call at Somerset House to obtain Mr Torris's release. The record of George's captivity was noted in the release request in the Admiralty records in London:

> Letter from Mr George Hall, late Master of the Enterprize of Hull regarding the release of a Prisoner named Edward Toris [sic], the Relation of a Person at Dunkirk who facilitated his Escape from a French prison. Referred to Transport Board. Reply from Transport Board proposing that he may be released on his Parole. Orders accordingly. Applicant informed.[34]

George duly secured Torris's freedom along with the Admiralty's request to Torris never to mention the name of his benefactor. They did meet later, in 1834, when George, loading cargo in the Charente *départemente* decided to enquire of the Torris family in Dunkirk. Copies of Torris's letter of thanks, written from Mill Prison near Plymouth, were pasted in the back of the second edition of *Journal of Two Escapes*, perhaps to convince readers of what might seem to some an unbelievable story. For Torris, 'Each and every day of my life could never be enough to show you the proofs of my gratitude.'[35]

Prisoner number 836 in the Verdun Register of British POWs in France was exceptional in escaping but also in securing the release of a French POW too.[36]

Younger Brother of Hull Trinity House 1812

Eighteen months after his return to Hull in 1811, George, now 30, was examined by the board of Trinity House on North Sea and Baltic pilotage. The warrant (see 1.6 (b) above) awarded him as a Younger Brother of Hull Trinity House on 18 July 1812 showed he was 'found fit and capable to take charge as master or pilot of any ship or vessel from the River Humber Eastward to Heligoland and the Red Buoy in the River Elbe'.[37] Heligoland, an island in the North Sea, had been captured by the British from Denmark in 1807. It was a forwarding depot for proscribed goods brought by British ships, carried up the Elbe to the Hanseatic port of Hamburg. It allowed the British merchant marine to break the French continental blockade which excluded British goods and goods brought into Britain from other parts of the world and re-exported, from Napoleon's controlled territories.[38]

Britain's triumph in the Battle of Trafalgar in Spain in 1805 had been effective in virtually stopping attacks on British shipping by the French navy. The British navy post at Trafalgar had expanded and by the year George joined the Younger Brethren of Hull Trinity House, trade was being re-established with former trading partners and British ships were sailing again to ports in the Mediterranean, Aegean, Adriatic and through the Black Sea. On the back of George's warrant is a description which served in 1812 as a passport photo would today: 'The within named George Hall is about Five Feet seven inches high, fair complexion, brown hair and has a scar on his left arm.'

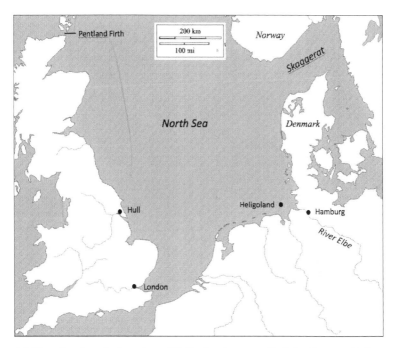

1.8 Map showing the location of Heligoland, now called the German Bight.

Between 1812 and 1814, after George's return to Hull and before Napoleon's downfall in 1815, he is recorded in the Hull Trinity House muster rolls going far beyond Heligoland to St Petersburg, then Malta, a British protectorate and trading station in the Mediterranean.[39] His command, the *Lord Wellington*, probably sailed in convoy with protection from a British man-of-war at a time when Britain was subsidising the Russian army through the profits of trade,[40] a strategy which led to Napoleon's ill-fated march on Moscow in 1812. Tsar Alexander rejected Napoleon's continental system as ruinous to Russia, causing Napoleon to assemble the biggest army in European history to invade Russia. The *Lord Wellington* carried a crew of 34 men, including Captain George Hall, and 32 other men, possibly soldiers. The crew signed on to the ship on 29 October 1812 and were discharged on 9 January 1814. Was George's ship

1.9 Muster roll of the *Lord Wellington*.

simply trading with St Petersburg whose port, Kronstadt, was the base for Russia's Baltic fleet during these crucial years, or carrying British soldiers to the garrison on Malta, which was much liked by the British navy for its prized harbours. Britain was supposed to evacuate Malta under the Treaty of Amiens (1802) with France, Malta's previous occupier. Britain's failure to comply with the Treaty lead again to war with France.

Married life, children and a ship of his own

On 21 October 1817 in Holy Trinity in Hull, at the age of 35, George married Grace Williamson, the 30-year-old daughter of Captain Thomas Williamson, a wealthy Hull merchant whose family had become enriched by importing iron from Sweden. This late courtship was not unusual at a time when England was recovering from war and men were in short supply.

All we know of Grace comes mainly from fragments of an 1814 journal she left, written when she was 27, in the year Napoleon abdicated and went into exile on the island of Elba. There are only very occasional references to her in family letters. Grace and her sister Mildred had been at school in York as young girls, taught by the wife of Dr Cammadge, the organist at York Minster. Her father, Thomas Williamson, like her father-in-law, John Hall, and her husband George, was a merchant and shipowner. Her uncle, Joseph Williamson, had been a surgeon on *HMS Marlborough*, part of the British fleet in the 'Glorious First of June' battle between the French and British fleets in one of the first naval actions of the French Revolutionary Wars. Her cousin, George Dutchman, like her husband, had been a prisoner of war in France and was officially released in 1814.

Grace lived a typically upper middle-class woman's life of social visiting, attending church on Sundays (devotion was a key part of her private and public life), evening soirées where she danced and sometimes sang, dining with friends, going to see 'fashions', watching closely for the mail, and enjoying the theatre and instruction in painting. In July 1814, she took tea with a 'Mrs C' and walked with her to the Sculcoates Refuge, established in Boteler Street, Hull, for the mentally disturbed poor.

George and Grace Hall began their life together in the Moira Buildings, 54 Prospect Street, Hull. Grace was fated to experience only ten years of marriage before dying in 1827, leaving George a widower with four children: George 9, Tom 8, John 2½ and Grace 17 months. A flattering, alluring portrait of Grace and her younger sister Mildred now hangs in the Terrace Station dining room at Hororata, Canterbury, New Zealand, where John Hall and his brothers emigrated in 1852. The women are dressed for a grand social occasion. They wear high-waisted, uncorseted, Regency gowns, their hair in fashionable ringlets, fans in their hands.

1.10 Grace and Mildred Williamson, sisters.

Destination	Master	Duration	Source
Malta via St Petersburg and London	Geo Hall, Master of *Lord Wellington*	Oct 1812–Jan 1814	Vol. 41, entry 283 (DSTR/39)
From Riga to Archangel to Riga	Geo Hall, Master of *Grace*	May–Nov 1819	Vol. 43, entry 41 (DSTR/41)
From St Petersburg	Geo Hall, Master of *Grace*	July–Nov 1820	Vol. 43, entry 141 (DSTR/41)
From Hamburg	Geo Hall, Master of *Grace*	Mar–May 1821	Vol. 43, entry 211 (DSTR/41)
From Limerick	Geo Hall, Master of *Grace*	July–Nov 1821	Vol. 43, entry 311 (DSTR/41)
From Sante Fé	Geo Hall, Master of *Grace*	Jan–Dec 1822	Vol. 43, entry 438 (DSTR/41)
London to Gibraltar	Geo Hall, Master of *Grace*	1824	Vol. 44, entry 236 (DSTR/42)
South America	Geo Hall, Master of *Grace*	1825	Vol. 44, entry 330 (DSTR/42)
St Petersburg	Geo Hall, Master of *Grace*	1825	Vol. 44, entry 331 (DSTR/42)

Table 1.1 Voyages of George Hall in ships *Lord Wellington* and *Grace* from 1812 to 1825. Source: Trinity House Muster Rolls, Hull History Centre.

Two years after his marriage, George acquired his ship, *Grace*, named after his wife, and built in Sculcoates, the family parish. It was launched on 8 February 1819, a square-sterned snow, the biggest type of square-rigged brig, of 157 tons.[41] George was the sole owner. He left Hull in May 1819, sailed to the Baltic port of Riga and then on a long trajectory round northern Russia to Archangel at the mouth of the River Dvina. Archangel's trade was in iron, hemp, linseed, grain, tallow from Siberia, tar and pitch. As early as 1804 the British were able to build ships using Russian fir for half of what a vessel the same size would cost in materials in England. George may have been bringing home fir timber from Archangel for the Hull shipbuilding industry.[42] By late 1819 he was the father of two boys, George Williamson Hall and Thomas Williamson Hall, their names commemorating the two conjoined families. In the next two years, he is recorded taking the *Grace* to St Petersburg, Hamburg and Limerick and then, as the table below shows, far further afield to North and South America.

Grace Hall is an intriguing and enigmatic presence in the family story. An early daguerreotype shows her in a dark Regency-style silk dress with a white muslin chemise for modesty worn beneath, and a low scooped neckline with a brooch at her bosom. She clasps a white wrap around her shoulders. This more informal portrait is likely to have been made by George to have with him at sea. It shows an enlarged pupil in her left eye which may have been the result of pressure from a tumour, possibly symptomatic of tuberculosis.

1.11 Grace Hall (1787–1827), wife of George and mother to George, Thomas, John and Grace.

Grace left a second journal fragment written four months before her death at 40 where she alludes to bleeding and coughing. She clearly saw herself as the plaything of an all-powerful God and/or the Devil. She was depressed. Mildred nursed her and was relieved by local women to shop and go visiting. There is no mention in the journal of her baby daughter and youngest child, Grace, born the previous year, whom Mildred cared for from the age of 10 months. There is no mention of her husband George, or her other children, George, Thomas and John. Her daughter Ann, Thomas's twin, had died just eight months before. Grace struggled with her difficulties, finding solace in her faith in God:

> 1 February 1827: My heart is very hard and I am full of evil passions, have much to lament, but can do nothing without divine help. Oh what a mercy there is such Saviour to apply to; may I ever place all my trust and confidence in him and that that *he is indeed precious to me*. [43]

In this year of Grace's death, George Hall is recorded in Lloyd's Register of Ships as master and owner of the ship *Grace*, sailing from London to British-owned Gibraltar, then to Rio de Janeiro, Brazil. The South American round trip would have taken at least six months and would have most likely begun in the spring or summer months following the journal entry above. The *Hull Packet*'s Shipping Intelligence column of August 1827 records George Hall in *Grace*, arriving from Liverpool at Bahia on the Eastern Atlantic coast of Brazil, bound for Rio de Janeiro. His wife's anger may well have been the anger of a dying mother of four knowing her husband had planned such a voyage. She died on 12 June that year in midsummer. It is notable that the *Grace* is recorded in the year December 1825 to December 1826, preceding Grace's death, in Buenos Aires, Argentina, commanded by a John Wilkinson. [44] George may have been a solicitous husband when Grace fell ill, by delegating command of his ship to another, but it seems likely he was absent at her death or soon after. At 45, he then gave up long-haul voyages, 'more on account of my family than for being tired of the sea'.

New markets in North America

One of the items George Hall gave Hull Trinity House in order that he 'be remembered' was the mantle of a native chief of the Chinook tribe 'of the vicinity of Columbia in North America' and a 'pipe of the same tribe curiously carved in black slate'.[45] The Chinook Indians were traders of the lower Columbia River, crossing its broad expanse in the warmer months in canoes, trading with each other, and sometimes making war. The mantle and pipe are evidence that George, like other mariners from Hull recorded in Nootka Sound at the time, was probably making an exploratory trip to the newly opened Columbia region. Captain James Cook, on his last voyage, had revealed the vast quantities of sea-otter fur to be found along the north-west coast of North America, and the high prices paid for it in China. By 1792, 21 different countries were trading in this commodity.

Venturing into unknown territory was beset with dangers. One of the stories circulating in Hull at the time was of the capture by a Chinook chief of a young Hull man, John Rodgers Jewitt, who had joined an American ship, the *Boston*, when it had been fitted out in Hull for a return voyage to the North American coast. Jewett was taken prisoner in Nootka Sound and the rest of the ship's crew were massacred. He was eventually rescued in June 1806 when a letter was smuggled out of the camp where he was captive, to visiting traders.[46]

There is no record in his own hand of how George Hall came to own the mantle of a Chinook chief, but the carvings on the slate pipe seem to reflect a friendly exchange with this pipe-smoking ship's captain, perhaps George himself.

1.12 (a) The mantle of a Chinook chieftain and (b) a black slate pipe given to Hull Trinity House by George Hall. The pipe reflects contact, showing carving of a sailor, a ship's wheel, a floral motif, a dog and perhaps a mirror.

At the mouth of the recently discovered Columbia River was the location of a centre of trade established in 1811 by the great German-born fur merchant, John Jacob Astor, America's first multimillionaire. In exchange for knives and beads, gunpowder, hatchets, cloth, snuff and rum, the Indians disposed of their pelts of mink, beaver and otter.[47] George may well have been exploring the prospects of supplying goods from Yorkshire's manufacturing industries to Astor's trading posts on the Columbia River.

On one exciting winter's day in Hull, I found evidence on a Trinity House muster roll that recorded George Hall returning to Hull from Santa Fé (spelt Sante Fé) in New Mexico on the *Grace*, in November 1822, on a voyage which began on 4 January. He was possibly transporting British goods to North America following the opening of the prairies in 1821. The Santa Fé trail, connecting

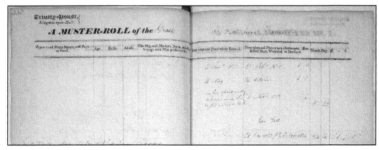

1.13 Muster roll showing 'Grace from Sante Fé'.

Franklin, Missouri, with Santa Fé, New Mexico, was the principal highway for goods coming from Missouri, Kansas and Oklahoma in the American West to New Mexico, the Mexican Gulf and thus to Europe. George could have left his ship in the Gulf of Mexico and gone by covered wagon along the trail to Santa Fé, and on return, retrieved his ship, sailed around the treacherous Cape Horn and up the west coast of North America to the Columbia River which debouched into the sea at Vancouver. According to the writer Washington Irving, Astor's early exploration parties to establish trading posts on the Columbia River in 1812 had found it was navigable for vessels of 300 tons, nearly twice the tonnage of the *Grace*, and traders had sailed at least 180 miles into the interior. The American painter, explorer and ethnographer, George Caitlin (1796–1872), famous for his portraits of the various Indian tribes who he spent time living among, claimed that 'the scalping knives used in the Indian country to the Rockies and the Pacific, bore the Sheffield mark'.[48] Caitlin's travels in North America began eight years after George Hall's but his remark shows that South Yorkshire traders had already made contact there.

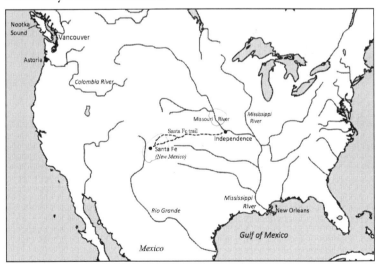

1.14 **Map of North America showing the Santa Fé trail, Nootka Sound, Astoria and the Columbia River.**

Opportunities in South America

Georges Hall's voyage to Rio de Janeiro in 1827 in the year of his wife's death, came at a time when Britain was making inroads into the markets of the newly independent states of Brazil and Argentina, especially for cotton textiles. Brazil, then, was the largest black nation outside Africa, its plantations run on slave labour, clothed mainly in cotton garments. Though Hull was proud of its anti-slavery history, spearheaded by William Wilberforce, there was hypocrisy surrounding Britain's attitude to slavery. During the eighteenth century, Britain was one of the main carriers of African slaves across the Atlantic. George's older brother John had died in the tropics in Jamaica, probably while transporting African slaves or the fruit of slave labour – sugar – from Britain's colonies to Europe. By 1845, the botanist, Berthold Seeman, showed just how much progress had been made by British merchants in Rio. The richest street, the Rua d'Alfandez, he said, was 'chiefly occupied by the agents of Manchester, Birmingham, Sheffield and Leeds' and the 'staid English merchants' were 'as well known as the heads of Government'.[48]

It is possible that George and Grace had fashionably named their first-born son George after a succession of German kings who had transformed Britain from a comparative backwater to a thriving global power. It is not surprising that George Hall then chose the free port of Hamburg, accessible by sea from Hull within 24 hours in fine weather, as the place to educate his two oldest sons and later their sister.

Notes and references

1. George Hall, *Autobiography of a Little Sailor Boy*, first published by John Mozley Stark in c. 1839. A second edition of the *Autobiography* was published in Christchurch, New Zealand, in 1907. It was later also included with 'Some Recollections of My School Days', written by his son, Sir John Hall, in the last year of his life and published as *Stories of Two Generations* in Christchurch in 1998 by Dryden Press, Terrace Station, Hororata. The quotation appears on p. 22 of this edition.

2. According to a note in the Hull Register of Apprenticeships, 26 February 1759 and cited in a letter from Jeremy Hall to G. Oxley, Archivist, Guildhall, 7 January 1995. An independent investigator, Mr W. W. Reader, commissioned by Sir John Hall to do some genealogical research, discovered that George Hall's father had been a Master Mariner and Younger Brother of Hull Trinity House and had served his apprenticeship with William Hill, Master and Mariner.

3. John Hall, father of George Hall, was buried at the original St Peter's, Drypool, Hull, where his tombstone lay. This church preceded one built in 1822 and bombed in 1941. Only a garden remains today. The tower of St Peter's had been a landmark for shipping in the Humber during the age of sail.

There is another Hall family in Hull descended from a William Hall (1703–1784) who was also a master mariner. Their story is told in a privately published book called *The Story of the Hallmark*, but it seems the two Hall families were not related. *The Story of the Hallmark* includes a genealogy which unfortunately mixes up the two families and has George Hall's line badly confused. There seems to be no connection apparent between the two families since our George Hall's grandfather was a cabinet maker called Richard Hall (1704–?) who was the son of Joseph Hall (1658–1713) a clergyman and Rector of Nettleton.

4. A. Storey, *Trinity House of Kingston upon Hull*, vol. 2, p. 156. George Hall presented to Hull Trinity House on 29 November 1859 a silver tankard belonging to 'Geo Dutchman', who he said was 'my Grandfather' (maternal side) and a partner of a Mr Robinson, a descendant of an earlier Warden of the Saint John the Baptist Guild of Merchant Tailors.

5. Elena Lazzarini, 'The Trade of Luxury Goods in Livorno and Florence in the Eighteenth Century', in C. M. Sicca and A. Yarrington (eds), *Lustrous Trade: Material Culture and the History of Sculpture in England and Italy, c.1700–c.1860*, Continuum, 2001, ch. 3.

6. George Hall, 1839 alamanac, TSA.

7. ibid.

8. George Hall, *Autobiography*, 3rd edn, 1998, p. 12.

9. ibid., p. 11.

10. ibid., pp. 14–15. George misspells HMS *Courageux*.

11. ibid., p. 20.

12. ibid., pp. 19–20.

13. R. I. & S. Wilberforce, *The Life of William Wilberforce*, vol. 1, p. 8.

14. A. Storey, 'Agreement of Younger Brethren to Serve on the Armed Yacht', Appendix III, Trinity House of Kingston upon Hull, vol. 2, p. 176.

15. ibid., pp. 49–50.

16. ibid., pp. 51–2.

17. Admiralty papers for *Enterprize*, IMG_4878.

18. Lloyd's List facsimile copies 1804, National Maritime Museum, Greenwich. The ship, at least on capture, was taken to Rotterdam.

19. George Hall, *Journal of My Two Escapes from French Prisons during the War with Napoleon*, 2nd edn, Truslove & Hanson Limited, London, 1860. I quote always from this edition.

20. Roger Boutet de Monvel, *Eminent English Men and Women in Paris*, trans. G. Henning, London: David Nutt, 1912, p. 22.

21. ibid., p. 44.

22. ibid., p. 55.

23. ibid., p. 23.

24. Antony Brett-James (ed.), *Escape from the French: Captain Hewson's Narrative 1803–1809*, London: Hodder & Stoughton 1981, p. 61.

25. George Hall, *Journal*, 2nd edn, p. 1.

26. ibid., p. 9.

27. ibid., pp. 62–3.

28. ibid., p. 91.

29. ibid., p. 85.

30. ibid., pp. 154–5.

31. ibid., pp. 156–8.

32. Francis Abell, *Prisoners of War in Britain 1756 to 1815*, Ulan Press, 2012, pp. 34–42.

33. R. Thorne, ed., biography of John Staniforth from *The History of Parliament, The House of Commons, 1790–1820*, Boydell and Brewer, 2006.

34. ADM 12/147, Digest of Admiralty and Secretariat Papers – 72-104, 1811.

35. Edward Torris to George Hall, 19 January 1811 (translated from the French). Insert at the back of George Hall's Journal, 2nd edn, 1860.

36. According to historian Peter Clark, George Hall was prisoner number 836 in the Verdun Register of British POWs held in France and he also appears in a list of Merchant Sea Masters who were prisoners of war held at Verdun on 4 September 1809, published in *The Times* of London on 23 October 1809 (p. 4, col. a).

37. Warrant issued to George Hall as a Younger Brother of Hull Trinity House, 18 July 1812 to show he had passed the necessary navigational tests in North Sea or Baltic pilotage, TSA. 42.

38. George Drower, *Heligoland: The True Story of the German Bight and the Island that Britain Forgot*, London: The History Press, 2002.

39. Muster roll of the Lord Wellington, vol.41, entry 283, DSTR/39, Hull History Centre: 'Malta via St Petersburg and London'.

40. Richard Woodman, *Britannia's Realm, A History of the British Merchant Navy*, vol. 2, London: The History Press, 2009, pp. 193–4.

41. CDPC/1/2/13, document, Hull Shipping Register, Hull History Centre.

42. J. Jepson Oddy, *European Commerce, Showing New and Secure Channels of Trade with the Continent of Europe: Detailing the Produce, Manufactures, and Commerce, of Russia, Prussia, Sweden, Denmark and Germany* ... (1804), pp. 93–4.

43. Fragment of the 1827 Journal of Grace Hall, written four months before her death, TSA.

44. CDSTR/4, Hull Trinity House Muster Rolls, vol. XLV, Book 45, Hull History Centre.

45. A. Storey, *Trinity House of Kingston upon Hull*, vol. 2, p. 182: extract from the 'vote' and 'order' books relating to articles in the House, entry 10 December 1853.

46. Robb Robinson, 'John Jewitt: An Indian slave in the Nootka Sound', in *Far Horizons, From Hull to the Ends of the Earth*, Hull: Maritime Historical Studies Centre, University of Hull, second edition, 2014, PFH Productions, p. 103.

47. Van Wyck Brooks, *The World of Washington Irving*, E.P. Dutton & Co. Inc., 1944, p. 290.

48. ibid., p. 290.

49. Bertold Seemann, *Narrative of the Voyage of HMS Herald During the Years 1845-51 Under the Command of Captain Henry Kellett, R.N., C.B., Being a Circumnavigation of the Globe and Three Cruizes to the Arctic Regions in Search of Sir John Franklin*, London: Reeve & Co., 1853, vol.1. pp. 14–16.

2

AUNT MILDRED AND THE DISRUPTIVE DOUBLE BIND

'You none of you see it in so strong a light as I do. This has been a growing evil for years past & be assured nothing is more sure than that Children were never so mislead as you all have been and without any good to yourselves, as you will find in the end. I do believe your Aunt is at present writing your sister in the way you wish but John the evil is done; your Sister is different to me at present.'[1]

In 1828, the year after Grace Hall died, George was made Warden of Hull Trinity House, a role he shared with another, serving for alternating three-month periods in the year. As an Elder Brother of the guild, he held a position that was central to the life of the port. The House operated as a significant arbiter and manager of the city's maritime affairs and there had been links to the royal household since Henry VIII first granted the House a royal charter. George Hall was a Younger Brethren and Steward during the years 1812–1813, after his return from captivity in France; he became an Assistant in 1820, effectively a member of the governing board; he was promoted to Elder Brother in May 1827, the month before his wife's death, and acted as Warden on five occasions – 1828–29, 1835–36, 1841–42,

1847–48 and 1852–53. In his personal life, as the quote above shows, he struggled with a near insoluble problem concerning his sister-in-law, Mildred, over how much influence she exerted on his four bereaved children, George, Thomas, John and Grace.

Mildred had cared for baby Grace, as she explained to John, 'from the age of 10 months from her poor Mother's Death'. She had 'devoted everything and many comforts in doing' until

2.1 John Hall (right), aged 4, unbreeched, and Grace, 2, with pet dog.

she married in 1832 when, 'she [Grace, then 6] was taken from her best friend'.[2] Mildred's husband, William Bean Fowler, reportedly a quiet and pleasant man, was a magistrate and shipowner from the nearby port town of Scarborough. Mildred and William, childless, continued their interest in George's family. It is difficult to know exactly how much Mildred's input was, but it was clearly substantial; enough for her to say to John when he was 28: 'After having brought you all up from infancy [...] with my kind, affectionate Husband, I am supported [in his] affectionate kindheartedness to his dear Sister's children.'[3] From allusions to other carers in the family letters, whether female relatives, nurses or housekeepers, it is clear she was not the only feminine presence in their lives, but Mildred saw her input as paramount. When the brothers announced their emigration plans to her she claimed that 'the trial of [...] having to part with you all has nearly got my life'.[4]

His sister-in-law's influence was excessively threatening to their father. Many of his letters to his children are concerned with explaining this unusual relationship. Today the conflict between their father and surrogate mother would be recognised as a clear case of 'parental alienation', thought to be exceptionally harmful to children by the family court advisory and support services dealing with divorce, except in this case the alienation of George from his children was directed by an aunt not a divorced wife. It was a difficult double bind for the children, for both father and aunt had given them love and care but to indulge one was to risk incurring the other's insecurities and wrath.

It is possible that Mildred's antagonism to George might have stemmed from feelings of rejection; perhaps she expected to replace her deceased sister as George's wife as well as carer of his children. From his correspondence and almanacs, he appeared to have two addresses in Brook Street. Possibly he was based in one, while the other was where Aunt Mildred and the children lived after their mother's death, until she married William Fowler five years later.

Mildred's willingness to adopt the role of surrogate parent was fortunate for seafaring George, but the bitter disappointment that his wife had willed her estate to her children through a trust administered by Mildred rather than through him led him to suppose that his wife and her advisors did not have confidence in him to exercise the legacy in their favour. This particularly soured his relationship with Mildred. He was determined to retain his primary rights over his children whom he loved dearly ('I always loved Children, my father before me')[5] and to ensure that they in return had the appropriate dutiful approach to him as their father. This was sometimes difficult to achieve in the circumstances. He devised a method of educating his children, once they were old enough to leave home, which distanced them from Mildred, allowing him a degree of freedom in his personal life and direct contact with them away from his bête noir.

The purpose of schooling abroad was not simply expedient in these ways. From his imprisonment in France and his maritime career in the Baltic and Mediterranean, George knew how valuable foreign languages were likely to be to his children's education and their chances in life. John began school in Hull and it is probable that his older brothers George and Thomas did so too, before attending a German school at Klein Flottbeck, near Hamburg[6] aged 13 and 12. In

2.2 George W. Hall (right) and Thomas W. Hall, aged *c*.11 and 10, as schoolboys.

1834, George was moved to a school in Bordeaux, while Thomas was at school in Saintes, near the mouth of the Charente River. The town was a base for transporting locally produced cognac from warehouses to ships at the mouth of the river and thence to destinations like London or St Petersburg. Both towns were located on George Hall's wine-trading routes. John went to school in St Gall, Switzerland, to learn German, before being moved to a school in Paris.

George's efforts to give his children a better education than he had himself is touching and admirable. In doing so, he did not neglect his youngest, Grace. She first went to Mrs Moon's in Hessle, a village on the north bank of the Humber estuary, then at the age of 13 to Miss Stockdale's in Albion Street, Hull, considered to be one of the best schools in the town, according to her father. From there she went on to a finishing school in Hamburg. She and John corresponded sometimes in German while at school.

The children were brought up to be good Anglicans, as George was himself, but to have tolerance for other religions, whereas Aunt

Mildred detested Catholics, something that caused division when at 14 Grace was sent to her Hamburg school, where Catholics were present. George was clear in his reasons: 'I wish to break her off from her Aunt who will (if left to her) spoil her, time she is with me she is a good Girl but the moment your Aunt comes in the way, unpleasantness is sure to arise.'[7] Grace's previous Albion Street school had also caused upset with Aunt Mildred who had not been informed of the choice beforehand. George received a visit from an irate Mildred accompanied by her husband, but George was prepared and from this time onward appears to have no compunction in cutting ties with Mildred as far as he could:

> Sufficient was said by me to convince them that any further interference in my family on their part would not be permitted by me; our interview was not long, and on parting it was in a way that we are not likely to be again reconciled for a long time. I have not spoken to her since; your Uncle and I speak when we meet; he is a good man and seeks for peace but I am fearful he will not find your Brothers go to see them, also Grace on a Saturday afternoon; but on a Sunday my Children all remain with me; all this has given me much pain and grief of mind, but I could not live in the way I was doing any longer; and I say to you as a Father, who has been at much expense and great care of mind in bringing you all up, without the aid of your dear departed mother, who alone would have shared my anxieties with you. I wish you to live in love and friendship with your Aunt and Uncle, but never to let your mind be biased from what your father considers to be your duty.[8]

The children, particularly the younger John and Grace, were pressured on both sides by their tortured father and his enduring entanglement with their aunt who still corresponded with them, though once they were at schools abroad she was prevented from seeing them except in their school holidays. John and Grace proved able to cope with the conflict between their father and Mildred. It no doubt taught them invaluable skills in compromise and mediation. John, at 15, handled the emotional tug-of-war with equanimity. In one letter from his school in Paris, he draws his father's attention away from the conflict to his own difficulties in the classroom, but also reminds him of his continued affection for Aunt Mildred who he hoped would visit the Paris Exhibition in 1839: 'it grieves me much when I think how much it would have pleased Aunt to see Paris' and 'I trust I may hear something tending towards a reconciliation'.[9]

The relationship did not improve and was becoming extremely divisive as George struggled to retain influence over his children. 'If I find that when you pay the respect due to your Uncle as a friend and to your Aunt as a near relative, that if either the one or the other should speak a disrespectful word of your father & you with indifference pop it over you will *John* incur my sworn displeasure, now take this warning.'[10] He thought John was old enough to have learned the nature of what George regarded

2.3 Aunt Mildred (Fowler), religious fundamentalist, surrogate mother, and bête noir of George Hall, with her husband William.

as true friendship, what would unite and what would disunite 'the most sacred ties of nature' and he regarded Aunt Mildred as 'more dangerous to trespass on laws common to all'.[11]

Mildred's attempt to exert a dominating influence on the children in their developing years against his own beliefs and experience was anathema to George, particularly when expressed in a way that denigrated him. Aunt Mildred thought the children were influenced for the worse by George's advice and the friends he associated with, as her following message to John shows: '[Grace] is very affectionate which counterbalances in some measure the evil advise [*sic*] she has always had given her by those around her.'[12]

An example of the influence Mildred tried to exert can be seen in a letter she wrote to John a few days before Christmas on 16 December 1841, at the approach of his seventeenth birthday. It might appear today as a rather gruesome and sanctimonious attempt to warn him of sexual or other sinful temptations that might befall him and to remind him that his father (not pious enough) should have written him such a letter to guide his moral behaviour. She forwarded the 'beautiful letter' written by a 'pious Father to his Son on his Birthday' which requests that the contents 'sink deep' in the son's heart (he is also motherless), and reminds him he will more and more see 'the snares and temptations of this *wicked world*'. She adds, pointedly, 'I am aware you have only me to remind you of such things'. The enclosure from the anonymous father to his son reads:

> This will probably reach you on your Birthday. It is a day which should remind you of the importance of time, and the swift approach of eternity [...] Have you seen yourself a sinner, and gone to the blood of Christ for pardon? Forms and notions never yet saved a soul [...] it is no trifle whether you have real grace or not: it is everything

to ascertain this point, and to act upon it [...] It is full time my dear that you shew a decision of character.[13]

The children's bond with Mildred was close but her anxieties about her role – she remained childless herself – and the tensions it caused, went with her to her grave. On her tombstone in Scarborough are the words: 'Father I will that they also whom thou hast given me, be with me where I am that they may behold my glory – John 17 v. 24'. The Hall children responded with a commemorative window in St Mary's, Scarborough, dedicated 'To the Glory of God in memory of Mildred the wife of William Bean Fowler who died 26 July 1861 aged 69 by her nephews and niece'. This window was destroyed by German bombing in 1940.

Schooling and trade

Eleven surviving small Goldsmith almanacs or diaries belonging to George Hall and dating from 1829 to 1839 show he was an energetic merchant during the decade after his wife's death when his two older boys were at school abroad and then beginning their apprenticeships at sea. He travelled the traditional trading routes between Hull and the Mediterranean, Hull and Hamburg, Hull and the Baltic port of Riga, and also the cognac-producing department of the Charente River in France. When at home, he kept himself abreast of the latest Enlightenment ideas through visits to the Hull Literary and Philosophical Society to listen to talks on philosophy, literature and science, as mentioned in his 1834 almanac.

George Hall's business trips were organised outside his Trinity House duties and planned to achieve maximum contact with his sons at school:

9 May 1832, 'Arrived in Hambro'
10 May 1832, 'Saw my two sons'
11 May 1832, 'Had my two sons on board'

In 1835, when he took John to St Gall, Switzerland, a main centre for goods passing from Germany into Italy, they enjoyed some educational sightseeing on the way.

[My father] took me in a steamer from Hull to Rotterdam. [...] From there we went in river steamers up to Cologne, and so on up to Heidelburg, Mainz and Mannheim. From thence we had to proceed by land, and, as was customary in those days, my father joined with two other travellers in hiring a carriage to take us all the way to Basle. [...] From Basle we went to Aargau, calling at [...] the old birthplace of the Hapsburg dynasty. We paid a prolonged visit to the old Castle [...] From thence we went to Zurich, and by diligence [coach] to St Gall. Here I was placed in a large school kept by Mr Tobler [...] I was the only English boy. Except for one master who knew a few words of English, nobody could speak it. The consequence was, in a fortnight, I could speak German pretty well.[14]

2.4 The schoolboy, John. 'At ten years of age my father took me to the Continent.'

In 1834, George Hall records a voyage made in April

from London to Charente, then to Cognac. It accords absolutely with the signed record in the Hull Muster Rolls of such a trip in his vessel *Grace* taken between 1 April and 20 June with a crew of eight men and a servant. On 5 June 1834, his almanac shows that he 'Left Charent for Isle of Aix', the small island at the mouth of the Charente River. He visited his son Thomas at school in Saintes and took him on the initial stage of his homeward journey, dispatching him back with the pilot from the Isle of Aix. By 11 June, George had 'brought up under Bell Isle in Pallis Roads'. Belle-Ile was the French island off the coast of Brittany, Le Palais its chief town and Palais Roads the anchorage. George's erratic and phonetic spelling reflects a time when spelling had not been standardised and Samuel Johnson's dictionary was comparatively new. By 27 June he had 'arrived in London' and by 19 August was on his way to Memel in East Prussia before sailing back to Hull via the Sound or strait which now forms the Danish-Swedish border.

The Trinity House Muster Rolls, from which I was able to match George Hall's almanac entries with voyages made, were loaned to the Hull History Centre in 2012. An Act for the Relief of Disabled Seamen, passed in 1747, made it mandatory for ships' masters to take six pence from each crew member at the end of a voyage after Parliament had become concerned at the terrible toll on seamen's lives in the dangerous waters around the coasts of Britain and beyond. The money was then given to collectors provided by Trinity House at the point of arrival and discharge before the ship's muster roll was filed. It was an exhilarating day for me when I found George and his ship *Grace* in these ancient records, recorded on parchment in copper-plate script. All the entries in Table 2.1 overleaf were signed by 'Geo Hall', their respective dues paid and recorded.

From	Master	Duration	Source document
Malta	John Irwin. TH dues signed by Geo Hall	10 April 1827–20 Feb 1829	CDSTR/44. Book 46
Cadiz, Spain	Geo Hall	2 Sept 1831–6 Dec 1831 AND 7 Nov 1831–6 December 1831	Source CDSTR/45 Book 47
Riga	Geo Hall	26 July 1830–14 Sept 1830	CDSTR/45, Book 47
Leghorn, Italy	Geo Hall	24 Feb 1831–24 June 1831	CDSTR/45, Book 47
Leith to Hambro and Hull	Geo Hall	27 April 1832–15 Aug 1832	CDSTR/45. Book 47
Charente, France	Geo Hall	3 June 1833–11 Sept 1833 AND 16 Sept 1833–6 Nov 1833	CDSTR/47, Book 49
Charente, France	Geo Hall	1 April 1834–20 June 1834	CDSTR/47, Book 49
Memel to Oporto Portugal	Thomas B. Smith. Dues signed by Geo Hall	6 Aug 1834–20 Dec 1834	Bailiff C to 20 June 1834

Table 2.1 Voyages of the *Grace* 1827–1834, all but two commanded by George Hall. Source: Trinity House Muster Rolls, Hull History Centre.

While George was doing business on the Continent, travelling by steamer and coach, his ship *Grace* might also be independently carrying goods commanded by another. For example, in April 1835 the Hull Muster Rolls record it sailing between Hull and the Charente while George, as his almanac records, was in Dresden seeing a Mr Brooks, or at 'Wefssehot' visiting 'Mr Wefsellhach', the British Consul, or staying at the 'L'Hotel Dest, Petersburg unter der Lynden, Berlin,' where he saw 'Kaenig von Prueder'. Likewise, when he records 'arrived at Memel' on 19 August in his almanac, Thomas B. Smith appears to be sailing to Oporto in Portugal (Table 2.1). His letters to his children show he also used friends, such as Captain Bouch of the *Gazelle*, who appears often in the Hull Muster Rolls, to carry mail to his sons at school or post letters to them from a French port.

Grace W. Hall in Hamburg

Grace was 15 when George took her to Hamburg to a finishing school. Nicknamed 'Puggy' by her brothers, she was not a great beauty and her father and brothers were likely to have been concerned about her prospects of marriage, the single most reliable avenue to a secure future for a woman in the nineteenth century. John reported to young George in the summer of 1842 that Grace 'is much improved in looks' – she was 16 – and 'I think father intends [...] to take her to see the Continent'.[15] Perhaps George Hall and Grace, on this holiday together from Hamburg, took a steamer up the Elbe River to Dresden where Richard Wagner was then director of the city's opera house. The holiday may have had an ulterior motive to discuss Grace's future, because in the September following she disabused her father of any intention he might have that she would settle down and look after him as an unmarried daughter, and had returned by steamer to school

2.5 Grace Williamson Hall as a young woman. '[…] my heart sinks often when I think of my own prospects […]'

in Hamburg. He wrote to John in September 1843 to say that Grace 'ought to study my comfort' and 'my love has cooled down in a way to her she little thinks […] all I can say is that never man was so deceived in hopes he had long flattered himself with'. He asked John to keep corresponding with her because 'tho her temper may lead her a little wrong at times, yet she has an affectionate heart'. George Hall, from this time on, planned to remarry for, 'being alone is so distressing'.[16]

In the time between leaving her finishing school (probably 1844) and before her marriage in 1862, Grace seems to have re-established a relationship with her father, as she moved between the family home in Brook Street, Hull, to his summer cottage in Elloughton, to her married brothers George and Thomas in Hull and to Aunt Mildred and Uncle William in Scarborough.

Their mother's legacy and its depressing consequences

In his moments of blackest despair over the family conflict with his children and Aunt Mildred, George saw himself as a victim:

At her [his wife, Grace Hall's] death I stood in the situation of a deserted husband with deserted children. Your mother will'd the direction of her children and her property in a way that will not bear reflection, and what has been the issue? Time will tell it, and what is past is past would be well if it could be forgot but that cannot be. While the same object [Mildred] remains alluring you all in the way she has ever done.[17]

Perhaps his wife's advisors felt that Mildred might have to take on the greatest burden of responsibility in bringing up George's children if their father continued to make a living at sea and whose life was therefore precarious. Or perhaps the arrangements Grace agreed for her estate, so shocking to George, were simply to ensure her inheritance remained within the control of her own family, the Williamsons, not uncommon in maritime ports like Hull. She may have had other reasons to exclude her husband from the inheritance, but these must remain speculative.

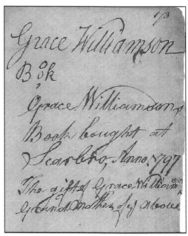

2.6 Inscription page of *The Great Importance of a Religious Life Considered* by Dr John Disney (LLB Cambridge), given to Grace Williamson, aged 10, by her maternal grandmother.

She and George had enjoyed ten years of marriage before her health deteriorated at the age of 40.

While George saw himself as a deserted husband at her death, I initially understood this to be the desertion death brought, not that Grace had literally deserted him as wife and mother, though he clearly considered the terms of her legacy were a desertion and betrayal. If we revisit the 1827 diary fragment she left behind, bearing in mind George's description of his state at her death, this dying woman clearly saw herself as the plaything of an all-powerful God and/or the Devil:

My heart is very hard and I am full of evil passions, have
much to lament, but can do nothing without divine help.
Oh what a mercy there is such a Saviour to apply to; may I
ever place all my trust and confidence in him and find that
he is indeed precious to me.[18]

Another reading of the desertion mentioned by George is
that possibly Grace, who even as a child had been schooled in a
fundamental type of Christianity, was deserting her husband and
family for religion in her increasingly tortured last days. Hull at
the time was a hotbed of a new evangelical Protestantism called
Unitarianism. It supported the abolition of slavery and freedom
for Jews and Catholics to practise their own religions. It favoured
education for the poor and was instrumental in setting up charitable
trusts for the poor and old. The evangelical creed posed difficulties
for its disciples who had to spread the gospel, be good (difficult to
achieve when they were stained by original sin), repent their sins
and honour the commandments of the Old Testament. Grace was
probably an evangelical Christian before her marriage to George Hall
in 1817. An entry in her journal of 1 June 1814 suggests she was,
since she attended church to hear 'Mr Dikes' or Revd Thomas Dykes,
a Unitarian preacher and friend of William Wilberforce, who built the
church of St John the Evangelist in Hull in 1791. If this was so, her
later struggles to assimilate the evangelical strict code of obedience
to God, which included philanthropy and her wifely duties, while
reconciling herself to the notion that God had willed her premature
destruction, must have been a personal torment.

On 5 February 1827, Grace records in her journal, four months
before her death, that Mrs Chatterton sat with her and they read
the life of the Revd John Newton, Bishop of Lincoln (1725–1807)
who, like George Hall, had begun his working life at sea as a cabin

boy, and had gone through various incarnations as merchant seaman, journalist and college tutor, before becoming an evangelical preacher and the founder of various missionary societies. He was also the composer of the hymn, 'Amazing Grace'. The sinful part of his life related to an episode as a slave trader and slave shipmaster. He admitted to being indifferent to the Africans he traded, submitting them to the lash and to the thumbscrew to subdue them. After his conversion, he influenced the young William Wilberforce, advising him not to become a preacher but to remain in parliament and fight for the abolition of slavery. His pamphlet, 'Thoughts About the African Slave Trade', had a direct impact on Wilberforce. To Grace Hall, Revd Newton's life of sin and repentance showed the 'forebearance of the Almighty to the most reprobate sinner and that nothing is too hard for him to perform. It also shows his exceeding great love and mercy in bringing such to repentance.' Following her immersion in Newton's vivid life, Mr Chatterton read to Grace from Psalm 40, the Psalm of David, to the Chief Musician:

> Withhold not thou tender mercies from me, O Lord, let thy loving kindness and thy truth continually preserve me. For innumerable evils have encompassed me about; mine inequities have taken hold upon me, so that I am unable to look up [...] therefore my heart faileth me [...] Let them be ashamed and confounded together that seek after my soul to destroy it; let them be driven backward and put to shame that wish me evil.

This is very heavy reading for a dying woman, and again there is no mention anywhere in this journal of her husband or her children. It ends on 22 February 1827 and Grace died in June. In August George is recorded in shipping records in Bahia, Brazil.

The reckoning

The final settlement of Grace Hall's estate came about when Grace, her youngest child, reached the age of consent. George called his sons to a meeting in London, but they had already discussed the fraught implications among themselves in advance. Thomas, it seems, had already taken his share of the legacy with the blessing of Mildred and her husband, William Fowler, probably to purchase his ship *Dauntless*. It fell upon George Williamson Hall, as the oldest son and recently returned from a voyage to Buenos Aires in September 1847, to complete the resolution of the family trusts. He met with the executors of his mother's will – Aunt Mildred and Uncle William Fowler, and their legal representative, William Dryden. Also present was his father's legal representative, a Mr Bunny. Prior to the meeting, George senior had made a proposal to Mr Bunny, based on a charge of ill-treatment by Grace's family, that property given by him to his wife in her marriage settlement be retrieved by him so that he might then disperse the capital gained from it. From comments his father had made in the past, his son George thought this would be to other relatives, not to his children. Their father's explanation about his proposal to John on 20 January 1848 was that 'I wish'd to disunite you all from the illiberal act of your mother & my wife. I gave it [property] unasked for, to your mother, for our mutual protection for life, and that impression will never be obliterated from my mind.' His proposal was rejected by George W. as 'a complete condemnation of mother's will'. John agreed. He told his older brother in a letter written on 26 January 1848 that he could not be party to any proceeding which would discredit his dead mother's memory. He felt that children who could consent to discredit their mother's reputation would not be likely to have much respect and affection for either parent. He valued a peaceful settlement with his father over the amount of property in question.[19] George and

John agreed that they 'must offer by letter' to their father 'conjointly on receiving the property', a proposal that 'if father thinks he has not been fairly done by, to secure to him the entire income [of the property] for life' and 'in case he declines that' to refer the matter to a third party irrespective of their own lawyers, and to abide by his decision if 'he thinks we might or ought to have acted otherwise'. This generous offer by two of his sons, was withdrawn after George met with his father to discuss the matter. George senior became enraged. George described the event to John in a letter:

> This morning Father commenced about it & my dear John such a violent scene ensued as completely upset me. He reproached me with everything, cant, ingratitude, baseness, selfishness, and told me if I had had my swing I should have turned him out of his own house and from his own table. Ordered me and my things out of his house – in short my dear John he cut me to the heart [...] On me he has vented his full violence [...] The proposal as it formerly stood, originated not from Mr Bunny but from him.[20]

Wounded, George wrote to John that 'I have loved him as my Father and do still, tho' perhaps he has never believed it [...] I feel but little tie to my native land, only that our dear Grace must still and ever be an object of solicitude.'[21]

Presumably, Grace, too, had followed her brothers' example, because on 24 February 1848 she reported to John that she had been told to leave the family home and go to her aunt:

> I am at Tom's for the present [...] There was no unpleasantness, but on Monday after going home from

meeting Aunt at the train Papa called me into his room and enquired if Aunt had arrived, he then said he had brought me up from infancy but had made up his mind he would live with me no longer, that he had waited until Aunt came and I was to now do as I liked. You may suppose I did not wait to answer but was only too glad to get away: grievous as it is, it is not near so great a trouble to me, now the first blow has subsided.'[22]

John wrote to his father about Grace's forced departure and received a despairing reply: 'Your sister ought to have been my stay in life [...] I still love her, & you all and ever will.'[23]

Despite his passionate feelings about his wife's legacy and her apparent betrayal, George Hall was a charitable and generous man. He paid a pension to the sailor who transported him from captivity in France to England, and supported his uncles, William and Nathaniel, old sailors, who were 'for a long time pensioners of my father', according to John. He coached his children to make integrity their guiding principle in dealing with others.

John, like his siblings George and Grace, had also experienced a paternal rebuff three years before these turbulent events. It concerned his second older brother, Thomas, and revealed further family divisions. It had occurred after a period of prolonged activity by George Hall in 1845 to find John a suitable job. He and Mildred's husband, 'Uncle' William Fowler had worked hard to assist John, now 21, in finding a permanent position in the Post Office. Patronage was the path to success. William Fowler had used his influence with Sir Frederick Trench, MP for Scarborough, on behalf of John. His brother George had assisted in writing a letter of application and his father had approached Sir Walter James, a Hull Tory MP and friend of Gladstone. Despite all these efforts, John was passed over for the desired position, though Frederick Trench had applied to have John made permanent and said he bore the highest possible character for intelligence and good conduct.

John was lodging at Wapping in the heart of London's dockland at the time of this job-seeking, with an allowance of £6 a month from his father. He discovered by chance that Thomas had married. He wrote at once to tell his father whom he suspected was also in the dark about the event.

London, Sunday, 4 May 1845

> I have a very painful duty to perform in writing the present letter, insomuch as it conveys to you intelligence which will grieve you much, and of which I fear you have not yet had any intimation.

> Returning from church this morning I met Mr Young who informed me to my great surprise that Tom was married yesterday. Beyond informing you of this occurrence I think it will be better for me to treat only at present, of how it ought to influence my conduct.

> The matter appears to consist of two parts. —

> Firstly, Tom's entering into this connection against the injunctions of his father & without letting his family know one word of his intention — in reference to this part, I as in duty bound, ask for your instructions how I am to act; whether you wish me to renounce all communication with the family or whether you do not think such a step is called for.

The second part of the business is Tom's getting married within 500 yards of where I live, without thinking it worth his while to mention a word to me about it, & me having to hear of it thro' a second party. This is a personal insult to myself & such I must treat it. Tom may be able to give a satisfactory explanation of this extraordinary conduct, & if so, I shall be very happy to forget it; even if he cannot do that, but express his regret about the matter I will readily overlook it. […]

John received a sharp rebuke from his father:

Hull, 6 May 1845

It has not surprised me nor do I think it of such great moment to your self; so don't think that Tom is going to make any confessions to you, nor is it in your place to make such an alarming affair of the matter; as to what you are to do, think for yourself for, you are not going to commit me; but of this beware, not to fail in respect to your Brother, or he will soon show you your error. If you have been in the habit of visiting the Youngs and seeing what I anticipated and told you all when last in Town, you must have prepared your mind for the event & John, let me tell you, when you say that certain conditions must be completed by him or you will drop all connexions with him, I can but smile at your remark on a Senior Brother. If he has offended me it is not for you to make the breach wider, you have much to do yourself to govern your actions. In writing me you have done your duty, but what would Tom say if he knew the contents of your letter. In regard to not asking you it is a necessary conclusion that they wish'd it to be privat. When I have warned any of my children of what they ought, or ought not to do, if they act contrary, it does not affect me, and [I] shall wait in the present case all its events with composure.

By June, John had left his lodgings in Wapping and taken a trip into the country for his health. These snubs from Thomas, then his father, affected his feelings about Wapping and he no longer wanted to remain there.

An earlier conflict over his future had also been unsatisfactory. George Hall thought that his own 'friendly counsel' had been 'met [...] with a proud heart' by John. Perhaps Aunt Mildred had misinformed her nephew about his chances of receiving a fortune from his mother's legacy because as early as November 1843 George Hall had to explain the reality of his situation when John proposed being further financed by him to study for the Church. His father told John, '[your] expenses are more than I am justified in continuing unless I have some positive assurance that you'll refund such part as you [are] receiving from your father more than his other Children when you receive your fortune.'

John do you know what this great fortune is? I'll tell you. You will find it to be but little more than the enormous expense I have been already for you. [...] Many a father would have left his Children altogether. I have been a different man; tho not a fool by my rigid economy. I have accomplished my wishes independent of your mother or yr Aunt to whom you cling with so much affection. John it was your father who merited & you are indebted, for all that you have yet enjoyed. I am not going to enter into such a wild scheme for the sake of your passing a few more years to gain a poor lunatic's salary of £50 a year at the expense of the family who you have greatly overreached in expenses by hundreds. You mistake me very much.[24]

George felt John held him in the same light as Mildred did. He told John that however high in the world he had been led by his aunt to think his mother's family – the Williamsons – were, none could produce such an example of duty to children as their own father. All they had done was to break the happiness of his union by disparaging him to his children and the world.

Grace Hall's legacy and Aunt Mildred's influence had undoubtedly caused considerable disruption to family relations. With all the tension over John's future and the existing animosity between his father and aunt, and father, brother and sister, Thomas and Sarah probably felt that to have all present at their nuptials would be a disastrous mix.

The reference to his father's injunctions to Thomas not to enter into a connection with Sarah, and John's seemingly priggish approach to learning of his brother's wedding is significant. Perhaps the Williamson family thought Wapping was not an appropriate background for George's second son's wife. At 29, Sarah was three years older than Thomas. William Young, her father, previously a mariner, had 'swallowed the anchor', settled on shore, and established a respectable chandler's shop in Wapping High Street. In an early edition of *The Nautical Magazine*, which kept the shipping fraternity in the royal and merchant navies up-to-date with all maritime matters, Sarah's father is first on the list of recommended people to supply a new 'screw fid', an item which assisted in securing a topmast on a ship.

The fids may be seen at the office of the patentees, no 7, Hurst Street Liverpool, and at the following places, Mr

William Young, no 268 Wapping, near the Docks, London
[…][25]

Jean Garner, John Hall's biographer, describes Sarah as working class and found it remarkable that her parents had the inclination and resources to spend on her education. This classification seems misplaced as her father's occupation in the Wapping of the time could just as well point to prosperity as to poverty. A history of Wapping, written by Derek Morris and Ken Cozens, explains:

> Many of the merchants based in Wapping and St George in the East were deeply involved in these naval contracts. Whether it was ships, timber, biscuits, meat, bear, spirits, flags, gunpowder, slops or many other necessary supplies, Wapping merchants were bidding for and obtaining significant contracts that had an important impact on the area.[26]

Sarah's letters also demonstrate that she was as literate as her husband and his brothers. The school nearest to where she was born, St John of Wapping, is next to the church where she married, St John's. Since it is still customary for English school girls from Anglican schools to be offered the chance to marry in the church associated with their school, it is possible that this was her school. Furthermore, Wapping itself provided a colourful and lively education simply in the variety of those who lived there and passed through it. A doughty recorder of Wapping, the Reverend Harry Jones, Rector of St George-in-the-East where Sarah had been baptised, provided a wise account of the benefits of living in a cosmopolitan port. He wrote of the many languages spoken, the 'men in all colours of skin', the 'mixture of land and water, of homely trucks and foreign traders' the 'huge ocean-going ships' and 'that sense of space that characterises this part of London'.[27] Sarah had grown up in a teeming world peopled by those who supported a busy port, described by the Victorian journalist Henry Mayhew as 'decayed and bankrupt butchers, master bakers, publicans, grocers, old soldiers, old sailors, Polish refugees, broken-down gentlemen, discharged lawyer's clerks, suspended Government clerks, almsmen, pensioners, servants, thieves',[28] all, in short, who came for employment when denied it elsewhere. As a man about to take on his first command in the merchant marine, Thomas would have been attracted to someone whose father was a former mariner and now ran a business associated with shipping. It also showed good sense to marry a woman who was familiar with the excitements and challenges of a seafaring life and the long periods of absence these entailed.

George Hall marries for the second time

After the falling out with his daughter, the painful disruption with his eldest son over the legacy due to his children, and his exclusion from Thomas's wedding, George Hall resolved to find a wife before the coming winter, if only he could find 'a respectable and clever woman',[29] a family friend, Mrs Holmes, informed John. His father had admired Miss Mary Ann Packman in coming out of church 'some three or four years ago', she told him. Her letter is a telling description of the kind of matchmaking a family friend might be helpful with and also the kind of expectations a man of George's age (66) and accomplishments might have of a wife at that time: 'I said he could walk with me [...] and have another look at the Lady and if she did not please him there would be no harm done to any one as she had not the slightest suspicion of your Father's object.' George Hall was 'very much pleased with [Miss Packman] and made up his mind to propose to her [...]'.

George and Mary Ann were married in November 1848 in the elegant Georgian church of St James, Islington, London, 11 months after the fallout with his children over their mother's legacy. The register describes George's age as 'full' and describes him as a 'widower and gentleman'. Mary Ann declined to give her age (actually 47), but is described as the daughter of Harrison and Sybella Packman of Horndon-on-the-Hill, Essex. The couple retired to the family home at 17 Brook Street, Hull, and George redecorated his summer retreat, Rose Cottage in Elloughton, for his new wife. Mrs Holmes commented soothingly to John, presumably still estranged: 'he could not have made a better choice as she is every way equal in point of respectability and bears the character of being very sensible and a very sincere Christian, therefore I think there can be no doubt she will do her duty [...] to promote the interest & comfort of your Father and his family.'[30]

2.7 (a) George Hall *c.*1848. 'He was fully resolved to have a wife before the coming winter if he could only meet with a respectable clever woman.' (b) Mary Ann Packman, date unknown.

Family relations repaired

George Hall's rupture with Grace over her independence and her mother's legacy was temporary. Thomas and Sarah as well as Grace stayed at Rose Cottage in Elloughton the summer before his marriage to Mary Ann. Thomas was back from a voyage to Rio de Janeiro and at the cottage with Sarah and their baby, little Tom, 'brown from being out so much'. Their father had recovered his good spirits and was delighted to be requested, as Warden of Hull Trinity House, to retrieve the House's cutter, *Ariel*, from Cowes in the Isle of Wight, where it was being repaired, and have command of the yacht at the Hull regatta that summer.

2.8 The Trinity House yacht *Ariel* at the mouth of the River Hull inspecting the dolphin, a floating aid to ships entering or leaving the harbour when the wind and tide were unfavourable. One of its duties was to wait at the mouth of the Humber, at the request of the Admiralty, in readiness should the squadron escorting Queen Victoria along the coast to Scotland require the services of the Trinity House brethren.

George had seen his father after their fracas and he had not been 'unkind', but had only discussed 'indifferent subjects'. John, meanwhile, had recovered his composure, found a job as a private secretary to the head of the Post Office and, by the early 1850s, was utilising his brothers' experience and knowledge to research the subject of emigration, a notion full of possibilities for all three brothers, including separation from their father and aunt.

Notes and references

1. GH to JH, 4 April 1842.
2. MF to JH, 18 December 1852.
3. ibid.
4. MF to JH, 11 February 1853.
5. GH to JH, 6 June 1856.
6. GWH to JH, 4 January 1884. ('In 1831 when Tom and I were small boys at Flottbeck')
7. GH to JH, 19 May 1840.
8. ibid., 13 May 1837.
9. JH to GH, 26 February 1839.
10. GH to JH, 8 Mary 1844.
11. ibid.
12. MF to JH, 18 December 1852.
13. MF to JH, 16 December 1841.
14. 'Some Recollections of my Early School Days' in *Stories of Two Generations*, printed by Dryden Press, Terrace Station, Hororata, Canterbury, New Zealand, p. 29.
15. JH to GWH, 30 June 1842.
16. GH to JH, 11 September 1843.
17. ibid., 18 January 1844.
18. Grace Hall (mother) Journal fragment, 1 February 1827, TSA.
19. JH to GWH, 26 January 1848.
20. GWH to JH, 19 December 1847.
21. ibid., 27 December 1847.
22. Grace Hall (sister) to JH, 24 February 1848. On George Hall's gravestone at Elloughton there is no mention of his august career in Trinity House, or his escape from France as a prisoner of war, exceptional by any standards; he is simply styled as a gentleman, denoted by the abbreviation 'Esq.'. This stone he shares with his second wife and it may have been erected by her relatives since she died first. Grace rebelled against his last wishes stated in his will to be 'interred in the Church yard at Elloughton', and buried him with her mother and sister Anne in the Sacristy at Sculcoates (demolished in 1964). Her husband informed John that 'it was suggested to have Elder Brother [of Trinity House]' named on his memorial

stone there, 'but Grace preferred not'. These unusual events suggest that Aunt Mildred's influence lingered on.

23. GH to JH, February 1848.

24. GH to JH, 23 November 1843.

25. *The Nautical Magazine*, vol. 2, 1833.

26. Derek Morris and Ken Cozens, *Wapping 1600–1800: A Social History of an Early Modern London Maritime Suburb*, East London Historical Society, 2009.

27. Revd Harry Jones, *East and West London*, 1875, Smith, Elder & Co., p. 9. Though writing more than twenty years after the departure of Sarah and Thomas, Jones nevertheless gives a very colourful account of the Wapping they left.

28. Henry Mayhew, *London Labour and the London Poor*, selections by Victor Neuburg, Penguin Classics, 1985.

29. Mrs T. Holmes to JH, 30 November 1848.

30. ibid.

3

GEORGE WILLIAMSON HALL'S
MARITIME CAREER, 1834–1849

'Alas life, at least a life like ours, is but a series of partings'[1]

While George Hall was fretting over his children's legacy and his helplessness in the face of his wife's family's arrangements for it, worrying about his younger son John's job prospects and determining to remarry himself, his two older sons were developing their maritime careers. They were both commanding ships by the age of 26.

The Merchant Shipping Act of 1835 for the first time established a central register of seamen. By 1845 the Board of Trade began to better regulate the men who shipped Britain's trade goods and who played a crucial role in its expansion abroad, by examining and certificating its master mariners. Hitherto, masters were often appointed by shipowners, merchants, importers and agents and were not necessarily more competent than their sailors. Examination of new entrant masters and mates became compulsory, the examiners drawn from brethren at Trinity House London, Hull, Newcastle and Leith and some from Shields and Dundee. Both George and Thomas Hall, having proof of long service prior to 1850, simply had to apply and were granted their Master's Certificate of Service swiftly. At the time, politicians were also concerned that the rapid development of the Atlantic packet or passenger and mail-boat trade between England and North America was resulting in lost business for Great Britain, threatening British marine superiority and attracting British seamen to work on them. The American packets had more sail capacity then English brigs and barques, kept to regulated schedules in shorter times and were under sail day and night.

On 14 September 1850 at the Port of Scarborough, George, aged 32, made a Master's Claim for Certificate of Service which was issued in December 1850.[2] The claim was an invaluable document for my purposes because it outlined his career from apprentice to master. It named the ships he sailed with and in what capacity – as apprentice, seaman, mate or master – their port of origin and tonnage, the trade they were engaged in (given by destination – South America, Mediterranean, Baltic) and the years they sailed. The tonnage of the ship determined the crew size, and the bigger the crew, the greater the responsibility he had. Sailing to Calcutta and Bombay in ships like the *Lady Nugent*, and *Sam Boddington* would have tested his skills to the utmost as chief navigator. These were smaller cargo ships, unlike the bigger 400-ton East Indiamen which could stow up to 1,000 tons of tea on the return voyage and take passengers to and from the East India Company. They were a marvellous training ground for his first command on the *Mary Miller* on its voyages to South America.

George's five voyages into the tropics in the East India trade would not have been easy with heat and tropical diseases to contend with, but at least he would have been quartering with the first mate and master rather than the rest of the crew. It is apparent from the *Lady Nugent* papers that some of the crew became ill and others ran away. Though malaria is not contagious it does result in high fever and sometimes hallucinations and brain disorder, enough to scare any crew member. After escaping malaria and plague in his maritime adventures, George spent the rest of his life suffering from digestive illness.

3.1 George Williamson Hall's 'Master's Claim for Certificate of Service'.

Whereas the maritime careers of the brothers' father and grandfathers had been largely locally based in the Baltic, Black Sea and Mediterranean, as had their own apprenticeships, the later careers of George and Thomas reflected the development of overseas markets through Britain's command of the seas and broader exploration. Both men became involved in trade with India and South America and from greater ports than Hull – those of Liverpool, facing out to the Atlantic, and London. Liverpool already had a long-established trade with North America and the East Indies. Hull could not compete in terms of commerce with these two great port cities and even the advent of the railway from London to York did not help much because Hull was 35 miles away from the main link at York to the developing northern industrial cities.[3]

Apprenticeship

Most of George's voyages began in the spring or summer. The earliest record of his apprenticeship is a voyage in the *Aurora*,[4] which sailed in 1834 from London to the Mediterranean, probably carrying textiles or rope. George, back from school in Bordeaux, was 15. Hull had been active in the trade with the Mediterranean in the eighteenth century before Napoleon's campaigns disrupted the flow of goods, and likely destinations were Gibraltar or Leghorn (Livorno) in Italy where Hull sourced marble for its grand Georgian merchant houses. George's grandfather John Hall (1752–1816) had been active in the Italian trade so this was a safe choice for a first voyage.[5]

In George senior's almanac for 1835 a mid-winter entry states, 'Geo was bound apprentice for 3 years' and 'George went to join the *Toronto*'.[6] George's claim for his master's certificate confirms this was his first long-haul voyage to North America, where Hull was sourcing timber. As a boy or deckhand he would be bound to a ship's master for a number of years. He would act as cabin boy to the master of the ship, but also receive training and learn the basics of navigation, ship-handling and shipboard life from the master and mates. His father would pay between 40 and 50 guineas per voyage to the shipowner or handler, for his upkeep and training. An apprenticeship could last four years; his lasted three. It was the practice his father had followed in going to sea and it was the customary apprenticeship for anyone wanting to achieve certification in the nineteenth century in the merchant marine. With two generations before him experienced in seafaring and sail, George would have been familiar with sailing terminology and talk, an advantage when it came to 'learning the ropes' under the supervision of a good master and crew. In Hull, the Hall boys would have seen a harbour full of sailing ships, have listened to tales from their father George of his maritime life and imprisonment in France, and seen British ships leaving Hull and returning from the Baltic states, Russia and the Mediterranean. They would have heard stories of the larger whalers, reinforced against the risk of getting imprisoned in the ice, returning from expeditions to Greenland and the Davis Strait. At home in Brook Street, Hull, were portraits of their grandfather, Captain John Hall, standing proudly before a chart with his compass poised above it, and Captain Thomas Williamson, their mother's father. George had marvelled at 'an old painting of a ship' in the attic at Brook Street as a boy, 'with lofty poop and forecastle, and a round tops and strange old rigging and sails, which I have a notion had been commanded by a forefather or ours,' he wrote to John in 1884.[7] Their mother's Williamson family had long been associated with the foreign trade in Sweden.[8]

A life at sea offered interest, drama, enterprise and satisfaction. As a privileged boy from a long-serving maritime family, George would have been placed with the best possible master from his home port. In 1836, aged 18, he made two three-month voyages to St Petersburg, the first in July as a 'boy' or deckhand in the Hull ship the *Marys*, commanded by William Tucker, a man of 40, with 11 other crew members.[9] A month after his return, George again sailed for St Petersburg and his father saw him off on the *Marys* under the same master.

This great northern city was already elegant with its Admiralty and Winter Palace, its canal and bridge system which had inspired writers to compare it to Venice in European outlook and refinement. In the winter of 1829, seven years before George's visit, Thomas Raikes, a British diarist wrote:

A stranger is almost tempted to believe that the wand of a magician could alone have conjured up such a magnificent pile of buildings in one of the most desolate and uninhabitable corners of the globe [...] her maritime communications with [Europe] have introduced all the arts and refinements of modern life. [...] One of the first inconveniences is the [...] impossibility of finding any suitable accommodation at a public inn or hotel. Their number is very limited [...] they are deficient in every comfort, all equally dirty, ill-furnished and ill-attended. It can only be attributed to the scanty number of foreigners who visit this part of the world.[10]

Raikes, an Eton-educated dandy, found the women wearing French fashion, Tsar Nicholas I holding suppers in the Winter Palace seating 1,100 people, a currency inflated through the printing of money, and the tradesmen roguish and asking high prices for their goods. He was similarly unimpressed with the possibilities of the Russian navy, particularly when the tsar had designs on Turkey. Russian ships were good but because the fleet was laid up in winter for eight months of the year, and the Baltic and Black Seas were 'mere lakes when compared with the great ocean' he thought the present generation of Russian crews must become worn out before they could 'acquire half the experience of a common English sailor who is still in the prime of life'.[11] Is it too wild to imagine from the later evidence in his letters of George's literary tastes that this uncommon English sailor would have been reading poetry and novels during this journey if there was time, perhaps translations of Pushkin and Gogol, since Tolstoy had not yet been published?

The Lloyd's Register record of this voyage to St Petersburg in 1836 commanded by Master Tucker has beside it the words 'Lost'.[12] George recalled the drama years later in New Zealand. '[...] it was once my fate, on my third voyage, to be run down in the middle of the night in the North Sea, when we saved ourselves (with the loss of one man) with difficulty in two small boats and were picked up the next day by a passing vessel.'[13] The number of badly lit vessels plying the North Sea in the early nineteenth century led to numerous collisions and losses. His father passed the news of the near disaster to John at school in St Gall, Switzerland: 'George had a very narrow escape of his life, as the ship he was in was sunk in the Night by another Ship.'[14]

George W. Hall's inscription with the sovereign he earnt on this voyage says: 'This enclosed sovereign has been kept for my sake many years by my dear Aunt and only returned to me on her death. It is my desire that my wife keep it [as] a token of the love [brought] her and only part with it to my daughter. Geo W. Hall.'[15]

3.2 The emblematic sovereign from George's earnings on the fated *Marys*

Seaman

Shipboard life was demanding, dangerous and thrilling. In his apprenticeship, living in the ship day and night for months on end, George, would have learnt the ship's gear, its rigging, the precise position of every item in the ship's construction and every manoeuvre of sailing. With no lighting on board, understanding was critical, particularly in bad weather, sometimes a matter of life or death. At the end of his three-year apprenticeship he would be a competent seaman, able to work aloft reefing sails, knotting and splicing ropes and steering the ship. These early years would have been harsh, entailing cramped and damp living quarters, the aroma of wet clothes and sweat, bad food and very little privacy. If the topsail snapped in a strong wind it might carry several seamen with it, one of the numerous ways in which a sailor could lose his life. Watches changed generally every four hours, and while not on duty an able seaman had only the shared sleeping quarters on the forecastle to catch a nap in or sit on his sea trunk to write a letter home. He had to make hooks and rings for the blocks and perhaps even know some carpentry to make a jury mast out of a yard in an emergency. He would have been familiar with the watch, under the command of one of the mates, day and night, standing at the helm keeping the ship on course – or at the bow to watch out for signs of weather change or other ships, icebergs, or land. As a seaman, he would also have regularly swabbed the deck or done essential maintenance like rubbing the main topmast with a substance extracted from meat to keep it from drying out.[16]

In March 1837 George, aged 18 and now a seaman, joined the *Andromache* at Hull for its round trip to Constantinople (Istanbul) and Odessa, returning to Hull nine months later, in December, in time for Christmas.[17] The ship, according to its Lloyd's Register record, was 'Hull-coppered', or copper-bottomed to preserve its timbers. It needed to be. In the years 1829–1830 it sailed twice between Liverpool and Charleston in North America and back to London; sailed from London to Kronstadt, St Petersburg's port in north-west Russia and back to Liverpool; and from London to Archangel in northern Russia, returning to Hull.[18]

Odessa, a commercial port and naval base, was on a bay formed by the Black Sea. Its deep water meant it was seldom closed by frost, a great advantage in terms of trade. The passage from Odessa to Constantinople took from two to five days.[19] The British possession of Malta prevented France and Spain from getting command of trade between Russia and Turkey, and having Russia as an ally had been an effective check on France's ambitions under Napoleon. Trade with Odessa had developed considerably since 1803 when six English ships had arrived there. Soon the port was exporting grain, oak timber, masts for ships, hemp, flax, sail cloth, tar – all valuable for the British shipbuilding industry – tallow for candles, hempseed oil and iron. Goods exported to Odessa from Britain were woollens, refined sugar, cotton, lead, tin, tin plates, earthenware and glass, iron and steel-ware, brass wire, stockings, salt and coal.[20] The British were pleased about this new trade with Russia and the feeling was likely to be mutual for, as J. Jepson Oddy who reported to a parliamentary committee on trade at the time remarked, 'we cannot help observing how amazingly advantageous [Russia's] trade is with the British dominions. Not only the amount of its sales is equal nearly to those of all other nations, but it is from Britain only that Russia receives a balance of cash.'[21]

George, as was customary, sailed from Odessa in the spring, faithfully recorded by his father in his 1837 almanac: '20 April: Andromache of the Humber bound for Odessa.' He sailed from Constantinople for Hull on 31 October and, by 5 December 1837, had arrived in the Humber, safely home for Christmas.[22]

Britain's trade routes were also conduits of disease such as cholera, plague and yellow fever. In 1835, two years before George's voyage to Constantinople, the port city of Alexandria in Egypt, under Ottoman control and by 1838 accessible to British trade through the Anglo-Ottoman Treaty, had lost half its population to the plague. Rats were the conveyors of the disease carried by fleas. Dogs running wild in the streets of Constantinople were blamed, but the fleas on rats which they killed were the real culprit. The dogs lived and foraged on the streets, keeping sleepers awake with their howls. Europeans living in the city kept the disease at bay by using sticks to avoid contact with others in the streets, refused strangers in their houses, and changed their clothes on returning home from any excursion.[23]

Aunt Mildred, George's surrogate mother, may have known about the plague scare from newspaper reports. She was anxious about him being in the infested city and wrote to John at school in St Gall: 'George is gone to Odessa, may the Almighty preserve him to return home in safety.'[24] It is likely that the *Andromache*, while in Constantinople, completed its business as swiftly as time allowed before sailing for Odessa. We don't have George's own account of how the city appeared to him but Claridge describes it vividly, not curbing his prejudices about the Ottomans:

> For the purposes of trade and commerce, Constantinople stands in a pre-eminently advantageous position, and has one of the finest ports in the world. These advantages, however, are thrown away upon the proud and indolent Ottomans; and their capital maintains but a low rank among commercial cities. The streets are without names, and the houses without numbers; nor is there any register to supply these defects, or a post-office establishment to facilitate the transmission of letters [these had to be posted via the Austrian consulate]. The total absence of carriage-wheels [streets too narrow], clocks, bells and all sonorous occupations, leaves the whole city wrapt in almost unbroken silence; while the people appear to be mute, and desirous of passing along the streets without being seen.[25]

If time allowed George might have visited the sights, including the Blue Mosque, walked the narrow unpaved streets with their painted wooden houses, changed his money at the English store, and perhaps been shocked by the slave market where, according to Claridge, Nubian and Abyssinian boys and girls were sold from between £10 and £20 as servants. Constantinople, to an impressionable 18-year-old, would have appeared as exotic a place as he could possibly have encountered outside the pages of the *Arabian Nights*.

Travellers going from Constantinople to Odessa had to be quarantined for 14 days on arrival in an area called the Lazzaretto. Sailors were stripped for inspection before the director of the Lazzaretto and a surgeon, had their clothes fumigated and were quartered in cells until release. The port flew a red flag to warn ships that plague was in the city.

Second mate

In the year when his younger brother John was experiencing grave disappointment in being passed over for the position he

3.4 Odessa's quarantine area, the Lazzaretto, 1839.

wanted in the post office in Brighton, George was sailing in the *Princess Victoria* from London to Calcutta and back to London, his first voyage in the East India trade. He joined the ship, aged 21, in March 1839 as second mate, and part of a 24-man crew. The expectations of a second mate at the time are described in Lloyd's Captain's Register: he had to have four years' experience at sea and be 17, understand the first five rules of arithmetic and the use of logarithms, including the bearings and distance of the port he was bound to, by Mercator's method; be able to correct the sun's declination for longitude, and find his latitude by meridian altitude of the sun; and to work 'such other easy problems of a like nature as may be put to him'. He must understand the use of the sextant and be able to observe with it and read off the arc. In seamanship he must understand the rigging and unrigging of ships and the stowing of holds; must understand the measurement of the logline, glass, and leadline; be conversant with the rule of the road before entering port as regards sailing vessels, and the lights and fog signals carried by them, and understand the commercial code of signals for the use of all nations. He must be able to work a 'day's work complete'.[26]

The crew list of the *Princess Victoria*[27] reads like a directory of the main ports in the kingdom, with sailors recruited from Yarmouth, Dover, Hull, London, Dundee, Jersey, Inverness, Dublin, Dumfries and Southampton. This accorded with the regulations of the Navigation Acts[28] which stated that a high proportion of crews in the foreign trade leaving British ports had to be British. It left the port of London on the 18 July, under the command of Frederick Blackmore. The third mate and one seaman were discharged sick at Calcutta on 1 December 1839 and the steward 'ran away' on 26 September at Mauritius, perhaps to escape contagion. George's father's notes in his almanac of 1839 state that the *Princess Victoria* picked up a cargo in Bordeaux first, possibly goods for the expatriate community in Calcutta employed by the East India Company:

Jan 12 Capt Blackmoor [*sic*], Victoria, Princess
9 March George sailed for Bourdeaux
16 March George at the Downs
3 April Capt Blackmoor sailed from Bourdeaux[29]

At the time Bordeaux was an entrepôt and specialised in the handling of colonial produce such as sugar, indigo, cocoa, coffee, silk and cotton, much of which was shipped to Holland and Northern Europe.[30] Captain Blackmore was likely receiving orders for material such as silks which could be dyed, spun and woven into pieces, stockings, ribbons and fringes back in Yorkshire, or cotton to be made into stockings, calicoes, muslins, even 'dimities, fustians [...], many of which are sent to the

Baltic and North and South American markets', as described by Thomas Allen in his *New and Complete History of the County of York*, written in 1828. As second mate, George may have assisted in provisioning the ship for departure.

The *Princess Victoria* sailed to the Azores and Cape Verde Islands in the North Atlantic, a traditional provisioning point for fresh water and fruit, then down to the South Atlantic and around the Horn of Africa to Mauritius in the Indian Ocean and up to Calcutta in the Bay of Bengal. The ship also stopped at Tenerife for water and provisions. George reminisced about this voyage during the spring of 1889 in a letter to John, who was returning from England with his family via the Cape to New Zealand and had visited Tenerife: 'My first acquaintance with Tenerife dates back as far as 1839. Santa Cruz was a small place then. I thought the boys [John's sons] would have been interested in the first Spanish town they had ever seen. I was immensely so [...]'[31]

On the *Lady Nugent*, 1842-1843
George experienced a hiatus with his next ship, the *Lady Nugent*, in which he had again sailed to Calcutta. As John related to Grace, it had been damaged by a terrific hurricane that took place on 8 June 1842. The ship was still laid up in dry dock in January 1843 in Calcutta for repairs. His father embellished the account in a letter to John the same month. George and his crew had all 'suffered a great deal' but he was now in perfect health, verified by Captain Hawkins whose wife had just 'stept in' to tell him he had seen George in Calcutta. He was looking for a returning ship and as soon as he had a situation would be on the high seas.

The *Lady Nugent*, after its rebuild, transported convicts to Australia and immigrants to New Zealand, notably carrying Edward Gibbon Wakefield's only son, Jerningham, on a reconnaissance trip

3.5 Tattered remains of the Lady Nugent's crew list, showing George W. Hall as 'second officer'.

to New Zealand with the advance party for the Canterbury settlers under John Robert Godley in 1850 (see image 5.5).

On the *Samuel Boddington*, 1844
George was recruited onto the *Samuel Boddington* as second mate at Calcutta, due to the dry-docking of the *Lady Nugent*. It was a Whitby barque more than twice the size of the *Princess Victoria* and bound for Bombay under the supervision of Master Edward Noakes, aged 33, with a crew of 39 men.

The voyage was eventful. The crew list shows that 11 men left the ship in Bombay, five left at the Cape and seven left at Calcutta, again implying disease on board. Master Noakes had to recruit nine further men in Calcutta in November 1843, mostly seamen. It was here that George joined as '2nd officer'. The second mate's responsibility was usually the sails, masts and rigging and, if necessary, he had to climb aloft to tend to them with the other crewmen. His reward for this dangerous responsibility was to live aft with the master and the first mate.

The family was concerned when they heard that the *Lady Nugent* had been badly damaged, but the network of Hull men returning from the East had again reported a sighting of George in Calcutta, and his father reported that he would be returning with passengers from Calcutta and Madras on the *Samuel Boddington*. On his return, George stayed with his father and his sister Grace in the family's country cottage at Elloughton, recently purchased by George Hall. He was 'not well the whole time he was at home' Grace reported to John.[32] This may have been due to his setback on the *Lady Nugent* or perhaps the beginnings of the digestive problems that were to weaken him for the rest of his life.

By 1844 George was master of the barque *Mary Miller*, sailing to and from South and North America. By the time of this first command he had handled ships on the Atlantic, Mediterranean, Baltic Sea, Black Sea, and the Indian Ocean as an apprentice, able seaman, first and second mate. His extensive experience in

3. 6 Captain George W. Hall. 'The port of Copiapo, in contradistinction to the city, appears to conist of some eighty or a hundred houses, a few of which were tolerable, the rest, Oh!'

the East India trade gave him the necessary boost to apply for his own command, and now began an adventure lasting five years when he became part of the expansion of British trade to South America at the height of Britain's industrial revolution.

Captain of the *Mary Miller*, 1845–1849

Joseph Conrad described the copper-ore trade between Swansea, Wales, and the Chilean coast as 'manned by hardy crews and commanded by young masters',[33] an accurate description of George W. Hall's first voyage to Valparaiso in 1845, the main port of independent Chile. In the 1840s Swansea was smelting 90 per cent of the world's copper and was the centre of a thriving metal works industry.[34]

The *Mary Miller*'s destination was ports on the west coast of America, returning to Swansea. On its outward voyage it would have carried manufactured goods from Hull, its port of departure, since Valparaiso was highly dependent on British imports. Britain was the country that arranged most of its borrowing. Copper ore in the form of ingots was increasingly sourced from Chile since the depletion of resources in Cornwall. Copper was in great demand for British industry as piping and also for protecting ships' hulls from worm and general deterioration.

As was usual at the time, ownership of the *Mary Miller* was divided into 64 part shares, the majority owned by a mine proprietor, Joseph Macs of Lea near Matlock in Derby, who had 48 shares. The rest were owned by merchants, Henry Hubbersty from Hull, and Marmaduke Brown of Spursholt, Hertfordshire.[35] The ship of 290 tons had been built in 1842 in Hull. It was surveyed before departure and was described as a three-masted, square-rigged vessel, square-sterned with a carved

3.7 *Mary Miller* on the high seas, 1847.

female figurehead.[36]

As master, George looked after the accounts, the insurance and any legal matters relating to the *Mary Miller*, recruited and managed the crew, authorised repairs to the ship and sold its cargo. The journey from Hull to Valparaiso was approximately 7–8,000 miles and took up to three months. His salary was about £20 a month but he could take primage (a percentage of the cargo's income) if he arranged it himself, and a fee for carrying mail.

According to the ship's papers, the crew of 13 men included a mate and junior mate, a cook, steward, six able seamen, and two apprentices. Most were British, coming from Hull, Cardiff, Plymouth and Melton. A Yarmouth man joined at Valparaiso and a Maltese joined at Talcahuano.

George took a leather-bound Bible[37] with him on this voyage inscribed 'Barque Mary Miller of Hull, February 1845' with the ship's library listed on its back cover. This

3.8 Map of South America showing ports visited by two generations of Hall mariners.

included five Bibles, three Testaments and six Common Prayer Books, Bunyan's *Pilgrim's Progress*, a biography of its author and a volume of sea sermons. Other books were a biography of the Revd John Newton, the Anglican clergyman and former slave shipmaster whose life George's dying mother had been reading (perhaps the same book) and a biography of Colonel James Gardiner, a Scottish soldier who fought with British troops in the Jacobite Rebellion of 1745. Further biographies included one of Cyprian, the Bishop of Carthage; the Revd John Flavel, an English Presbyterian clergyman and puritan; the Revd Thomas Scott, Rector of Astor Standford in Buckinghamshire; Archbishop Robert Leighton, a seventeenth-century Scottish prelate and scholar who became Archbishop of Glasgow and Principal of the University of Edinburgh from 1653 to 1662, admired for his valuable instruction in the art of living a holy life; and finally, a biography of Napoleon Bonaparte. There was also a book of Miscellaneous Anecdotes, and one called *Wonders of Nature & Art*. There was a list of Bible readings suitable for particular situations George might face on board and suggested daily readings with the crew. This was a fairly intellectual and spiritual diet for a merchant sea captain in the foreign service. In his obituary published in the *Star* newspaper in early 1896, George was described as 'a man of cultured tastes and wide reading'.

George left Hull on 24 February 1845, sailed down the North Atlantic coast past Spain, across the equator into the South Atlantic, round Cape Horn at the bottom of South America and up to the Pacific port of Valparaiso. He had arrived by 25 May, a journey of three months. He then sailed to Copiapo, the mining town north of Santiago which was rich in copper.

We must imagine the *Mary Miller*, anchored in deep water in a roadstead inside the port and George being rowed to the Customs House on the quay to deposit the ship's papers which included apprentice debentures and seamen's register tickets. His shore rig would have been much the same as in the portrait of his father as a young man around the time he was pioneering the same trade route, a necktie, highly coloured, a broad gold watch-chain, smart boots and a jacket.

George did some coastal shipping from Concepcion and Talcahuano back to Valparaiso, before returning to Swansea in December, after an absence of ten months.

The Hull Packet and East Riding Times of 1845 recorded the *Mary Miller*'s progress in its Shipping Intelligence and Foreign Ports columns for the edification of family, friends, owner, merchant or agent.

HULL, Feb 19, sailed the Mary Miller for Valparaiso
DEAL arrived 23rd, Mary Miller, Hall, Hull, and sailed 24th for Valparaiso

VALPARAISO, May 25th – Mary Miller, Hall from Hull
VALPARAISO, June 30th – sailed: Mary Miller, Hall for Cophiba [Copiapo presumably]

One of the popular accounts of Chile at the time, much read in Britain and North America, was *Travels in Chile and La Plata*, by the English engineer and entrepreneur, John Miers, published in 1826, twenty years before George's visit. Miers had gone to Valparaiso in 1819 at the invitation of Lord Cochrane, then commanding the Chilean navy, to help develop Chile's mineral resources. The newly emerging independent states of Chile and Brazil invited him successively to command their navies. He was beset by obstacles in an attempt to set up a plant at Concon to produce rolling copper plate for sheathing vessels operating in the American and East Indian markets and warned of the dangers of setting up business in Chile:

> This insecurity of property in the possession of individuals, and the arbitrary proceedings of the government, may serve as a caution to other Englishmen against risking their property in any except mercantile speculations in Chile.[38]

George, too, may have been exploring business opportunities in Copiapo with Mr Miller, who accompanied him off the ship to visit mines and a flour mill (George later went into business importing corn to Hull), and a letter below to his sister Grace shows that he took a lively interest in his surroundings:

> July 6th: We got in this morning (Sunday) and came to an anchor in 5 fath. in the long looked for port of Copiapo. [...] In vain I looked for a glimpse of a town [...] nothing to be seen as far as the eye could reach, but one vast extent

of bleak, barren, rugged hills, swelling in the background into stupendous mountains, some of which appeared capped with snow but all defying my closest scrutiny with a good telescope to detect the slightest symptom of vegetation. Patience however – with a stiff breeze we close in at a rapid rate, and presently I almost fancied I could discern something moving on the tops of the ugly black rocks which skirted the bottom of the bay; soon my conjecture turns into certainty, a flag staff also made an appearance, but although Sunday undecorated with the lone star of Chile. [...] We soon had the Captain of the Port on board and one anchor down. The former, one of Lord Cochrane's officers as he took great care to let me understand, a consummate beggar and possessing a very fair share of English and a large share of impudence. Mr Miller and I went on shore, taking my carpetbag with necessaries for the journey up to the city of Copiapo, a distance of 18 leagues the greatest part thro one continuous desert.[39]

George and Mr Miller experienced a rehearsal for a theatrical performance by the locals. 'Every one in the place, tho' not Yankees, seemed well aware of their independence,' he told Grace. The whole scene impressed him as evidence of a people struggling after improvement and 'possessed at all events of civilized *tastes*'. Indeed, all Englishmen with whom he had conversed on the subject united in approving of the Chilean character, for although it was yet far from what he would wish to see, it was rapidly improving and the country with it.[40]

A month later, still exploring, he and Mr Miller started out at 2 a.m. to avoid the heat, implying a serious purpose. He concluded that the river water, though good, was not drinkable and the arable land he saw could only be used for producing fodder for mules and horses. They looked at silver mills worked by mules turning a horizontal wheel, regrinding the refuse of other mills, then returned to the ship and departed.

On his next voyage to Valparaiso in April 1846, George left from Liverpool and travelled via Gothenburg, the second city of Sweden, situated in the Kattegat at the mouth of the Gotha River, where he dropped mail. He wrote another long letter to Grace.[41] On board, he read the poetry of Byron and a novel by Walter Scott. He had a bird for company, a musical wind instrument and music copied and given to him by his sister. He was reminded of his grandfather, his father and brother Thomas, who as mariners all, like him, had to experience the pain of parting with loved ones and the possibility of not returning. He longed for a 'budget' of letters from family ('Oh! How eagerly I will seize them, and devour every line'), and became morbidly reflective:

> How many years have gone by since last I was this way [1836] [...] *many* are the changes those years have brought with them, changes wrought both on myself and all around me? Of many I then knew, some are dispersed through distant countries, some married – and some gone where ere none return; and not a few with ocean their grave and the cold blue waves their winding sheet.

The Hanoverian kings had transformed Britain from a comparative backwater to a powerful country, rich in colonies and trade, protected by the strongest navy in the world. George perfectly expressed how Britons perceived their global status as a civilising power at this time:

[…] it has been my pride to see the enterprising spirit of my country men pervading every corner of this habitable globe, and every where to feel its powerful effects. […] Has that same spirit of enterprise not extended to every thing, to art and science as well as to commerce, considering nothing too unimportant – nothing too vast and arduous for investigation? Has it not been the means of diffusing civilisation through every corner of the earth where it has penetrated?

In the last month of this voyage in 1846, and in the last month of the year, George encountered a death at sea. The *Mary Miller*'s folded and much unfolded 'Articles' for 1847 on which all his contacts with consuls along the way are recorded, and sealed with a red seal, discloses a handwritten paragraph by 'George Williamson Hall':

On the morning of 27 December last James Dent, Mate, was found dead on board of said ship believed to have died of asphyxia by reason of breathing Carbonized air because the Master had caused the ship's hold to be closed the day before.[42]

Any death on a British-registered ship had to be reported to the British consul in Valparaiso. Captains were responsible for their crews, and under the legal jurisdiction of the Board of Trade while away from Britain. This episode looks like an accidental death. James Dent was 29 and from Hull like his master. Perhaps he had gone to his sleeping quarters below deck after a watch and fumes from a cooking fire had not been adequately ventilated, or maybe he was asthmatic.

3. 9 The much annotated and sealed Articles of the *Mary Miller*, 1846, showing the death of James Dent.

There could be many reasons why a hold had to be shut in bad weather, sometimes to prevent water drenching sleeping quarters. A death certificate was obtained via the appellant lawyer of the firm of Hunt Collingwood and delivered to George W. Hall. The sad fact was that life was cheap on board ship, shipwrecks were a weekly occurrence and official recordings of any inquiries into such incidents did not occur until much later. George continued with another voyage on the *Mary Miller* to Valparaiso via Gothenburg in January 1847 with a larger crew of 29 men.

At home, his father had become concerned about the approaching coming of age of Grace, and wanted to discuss their mother's marriage settlement and legacy, hoping to persuade his children's legal advisors that he could execute it himself, not via Aunt Mildred, the trustee. George returned to these family issues in September 1847. The brothers intended to meet at Scarborough, the home of Aunt Mildred and William Fowler once George had discharged his ship.

George made three more voyages to South America on the *Mary Miller*, the first in January 1848, again to Valparaiso, and the second to Buenos Aires, returning via Cadiz, Beirut and Alexandria. British goods had been flowing freely into Argentina since 1817 and many British importers had agents in Cadiz, a usual port of call for any British ship going to South America. At the time of George's voyage, Beirut was the major entrepôt port of the Syrian coast, with a population of 27,500. Alexandria in Egypt had a bigger population of 104,000 and these Levantine ports were a part of Britain's economy. It is likely George was carrying mail to British merchants resident there as well as goods. Alexandria was a melting pot of immigrants from Greece, Italy and the Levant and the centre of Egypt's commercial and maritime expansion. It had good overland connections between the Mediterranean and the Red Sea and a healthy trade in Egyptian cotton, much desired in England and Europe.

In 1849, George took the *Mary Miller* to Buenos Aires on his last voyage. He had arrived there by June and left on his return for London and Liverpool by October. His father's ship *Grace* was among the early British ships to trade with Buenos Aires in 1827, when it became the capital of the Argentine Republic. By the time his eldest son was visiting, British merchants had been bringing general cargoes from Liverpool valued (on a typical ship of 230 tons) at about £18,218 in the currency of the time, and returning with ox hide.[43]

3.10 'Buenos Ayres from the Inner Roads', by J.E. May 1833.

George remained in Hull after this voyage, having set up his grain-importing business. His mother's legacy may have enabled him to do this. He had obtained certification as a master in the merchant marine by December 1850, aged 32. William Fowler, Aunt Mildred's husband, and a Trinity House brother, had signed and witnessed his application documents at the Port of Scarborough. The year was auspicious in another important way because he married a Cottingham-born woman, the daughter of solicitor William Dryden and settled in 27 Spring Street, Hull, the address where his daughter Agnes Mildred was born in 1851. His seafaring days were now over and he began to explore with his brothers the possibilities of another grand adventure.

Notes and references

1. GWH to Grace Hall, aboard *Mary Miller*, 21 April 1846.
2. BT 124/5, image 252, row 1.
3. K. J. Allison (ed.), 'Economy 1835-70' in Modern Hull (1969), British History Online, p. 217.
4. This might have been the *Aurora*, of 368 tons, built at Selby in 1782 for Francis Hall. Francis was the uncle of a John Hall (not our family) who established the ropery at Barton-on-Humber in the eighteenth century and was a significant man in Hull – one-time sheriff and chamberlain, and six times warden of Hull Trinity House. See *The Story of the Hall-Mark*, p. 2–5 with photo of *Aurora* p. 7.
5. Jeremy Hall, 'Notes for family reunion', TSA.
6. George Hall, Almanac 1835.
7. GWH to JH, 1 March 1884.
8. Gordon Jackson, *Hull in the Eighteenth Century*, published for the University of Hull by Oxford University Press, 1972, p. 123. 'In the middle of the eighteenth century Hull men were prominent in the English factory at Gothenburg. The papers of the annual meeting in March 1756 were signed by Robert Hall, John Hall, senior and junior, Robert McFarland and William Williamson, and there were others not present. [...] In 1763 factors mentioned in the Factory accounts included [...] Robert and Benjamin Hall and William Williamson of Joseph and William Williamson, the greatest iron importers in Hull [...]' While the Williamson family are connected through marriage to my Hall family, I am fairly certain the Halls mentioned are antecedents of the family in note 4 above.
9. Crew list of the *Marys*, BT 98/303 (July–Sept 1836) – the plural name is likely to refer to Mary, the mother of Jesus and Mary Magdalene.

10. Thomas Raikes, *A Visit to St Petersburg in the Winter of 1829–30*, London 1838.

11. ibid., pp. 109–10.

12. Lloyd's Register of Shipping 1836.

13. GWH to JH, 7 September 1883, Blighs Road, Christchurch.

14. GH to JH, 13 May 1837.

15. Coins given by John Taylor to the Terrace Station Archive with three associated annotations.

16. Sir William B. Forwood, *Reminiscences of a Liverpool Shipowner 1850–1920*, Liverpool: Henry Young & Sons Ltd, 1920, p. 13.

17. *Andromache*, Hull to Black Sea, Constantinople and Odessa. Source: TNA: PRO BT 98/301, Mercantile Crew Agreements – Hull-registered vessels – H-I – Voyages ending in 1838.

18. Trinity House Muster Rolls, CDSTR/45, Book 47.

19. J. Jepson Oddy, *European Commerce, Showing New and Secure Channels of Trade with the Continent of Europe*, London: W. J. & J. Richardson, Royal Exchange Publisher, 1 January 1804, p. 173.

20. ibid., p. 206.

21. ibid., p. 209.

22. George Hall, Almanac 1837.

23. R. T. Claridge, *Guide Along the Danube and Overland to India*, 1839, p. 185. A tour guide for travel down the Danube made possible by steam navigation.

24. Aunt Mildred to JH, 9 May 1837.

25. Claridge, pp. 183–4.

26. Captain's Register, Lloyd's, 1869.

27. Crew List of *Princess Victoria*. Source: TNA: PRO BT 98/346, Mercantile Crew Agreements – Liverpool-registered Vessels – J-K – Voyages 1835–44.

28. The Navigation Acts or British Acts of Trade of 1651, 1660, 1663 and 1733 formed the basis of English trade policy overseas for nearly 200 years and were repealed in 1849. They restricted colonial trade to England. The first, for instance, prohibited English colonies trading directly with the Netherlands, England's greatest commercial rival at the time, or with Spain or France and their colonies.

29. George Hall, Almanac 1839.

30. Gregory Stevens-Cox, *St Peter Port 1680-1830: The History of the International Entrepôt*, Boydell & Brewer, 1999.

31. GWH to JH 16 May 1889, St Heliers, Jersey.

32. Grace Hall to JH, 25 July 1844.

33. Joseph Conrad, *The Mirror of the Sea*, Little Toller Books, 2013, p. 27; first edn, Methuen 1913.

34. Lucille H. Campey, *Fast-sailing and Copper-Bottomed*, Natural Heritage, 2002.

35. Certificate of British Registry of the *Mary Miller*, PRO BT 107 298.

36. Shipping Register document CDPC/1/10/3, Hull History Centre.

37. George Williamson's Bible carried on the 1845 voyage of the *Mary Miller*, TSA.

38. John Miers, *Travels in Chile and La Plata* … 1826, vol. 1, p, 293. Digitised by Google from the library of Oxford University.

39. GWH to Grace Hall, 6 July 1845? [year omitted]. Letter given to Terrace Station Archive by Tim Rix, great-grandson of Grace Neall (née Hall).

40. ibid.

41. GWH to Grace Hall, 21 April 1846, letter given to TSA by Tim Rix.

42. Articles for *Mary Miller*, 1847, PRO/BT 98 1255.

43. Nicholas Twohill, 'The British World and its Role in the Relationship Between New Zealand and the Southern Cone Countries of South America, 1820–1914, Jun. 2010, *Historia* (Santiago), vol. 43 (1), pp. 123–4.

4

THOMAS WILLIAMSON HALL'S
MARITIME CAREER, 1835–1852

A ship is not a slave. You must make her easy in a seaway. You must
never forget that you owe her the fullest share of your thought,
of your skill, of your self-love. If you remember that obligation,
naturally and without effort, as if it were an instinctive feeling of
your inner life, she will sail, stay, run for you as long as she is able,
or, like a seabird going to rest upon the angry waves, she will lay on
the heaviest gale that ever made you doubt living long enough to
see another sunrise.

Joseph Conrad, *The Mirror of the Sea*[1]

Conrad's advice to seafarers to be one with their ships and all will be
well excludes all the other harrowing aspects of a life at sea in the age
of sail, such as grasping shipowners, bad food, disease, and reluctant
crews. But it was predictable, given his background, that George
Hall's second son, Thomas Williamson Hall, born the year after his
brother George in 1819, would also go to sea and experience all that
it offered, the highs and the lows of the 'heaviest gale' kind.

There were changes in local Hull shipbuilding and shipowning
during their father's maritime career which altered the career

trajectory for George Hall's two mariner sons. Hull in 1801 was second only to London in shipbuilding, with six yards active along the River Hull. In 1813, the shipping registered at Hull gave employment to 5,553 seamen[2] though this may have been an over-estimation it is thought. Over the next 40 years the bonanza in shipbuilding and repair diminished, exacerbated by new steamships built on the Clyde to serve the packet companies taking ships to St Petersburg and the

4.1 Captain Thomas Williamson Hall. 'Bye the bye, did you give those Shakespeare works of mine to George?'

Baltic ports. The East India Company had long monopolised British shipping to South East Asia, allowing only London-based ships in the trade, but the rise of a laissez-faire economic ideology in Britain led to the 1833 Government of India Act which removed the East India Company's trade monopoly. The company's decline freed up trade so other smaller British ships could take longer journeys to Britain's colonies in maritime South East Asia. All these changes were reflected in the switch by both George W. and Thomas W. Hall from short sea voyages closer to Hull to long sea voyages to the East and to South America, George to Calcutta in 1839 and Thomas to Argentina in 1842.

Boyhood

Thomas was a twin to Ann, who died aged six in 1826, a year before the death of their mother. Losing a twin closely followed by his mother must have been traumatic at such a young age. However, there are plenty of references in the family letters to his father's tenderness towards his children, and with Thomas's Aunt Mildred providing the warmth of a surrogate mother and additional contact with other women in the extended Hall and Williamson families as well as with family nurses and housekeepers, he grew up to be a confident and successful man.

Thomas was sent away to school at the age of ten with his brother George in 1829, probably near the village of Blankanese, on the Elbe River, now a suburb of Hamburg. He and George sometimes attended church services at 'a pretty little village' of Nienstedten, above Blankanese, playing in the riverside 'lustgarten' or pleasure garden nearby on Sundays and holidays, a good place to watch ships going by on the Elbe.[3] He then went to school in Saintes, near the port of Bordeaux, before leaving and beginning an apprenticeship at sea. I found only a handful of references in the family letters to Thomas's maritime career so what follows is from research undertaken in the National Archives in Kew, Lloyd's Register of Shipping, the Trinity House Muster Rolls in Hull, his father's almanac entries and British newspaper shipping reports. I was able to confirm what was stated on his Certificate of Competency as a Master, issued by the Board of Trade in April 1851 when Britain began to register its sailors, and to build a timeline of his development at sea when Britain's merchant marine formed the spine of Britain's maritime expansion and mercantile development.

Hull's own dock area had been enlarged following a speculative boom in 1825. With the opening of Junction Dock in 1829 connecting the Humber River to the Old Docks and increasing the port area to 23 acres, there were many more foreign ships entering the port. Many of these ships were from North America, since the increased duty on Baltic timber, so beloved of the thriving shipbuilding industries in Hull and Scarborough at the time, forced shipowners to find other sources of timber for shipbuilding and ships' masts.

We have an inkling of Thomas's apprenticeship from the almanac entries his father made in 1835 when Tom was 16. It is possible his apprenticeship began even earlier than this – his obituary says he went to sea at the age of 10 (in 1829) and is likely to have been a recollection told by Thomas to the author and no doubt reflected early experience in school holidays on his father's ship or ships of his Scarborough-based uncle, William Fowler. Since his older brother was apprenticed officially at 16 this is more likely to be the age at which his serious apprenticeship began. Fifteen was the age thought to be appropriate for boys to begin when their limbs were pliable and they were able to cope with going aloft in the rigging. By 18 they would be too old for this work and it would be even more dangerous. According to Professor D. Woodward, Honourable Archivist at Hull Trinity House, neither Thomas nor George attended the associated school for navigation and seamanship, despite their father's close association with the House. The school records are comprehensive and would have shown their attendance if they had been pupils. Their sea training was acquired as apprentices learning directly from first-hand experience on board ship.

In January 1835, when Thomas was 16, George Hall's almanac entry reads: 'My Tom went on board the *Diana*.' A Hull ship of this name which traded between Hull and St Petersburg's main port, Kronstadt, is recorded several times in the Muster Rolls for 1839–1849.[4] This Russian port near the head of the Gulf of Finland became the seat of the Russian Admiralty and the base for the Russian Baltic Fleet. *Diana* was commanded by Captain William Dalton. Thomas's father was active at this time in taking his ship *Grace* from Hull to Riga in the Baltic Sea and would have advised on which ships it was safe to serve and where the food and tuition was likely to be good.

In 1836, when Thomas was 17, his father wrote in his almanac for 17 June: 'Dauntless at Scarborough' and a month later, on 16

September 1836, he wrote, 'Tom went to Scarboro'. A ship of that name, commanded by William Wise, is recorded in the Hull Muster Rolls making three voyages to St Petersburg. Thomas was probably familiarising himself with the requirements of ships sailing between Hull and Russia because the first extant crew list recording his name is his voyage on the *Welton* to St Petersburg in the spring of 1837, under the command of Captain Francis Reimers, an experienced captain in the Baltic trade. It indicates that Thomas's previous ship had been the *Bravo*, a vessel that customarily sailed between Hull and Hamburg. Hull mariners usually sailed to Russia from April to September when the weather was warmer with no danger of ice. On 13 March 1837 his father recorded in his almanac: 'Tom went on board the *Welton*, Capt Rheims' and by 6 May 1837, 'Tom sailed for St Petersburg in the *Welton*.'[5] The ship crossed the North Sea, sailed up the Skagerrak and down the Kattegat, arriving at the Sound in Sweden on 2 June 1837.[6] From the Sound it entered the Baltic Sea and sailed up into the Gulf of Finland to Kronstadt, returning to Hull with a cargo of iron and timber, according to the *Hull Packet*:

> Welton of Hull, Reimers, from Petersburg, b 264 [burthen/ burden] 13 men [these included two indentured apprentices], 1549 bars of iron, 27c. 2 qrs deals, 17 battens, 4c. 20 deal ends, 4 ½ fathoms lathwood, 8 cwt oakum, ¼ fathom finewood, 3 bears. Wright & Co. agents.[6]

The Baltic states were fundamental suppliers of the hardwood necessary for building ships and their masts in Hull and neighbouring Scarborough. The *Welton* was probably carrying textiles to St Petersburg since other ships of that month were taking to the city bales of cotton twist and woollens, and returning with timber as described.

4.2 *Welton* crew agreement to St Petersburg, 1837, showing Thomas as 'seaman'.

The crew lists for the *Welton* show that Thomas made two voyages to St Petersburg on this ship in 1837, both in the capacity of seaman.[7] He was discharged from the first voyage in Hull in mid-July, then rejoined the *Welton* for St Petersburg again on 1 August, returning to Hull by 23 September, a voyage of 54 days. St Petersburg had an ever-increasing demand for woollen and iron goods. According to the *Hull Packet* this second voyage returned with rough hemp, linseed, skins, wool, lathwood, two masts and four casks of cranberries for Christmas. Thomas then joined the *Shamrock*[8] for a passage to Hamburg from Hull in October as a seaman. He was now 18.

Trade between Britain and the free port of Hamburg at the time was thriving with about a third of the ships in its port flying the British flag. Hull was one of the chief outlets for shipping British cotton, linen and woollen yarns as well as manufactured goods, hardware and machinery. The port is some 65 miles from the mouth of the Elbe River which flows into the North Sea at Cuxhaven, so British ships would have had to navigate up the Elbe to offload their goods.

As in other ports frequented by the Hall family during their maritime careers – Gothenburg, Riga, St Petersburg – merchant families often placed a son in a British enterprise in these ports. Hamburg merchant families would likewise send their sons to a British enterprise or to the London branch of a Hamburg merchant house. Thomas would have been speaking English as much as German in his transactions with the natives and merchants of Hamburg and probably encountering boys he knew from Hull.

Like his brother George, who had sailed to Odessa in the spring of 1837, Thomas next left Hull in February 1839 for the same destination, sailing this time via the British protectorate, Malta. He had been promoted. George Hall informed 15-year-old John Hall, at school in St Gall, Switzerland, 'Your brother Tom sailed on the 15th of this month for Malta and the Black Sea. He is second mate of a ship called the *Daniel Wheeler*.'[9] Crew agreements show that as a second mate, Thomas would have been earning about £3.10.0 a month, in charge of a four-hour watch in rotation with the mate. At the time, Odessa, like Hamburg, was a free port, attracting trade from Greece, Poland, Britain, France and Germany.

The correspondence of the Beswick family in Scarborough, who were family friends, shows that Aunt Mildred was also following Thomas's progress with interest. In a letter from Samuel Beswick to his son William, a friend of Thomas's, he says: 'Mrs W. Fowler desires her love to Thos Hall who is on board the Thos. [*sic*] Wheeler of Hull.'[10] William Beswick was also travelling to Odessa at the time but on the ship *Indus*. Since officers often dined with other officers on ships in the same harbour, and crew met crew, these greetings could be passed on and local news exchanged from letters received from home. Aunt Mildred wrote on 29 April 1839 to tell John: 'Thomas arrived in Malta.'[11] She wrote again to update him when, 'Tom at Odessa 7th November.'[12] This careful noting of arrivals and departures of loved ones was essential when mail was conveyed by sailing ship and a shipwreck might not be discovered until the next mail, months after the event, or read first in a 'Shipping Intelligence' newspaper report. The communities of the ports of Hull and Scarborough were intimately connected in their occupations of shipbuilding and seafaring and relatives and friends joined in keeping the flow of information moving. Any one of them could be a vital help or have a necessary connection should one of their own run into trouble on a foreign shore. On any of these journeys in the foreign trade there was the risk that a British merchant ship could be lost at sea, wrecked, attacked by pirates or caught up in a military or civil disturbance in the area where it was trading.

In 1842, Thomas had a family duty to perform. He accompanied his father to Hamburg to visit Grace, now 16, at her finishing school, to witness her confirmation, an important rite of passage. On a good sailing day, Hamburg was only 24 hours away from Hull. The ceremony would have taken place in the English church of St Thomas Becket, built in 1838. 'It was the most beautiful service,' Grace wrote to John, 'I can never forget it. When we returned from Church Papa presented me with a beautiful gold Watsch with a gold key.'[13] Grace, like her brothers, had frequent letters from her father and aunt. When her father visited Hamburg on business he would take a 'budget' of letters to keep her in the loop of family news. On one occasion Captain Hawkins, a friend of her father's, had visited and left her a little ivory comb in a segan case which she thought very pretty. After her confirmation service, George, Thomas and Grace probably celebrated with tea and cakes in this most British-influenced German city, where young men aped British fashion. Two months after this visit, a fire which started in a tobacco warehouse on Deichstrasse 42 was to rip through the central city, devastating seven churches, sixty schools, the Bank of Hamburg and the old town hall, as well as 1,700 homes. Grace's school seems to have been spared. William Lindley, a British engineer, would build the city's first railway and contribute to the plans of rebuilding its city centre after the fire, also modernising its water supply system and sewerage.

Opportunities beckon

On his return from Hamburg after seeing Grace, Thomas's next voyage was his first to South America on the *New Express*. It sailed from Blackwall, Port of London, to the Rio de la Plata in Argentina and back, a journey of nine months' duration. While his brother George's first command involved the copper trade with Chile, the crew agreement of the *New Express* is less specific about cargo but does reveal the broad parameters of the passage to be undertaken for the information of the Board of Trade, the governing body of any merchantman:

> London to the Island of Ascension and from thence to the Cape de Verde Islands to proceed to the River Plate thence back to Europe or Great Britain. If a return cargo cannot be obtained there the crew to proceed to Havanna, Mauritius, India or round Cape Horn with the ship as the Captain may find it most beneficial for employment and from thence to the Port or Ports of Europe and Great Britain.[14]

One of Britain's main objectives for trade with South America, especially after Chile gained its independence from Spain in 1818, was to provide security for British merchants trading in the area and to secure the opening to trade of the ports which included those on the river systems such as the River Plate and Amazon on an equal basis to all nations.[15] Thomas, now 22, joined the *New Express* in London as first mate. The ship was most likely one of the new Blackwall frigates, the three-masted fully rigged ships built between the 1830s and 1870s as smaller, faster ships intended to replace the giant East Indiamen trading between England, the Cape of Good Hope, India and China after the East India Company's hold on trade became more restricted. They were also used in trade between England, Australia and New Zealand.

To have achieved officer status by the age of 22 and to be the master's deputy should he be indisposed was good progress. Thomas could now direct the ship with the master and take his meals with him. The food would have been an improvement on the crew provisions for each man which included a pound of sugar and tack with 2 oz of tea and one-

4.3 One of the famous Blackwall frigates, the *Barham*, built in 1846 at the Blackwall yard, owned by Green's Blackwall Line.

and-a-half pounds of beef or pork a day. As for the conduct of the men, the crew list instructs: 'No spirits to be demanded; if any on board, to be entirely at the option of the Master.'[16]

It seems the *New Express* had received orders to proceed to Australia from South America because in late 1842 his father reported to John that Thomas had been sighted in Sydney and by mid-January he reports that George, then in Calcutta, was expected to arrive back in England at the same time as Thomas was returning from Australia. If Thomas and George had visited Australia on different ships in 1842, they would both have had foreknowledge of the Australian colony first-hand before they chose New Zealand as their preferred country for emigration.

The *New Express* was reported arriving in the British port of Deal on 7 January 1843 ('from the Mauritius') by the *Morning Chronicle*, and that accords with its crew agreement which says Thomas was discharged on 12 January 1843. It was an intense day for Deal on the Kent coast. Other ships arriving were three from Singapore, one from Calcutta, one going out via Deal to Tobago, Trinidad, one for New York, one for the Cape, one arriving from Honduras and one arriving from Valparaiso.

4.4 *New Express* crew agreement showing Thomas W. Hall as 'first mate'.

Thomas had already signed on to another ship within a month of his return on the *New Express*. He wrote from London to his friend William Beswick in Hull, and though he does not name his next ship it was his first voyage on the *Andromeda*, recorded for 1843 on his Master's Certificate of Competency.[17] He gives his reading preference too.

London
Feb 28th [18]43
Dear Wm
You will see by the writing of this that I have again made a move. I got up here on Wednesday last with the expectations of being soon at Hull again, but on the day of my arrival I found the vessel fixed and on the day following joined her to take her into the Tobacco Basin in the London Docks. We shall sail on Monday next for Lisbon and from thence proceed with salt to Buenos Ayres. I have not seen Sam [Beswick] since my return, I

have had very little time to spare, as I had got very few articles on leaving Hull having to join the ship so soon, have had no time except during the evenings, which I have had to myself, for the Capt. living on board with his wife, I am at liberty during the evenings. Bye the bye, did you give those Shakespeare works of mine to George or have you brought them back, should the latter be the case and you have an opportunity of forwarding them before I go, I will thank you to do so.

Remember me kindly to all friends; I hope to hear from you before I go, as you will have time sufficient; direct for the ship.

Yours sincerely

T. W. Hall

The *Andromeda* was a Hull-registered brig of 409 tons built in Sunderland, near Newcastle, in 1819. It was to sail from London to Lisbon then Buenos Aires. Thomas and John had arranged to meet before the ship sailed but John did not get out of bed early enough. He was searching for a position in London and wrote to Thomas to give his 'apology for not being on the Wharf this morning' for 'the servant did not wake me before a quarter to 8 o'clock, & although I was as quick as I possibly could, it had just struck eight when I got to the Wharf'.[18] They didn't have the chance to say goodbye.

Marriage

On 3 May 1845, aged 26, Thomas married Sarah Young of Wapping, the daughter of William Young, a former mariner and now ship's chandler whose name is mentioned in George Hall's almanac and who may have been a family friend or business contact. The marriage was witnessed that spring by her father and her brother-in-law, Samuel Dodd Chippingdale in St John of Wapping. She was 29, three years older than Thomas. At the time of her birth, her parents lived in Anchor and Hope Alley, a narrow street in the heart of old Wapping, lined with lodging houses and shops. At her marriage it is possible she was living above Mr Young's respectable chandler's business at 268 Wapping High Street, the main thoroughfare that ran parallel to the River Thames on its northern bank. Nothing is known of their courtship but it is even possible that Thomas had requisitioned materials from Mr Young for some of his voyages, or met Sarah at her church, St George in the East, in this teeming port. Perhaps they took a picnic on a boat along the Thames to the Royal Botanic Gardens, newly opened in 1841 at Kew; or strolled along the Thames Tunnel, one of the most extraordinary engineering feats of its time, completed by Isambard Kingdom Brunel. It was opened to foot traffic in 1843, with women selling trinkets from stalls along its way. They might have discussed the novels by Charles Dickens available at the new W.H. Smith bookstall on Fenchurch Street Station. This was the first station to be constructed in the City of London for the London and Blackwall Railway. It connected Minories in the City

4.4 Sarah, Thomas's wife, c.1853.

to Blackwall via Stepney, a line they may well have travelled together. It also connected some of the new docks reflecting Britain's massive expansion as a mercantile power – the West India Docks, via a branch line to the Isle of Dogs, and the East India Docks at Blackwall.

In the year of his marriage, Thomas received his first command in the foreign trade on the *Persian* of Liverpool. It lasted from 1845–1846, so may have entailed two voyages. Lloyd's Register of Ships records that a snow of this name, commanded by Master Hall, of 257 tons and built in Sunderland in 1834, was destined for Sunderland then London in the year 1846. Perhaps Thomas was picking up goods from Tyne and Wear before embarking. Whatever the ship's destination, the passage was disastrous because 'Wrecked' is appended to the Lloyd's entry. We know this is Thomas's command from various identifying details on the shipping records and because he mentions meeting up with another member of the *Persian*'s crew in a letter to his brother John in 1886.

> E. came on to dinner Friday evening. I had not seen him since I had command of the ship Persian in Hull & thirty-eight years is a long time to look back on [...][19]

INTERIOR OF LLOYD'S.

4.5 Engraving of the interior of Lloyd's, London.

Details listed in his application for a Master's Certificate for Competency show Thomas's command of the *Andromeda* is between 1846 and 1847 but the ship's papers show that on one voyage with her he left the Port of London for Honduras in July 1845 (three months after his marriage), and returned to Liverpool in January 1846. The *Andromeda* was bound 'to a port or ports or places of loading on the coast of South or North America for the purpose of procuring a cargo of Guano or other merchandise and from thence to her point of final discharge in the United Kingdom'. The crew of 20 men included a first and second mate, carpenter, cook/steward, sailmaker, eight able seamen, four ordinary seamen and two apprentices.

Guano, or bird droppings, was a major source of fertiliser for British agriculture. The discovery of major deposits on the Chincha Islands, off the coast of Peru, by a British ship's master, Andrew Livingston, created a new trade at a time of slump in British shipping in the early 1840s. The guano bonanza had only just begun with a first shipment in 1841 which was snapped up on the London market for £24 a ton.[20] Chinese labourers were used to cut the solidified guano from the mounds formed for loading onto ships and many died on the job.

British Honduras, Thomas's destination, had been independent from the first Mexican Empire from 1 July 1823 and from the Federal Republic of Central America since 5 November 1838. This land of tropical orchids, lowland rainforest and mangrove swamp was rich in natural resources, among them timber, gold, silver, copper, lead, iron ore and coal. One of the 'Mosquito States', beside the Caribbean Sea, Honduras' tiny offshore Swan Islands, north east of Honduras, also had guano but were perhaps a rest and replenishing point for the crew before venturing further south to Peru's three tiny Chincha Islands, which yielded the richest seabird guano amassed over hundreds of years from fish-eating birds like the cormorant, booby and penguin.

'Rio de la Hasha,' at the mouth of the Rancheria River and the Caribbean Sea in northern Columbia, was the *Andromeda*'s first port of discharge, according to the ship's papers. On 12 October 1845, three months after departure, the cook/steward named Davies Michael Venable left the *Andromeda*, by his own consent. Maybe his cooking was

4.7 A guano mound on one of the Chincha Islands.

not up to standard, or his manners serving captain and mates was under par. Perhaps he simply wanted to join another ship.

Thomas' second command on the *Andromeda* was ill-fated. Its outward voyage was fine and was recorded in Lloyd's List of 8 January 1847 as, 'Rio de Janeiro, arrived from Falmouth November 12, Andromeda, Hall'. At the time, Falmouth in Cornwall had a thriving packet service taking mail to Lisbon and Gibraltar, to Rio de Janeiro, Buenos Aires, Barbados, Jamaica, Halifax, and Malta and was the first port of call for international shipping for repairs, supplies and orders. The *Andromeda* began its return journey to Falmouth from Patagonia but had to be abandoned at the entrance to the Bay of Biscay, a notoriously dangerous place for shipping. There were severe gales that January resulting in numerous casualties, according to Lloyd's List. Thomas and his crew were rescued by a passing ship, the *Bangalore* from Madras. They came into Deal, Kent, as reported by the *Hull Packet,* on 19 February 1847.

> Deal, Feb. 10 – The Bangalore, Parsons [master], from Madras, has arrived and proceeded to the river, having on board the crew of the barque Andromeda, Hall of Hull, from Patagonia to Falmouth, for orders, which vessel was abandoned in a sinking state, Jan 28, in lat. 43.49N, long. 10 47 W. [21]

Significantly, the *Cork Examiner* further noted that 'Cholera broke out among the crew on 7th August' [and] 'fever prevailing on board the Andromeda'.[22] It is probable that with a diminished crew from illness, and the bad weather conditions, the ship ran into difficulties and had to be abandoned.

There are no records concerning either of Thomas's shipwrecks. The Board of Trade only became responsible for investigating wrecks in 1854 and did not begin to publish these until 1876, but it is most likely that Thomas as master would have written a report of the event and had his account signed off by the mate and second mate as senior officers. I was initially dismayed to learn that despite his first-class qualification as a master, Thomas had presided over two lost vessels. But further research in the Shipping Intelligence reports of contemporary newspapers and searches in Lloyd's Lists of the time showed an average of up to ten wrecks a day in the comparatively unregulated, poorly charted, under-buoyed and often dangerous local and international coastal waters. *The Nautical Magazine and Navy Chronicle* regularly published 'Bottle Papers' which typically had details of messages washed up in bottles on shore or picked up by poor fishermen with a last message by the captain of a wrecked or sinking ship.

The predominant cause of merchant vessel losses according to the Royal Commission into Shipwrecks which reported in 1873 was bad navigation – 65 per cent – and the next major cause was natural causes – storms – 30.5 per cent. Only 4.5 per cent of losses were caused by unseaworthy, overloaded vessels. The Bay of Biscay was notorious for its fierce storms and January was generally reckoned to be a bad month for them.

After his disaster with the *Andromeda*, and his return to Hull, Thomas and Sarah stayed near his father who had a month previously moved to his summer house, Elloughton, South Cave, near Hull, 'taking his servants with him'. Thomas, Sarah and his sister Grace took lodgings near to George and his new wife Mary Ann, since they 'had not room in the House',[23] then moved on to Scarborough and presumably Aunt Mildred.

Thomas wrote on 20 August 1847 to ask John in London a favour concerning the retrieval of a chronometer under repair, possibly a relic of the *Andromeda* voyage and wreck, which implies he was about to undertake another sea voyage in the spring. The letter also shows that George W. Hall, who had returned to England from South America at the end of August from a voyage on the *Mary Miller*, was not in robust health and was now living with Thomas and Sarah:

My dear John

[…] George & I have taken a house in John Street [Hull] & I am busy furnishing it at present so I am pretty occupied.

I will thank you if you have time to call at Parkinson & Frobisham & enquire how my Chronometer is going. It has been in their hands since February last, a much longer time than I at first anticipated. As I have not seen them since March it will be as well to let them know I am living by enquiring after it. I do not think I shall want it before the Spring, but can but tell.

George is much better than he was, he gets out after his business [grain] but has not yet recovered his strength. We are at present lodging in Story St but may most likely move and by Friday next, it will be then as well to address any letters to Brook St [Hull family home] as I am in there once or twice a day.

You will most likely have a letter from George before long as he intimated to me he intended doing so. Grace and Father are both well.

Now with kind love to you from all of us at Hull, I am, my dear John

Your affectionate brother

T.W. Hall

P.S.Parkinson & Frobisham's place is in Change, nearly opposite the Exchange. Respects to Mr McK. ...

On 24 January 1848, 11 months after Thomas's rescue by the *Bangalore*, a son was born to Thomas and Sarah, their first child, young Tom.

By 1849, Thomas had acquired his own brig, *Dauntless*, purchased in Van Diemen's Land (now Tasmania). It was one of the bigger ocean-going vessels, built in the yards at Blackwall Point, Tamar Valley, and probably constructed from the large specimens of eucalyptus that grew along the Tamar Valley river plains from Launceston to the coast of Tasmania. The tree is one of the tallest in the world and, according to the maritime historian Don Chambers, normal Launceston practice was to use New Zealand kauri for decks, masts and spars.[24] The money for the purchase is unlikely to have come from his father, since George Hall senior was notoriously careful with money and had been reluctant to assist his eldest son George by part-owning a ship with him.[25] It is probable that Thomas had extracted his and his sister Grace's share of their mother's legacy early to enable him to make a deposit on this ship because the ship's papers show he arranged that his sister Grace be a part-owner.[26] He may also have traded on his own account during captaincy of other ships.

It was on the *Dauntless* that Thomas and Sarah sailed to Buenos Aires in 1850. They left the port of Cork on 2 July. Sarah was again pregnant, and their first child Tom only two. On 4 October their second son, George Buceo, was born, named after the port of 'Buceo, Montevideo, River Plate', as Sir John Hall's genealogical chart indicates. Whether he was born on the ship or at the first port of call thereafter (Buceo) is not known. If on board, it is possible his father assisted at his son's birth because the crew of ten on the *Dauntless* were all men, including a mate from Bideford, a cook/steward and apprentice, both from the island of Jersey, a carpenter, five seamen, two of whom were Greeks from the Ionian islands and two others who were working their passage.[27] In the 1850s it was by no means unusual for a woman to give birth aboard a sailing ship since wives frequently sailed with their husbands who were active in the foreign trade. They were reluctant to lose husbands to long sea voyages and husbands were reluctant to leave wives with young families onshore.

John Hall on a ship passing the Bay of Buceo 'immediately to the east of M. Video' speculates in his 1885 diary that George Buceo may have been born in the 'large Saladero on the hill', a place where meat was dried, but he may not have known the exact details. The birth was registered in Liverpool on the family's return and George Buceo was baptised in March 1851 at the church of St Nicholas, Liverpool.

Thomas's voyages to South America were getting harder to justify in a time of economic downturn and increased competition, but he made one more voyage to Montevideo in the summer of 1852 when Sarah was again pregnant with young John ('Jack'), who was born in the month of Thomas's return on the *Dauntless*.

4.8 Montevideo from the Mount, 1850.

Notes and references

1. Joseph Conrad, 'The Weight of the Burden' in *The Mirror of the Sea*, Little Toller Books 2013, p. 68/Methuen 1913.

2. Joyce M. Bellamy, *The Trade and Shipping of Nineteenth-Century Hull*, East Yorkshire Local History Society, 1971, p. 13.

3. GWH to JH, 1 March 1884. ('In 1831 when Tom and I were small boys at Flottbeck').

4. CDSTR/44 Book 46. Hull History Centre.

5. George Hall, almanac 1837, TSA.

6. Shipping News, *Hull Packet*, 28 July 1837.

7. Crew List of the *Welton*, 1837, BT 98/308.

8. Crew List of the *Shamrock*, 1838, BT 98/306.

9. GH to JH, February 1839.

10. Samuel Beswick to W. C. Beswick, 27 April 1839.

11. Mildred Fowler to JH, 29 April 1839.

12. Mildred Fowler to JH, 3 December 1839.

13. Grace Hall to JH, 15 March 1842.

14. Crew List of the *New Express*, BT 98 375.

15. F. Kaufman and Jerome Elie, *Britain and the Americas: culture, politics and history*, California: ABC-Clio, 2005, p. 36.

16. Crew list of the *New Express*, BT 98 375.

17. The list of voyages associated with Thomas's Master's Certificate of Competency, 8 April 1851, was not as comprehensive as his brother George's: 'Master, first class, certification recorded at Hull Trinity House: 1. Andromeda, Mate, 30 July 1843 to 26 February 1844; 2. Of 2nd voyage in this certificate no record; 3. Verified as Master of the Persion of L'pool; 4. Verified as Master of the Andromeda from 10 February 1846 to 28 January 1847.'

18. JH to TWH, 3 February 1843.

19. TWH to JH 27 December 1886. Thomas' memory of this command places it in 1848 not as Lloyd's does, in 1846.

20. Neil Gow, 'Golden Age of Guano', www.saexplorers.org, 4 July 2016.

21. *Hull Packet*, 19 February 1847.

22. *Cork Examiner*, 1 January 1847.

23. GH to JH, 2 July 1847.

24. Don Chambers, 'Timbers used for shipbuilding in the Tamar Valley in the 1830s and 1840s' in Australian Journal of Maritime & Ocean Affairs, vol. 3, issue 3, 2001.

25. GWH to JH, 6 November 1844: 'I did just happen to say a word about Father's taking a small share in a small vessel with me, but without the smallest success; he declaring he had been very liberal to me; he never would of course ... it is the first time I ever named any thing of the kind, & of course the last.'

26. Transcriptions and transactions for *Dauntless*, PRO/BT 107.101, show he brought the ship for £1,900 and Grace had a part share.

27. Crew List, Schedule C, Transcriptions and Transactions of *Dauntless*, 1851, PRO/BT 98 2601.

5

WHY DID THE HALL BROTHERS EMIGRATE TO NEW ZEALAND?

'I am certain in a *new country* [you] have a *still* fairer
prospect before you.'[1]

The port of Hull was declining in the years preceding the Hall
brothers' emigration to New Zealand in the mid-nineteenth
century. Whaling in Greenland and the Davis Strait, which had
been a significant part of the city's economy, was now diminishing.
The port was also missing out on trading links that Liverpool and
London seemed to be exploiting better, such as trade with the East
Indies and with Australia. Some investors and merchants thought
that whaling had drawn too much capital to it, thus starving other
sources of potential development. In his *Picture of Hull* (1835),
the local historian, John Greenwood, summed up the widespread
anxiety that even trade which had been strong in the past was now
in deep decline and the merchants of Hull seemed unable to access
and exploit new and expanding markets:

> [...] The Mediterranean and Leghorn [Livorno] trade,
> from want of due cultivation, has here dwindled away

into insignificance and the American trade, that rich source of wealth to Liverpool, [is] in Hull of but limited extent. The West India trade has been attempted several times, but never established and two or three vessels have sailed hence to the East Indies, without as yet producing any profitable returns.[2]

In February 1840, Thomas Wilson, chairman of the newly formed (1837) Hull Chamber of Commerce, a shipowner and iron merchant, spoke at the third annual general meeting. He again decried the shameful lack of Hull trade with the East Indies, the lack of connection with Australia, the problem of locally produced manufactured goods being exported from London not Hull, and homeward cargoes (principally wool) returning via London 'to pass our very doors and to be consumed by places which ought to be dependent on us'.[3] He believed that a share of this lucrative trade might easily be obtained. He could recall the time when vessels sailed regularly from Hull to Genoa, Leghorn, Malta, Messina, Naples and Palermo and though extensive commerce since that time had begun with Egypt, the Greek Islands and the ports of the Black Sea, Hull was missing out. 'The Pacific Ocean, important as it is [from] a mercantile point of view, is to us a blank,' he said. And speaking of markets nearer home, 'Where is our trade with France [...] Portugal and Spain, all is gone – gone, as many other trades have done to Liverpool or to those who choose to take them [...]'[4]

This bleak picture of decline in the face of competition from bigger centres, gave no incentive for the Hall brothers to remain in Hull near their father, though it was clear that previous generations of their family on both the Hall and Williamson sides had benefitted from the port's earlier and more successful trading relationships. The brothers' grandfather, John Hall, had been involved in the Italian trade with Livorno. The trade with France, particularly for Charente wine, which was so much a part of George Hall's life in Hull, seemed now to be monopolised by Liverpool. Though their father had made two trips to South America at the opening of Argentina and Chile in 1822 and 1827, Hull had proved unable to capitalise on these possibilities. The port's shipbuilding and ship repair businesses were falling off after 1835 and faster steam packet ships were being built on the Clyde. While both George and Thomas had taken advantage of the burgeoning South American trade as captains in the merchant marine, it was in far larger ships than Hull was providing, and from the greater ports of London and Liverpool. Now, even the barques and brigs they had commanded were becoming uncompetitive.

5.1 The Hull they left behind: Whitefriargate Bridge and the Wilberforce Monument, erected in central Hull in 1834. The dock offices are to the right of the monument.

There was no shortage of adventurous genes in the Hall and Williamson families. Thomas Williamson, the maternal grandfather of George, Thomas and John Hall, like their father George, had been a mariner and shipowner and was descended from one of the wealthiest shipowning and merchant families in Hull. Their uncle, William Bean Fowler, had shares in Scarborough ships. They had knowledge gained from more than a century of commerce through the Hall, Williamson and Fowler shipowning and merchant families and trading contacts with Russia, the Baltic States and Sweden. The Williamsons were active in the importing of iron ore from Sweden to Hull which gave employment to many trades in Yorkshire whether in 'shipbuilding, nautical instruments, stoves, anchors, cannon, guns, bands, ramrods, chains, nail, hammers, gates, saws, sickles, sythes, screws, fire-grates [and] fire-irons'.[5] The family had helped to establish an English church in Gothenburg in the eighteenth century to serve the trading community there.

The three brothers spoke German and French after a boyhood education in Germany, France and Switzerland. They were widely read, as the library inventory at John Hall's New Zealand home at Hororata shows (John was a trustee for his brothers who predeceased him and he inherited some of George's books). George and Thomas, as captains in the foreign service, were both highly skilled men. John, the youngest, though overshadowed in worldly experience by his two older brothers prior to emigration, had administrative skills which were to enable his later success in New Zealand.

The leading merchants of Hull in the eighteenth century had sent their sons abroad to St Petersburg or Gothenburg as 'factors' or agents to facilitate trade. If Hull had been thriving commercially, at least George and Thomas might have been in a position to move into land-based occupations associated with shipping, whether in insurance brokerage, or as merchants or agents utilising contacts abroad. After his time on the *Mary Miller* (1845–1849), George had started a corn-importing business in Hull but the economic climate had been against him and his business had failed.

There were obviously other reasons which made the eventual decision to emigrate comparatively easy once the brothers' collective efforts and research fell into place. First, though George and Thomas had both success and adventure serving on vessels that had sailed some of the most demanding passages in the world, they were both now married with children. Thomas had married Sarah Young in 1845; George had married Agnes Emma Dryden, the daughter of the family solicitor, in 1850. This was no longer the time for foreign adventures on dangerous seas.

Another alarming development in the summer of 1849 in Hull was the cholera outbreak, supposedly brought from Hamburg by two sailors. In September of that year 500 deaths were reported in one week and in total the epidemic claimed 1,860 lives. It was mostly in the poorer districts of Hull, such as the Hessle Road area, but the Halls' parish of Sculcoates was also affected badly.[6]

The comparatively recent Fatal Accidents Act of 1846 had enabled dependants to claim damages for the death of a relative caused by negligence. As a shipowner, Thomas may have found the prospect of being sued by the families of his crew members for claims in excess of the value of his vessel a good reason to give up seafaring. Both he and George had by now experienced shipwreck and, in George's case, one death on board from what may have been his negligence. Britain's major ports like Liverpool and London were stuffed with sailing ships. Steam-powered ships were supplanting sail and Thomas had already indicated that competition was tough and a ship's captain couldn't afford to stand still if he wanted to pay his bills. George was struggling to make a profit from his grain-importing business in Hull and their younger brother John had been disappointed in his bid to become chief postmaster at Brighton.

Among personal reasons for emigration was the fact that George Hall had remarried in 1848, to Mary Ann Packman. This freed the brothers, knowing their father was secure in his domestic life and with a new focus. The battles with him over their mother's legacy had affected all his children. Grace would doubtless soon find a husband, but if she did not, Aunt Mildred and Uncle William Fowler were at hand in nearby Scarborough and devoted to her.

The 1840s and 1850s were decades of expanding horizons and new possibilities. At the family home in Brook Street, and in the taverns and streets of Hull, Liverpool and London, the Hall brothers would have known men whose enterprise had taken them far beyond Hull. Attitudes to emigration were also changing, as John later mentioned in a shipboard essay on his way to New Zealand:

> Hardly a circle can now be entered at home, of which some member has not a brother or other near relative at the Antipodes, and emigration, say rather *colonization*, is looked upon as a promising, albeit a somewhat bold and adventurous undertaking, instead of, as formerly, the resort of a ruined 'ne'er do well.[7]

From the late eighteenth century onward, scientific explorers had brought back from the New World concrete proof of what they had seen – maps, charts, sketches, watercolours and artefacts – and all of these no doubt fired the brothers' imaginations. A spirit of emigration was in the air, and an element of el dorado for those whose lives were oppressed by poverty or who felt they could not provide a similar standard of living for the next generation. Gold was discovered in California in 1848 and in Australia in 1851, causing populations in the new British colony to double. The brothers' decision to leave Britain was made at a time of peak emigration following the hungry forties when a sequence of bad harvests had resulted in high food prices, and industrial overproduction had led to severe unemployment. In the years 1850 to 1854, between 900,000 and one million Irish, in response to the great potato famine of 1845–1849 which impoverished thousands, emigrated to destinations other than Britain, the majority to the United States and British North America. About half a million went to Australia and New Zealand. The idea of emigration would oblige shipowners to turn to the faster clippers to take people to the new territories.

John had most reason to go. From 1845 he had improved on his job as an extra clerk in the post office and secured a more stimulating position as private secretary to Lieutenant Colonel William Maberly in the General Post Office, London. This had led him to become assistant to the post office surveyor in Gloucestershire. But he was tired of office life and was even considering training for the

Anglican ministry. In the summer of 1848 he had supported the Clerkenwell police force in keeping the peace by becoming a special constable to help quell Chartist rioters who were seeking to improve the working conditions of manual workers. He was restless. One friend was dismayed at his wish to emigrate and told him, 'You are the last person I should recommend to leave England as your prospects are far too brilliant to throw up.'[8] Regardless, John began to

5.2 John, aged 24, as a special constable in the Chartist Riots in London, during the summer of 1848.

research the possibilities of leaving. Between 1850 and 1852 his brothers gave advice and information from their own expertise, contacts and research as well as their direct experience, and came around to the idea of accompanying him.

On 4 April 1850, George wrote to John, six days before his marriage to Agnes Dryden,

> Tom says you are thinking of setting off to South America & turning Gaucho – at all events you had written to him to get you all the requisite information. Now I said to Tom that as I had a friend there – a most excellent fellow & a large Estancia Proprietor – if you would let me know more fully all the points on which you required information (I suppose for some of your friends) I would endeavor to get it for you from him or from some other practical men conversant with the country & business [...] so like a good boy drop me a line.[9]

John asked George about the commercial interests of British men in South America and considered Argentina as a possible venture, but George was unsuccessful in obtaining useful information:

> [...] many men may have lived as commercial men *for years* in the country, & yet are no more able to give the information we want, then if they had never been there. And this because they had never felt the least inclination or inducement to acquire any information out of their own line. Their only intercourse with natives or people from the country is often what their business compels. Their society [is] entirely English.[10]

He therefore, on John's behalf, had in his last letter to Thomas 'put a few more questions for him to *get answered'*, and asked, 'Could you get an introduction to the Argentine Consul, thro' any mutual friend? You might learn much from him.'[11] He sent John a Buenos Aires newspaper for background information. In this same letter, George recounted a darker story about Thomas's contact, the *estanciero*, or cattle-ranch owner, Henry Harratt, 45 miles outside Buenos Aires. A fortune easily gained had been lost by Harratt's brother, who went bankrupt and committed suicide.

George began to argue against South America and for Britain's own colonies, particularly New Zealand, which he thought were equally healthy but with more stability. 'Concerning them I have had a great deal [of experience] – I scarcely know to which I would give the preference – the religion is strong argument against South America.'[12] He advised John to read Frederick Weld's *Journal of a Journey between Nelson and Canterbury*. John also read Weld's *Hints to Intending Sheep-Farmers in New Zealand*, published in 1851, and wrote on it, 'This pamphlet more than anything else induced me to emigrate to New Zealand.'[13] Weld had estimated that if a man had capital of between £1,000 and £1,500, a sum well within

5.3 **Frederick Weld.**

the brothers' collective reach, a good beginning could be made in sheep farming.

George told his brother he preferred stock farming to agricultural or crop farming because it involved [unusually] 'more exercise and less hard labour'. He was sceptical of the proposed settlement in New Zealand promoted by Edward

Gibbon Wakefield, thinking it 'better meant than planned' and warned John that it might be a 'jolting affair'. He feared there would be 'pickings' for somebody. He knew New Zealand settlers paid a high price for land at £3 per acre and did not know how they could compete with Australia where, with 'less advantage', settlers only paid £1 an acre.[14]

For George, the prospects for his future health were a vital factor in weighing the decision to emigrate. He had long thought Hull 'horribly dull', a place where the sun shone about once a week. He had even been ill on his spring honeymoon in Chepstow and endured 'two large strong mustard plasters' on his chest and '5 dozen leeches,' so Agnes told John.[15] Her health was unreliable too. She had experienced a difficult pregnancy early in her marriage, and at the time wrote to John: 'You will have heard how little I am able to do my duties as wife or housekeeper but I hope soon to be allowed to go home & at least obviate some of the expenses of my long and tedious illness. [...] Walking has been prohibited me for months to come.'[16] Agnes gave birth to little Aggie in January, 1851, four months after this letter, and produced no further children.

Capital as well as health was important, but it was vital not to part with money until John had experienced the country and its ways, George advised. He sympathised with John in being passed over in his job prospects by royal patronage but was certain that if he made up his mind to 'make himself a country where he settle' he would get on, especially with capital at his disposal.[17] In the exodus to the Australian goldrush of 1851, New Zealand's prospects were overlooked. John made enquiries of the Colonial Land and Emigration Office about leasing land in New Zealand, the availability of land in the Middle [South] Island, and to clarify the government position on Māori land. He also went for an interview with the Canterbury Association which had recently published *Brief Information about the Canterbury Settlement*. It recommended breeding cattle, horses and sheep on the rich arable lands of the Canterbury prairies. Frederick Weld sent him a handwritten copy of his *Journal between Nelson and Canterbury* (1851), which helped to firm up his decision to choose Canterbury as a destination.

George was increasingly convinced by the persuasive evidence John was accumulating. In January 1852 he wrote to him: 'My mind is made up, if you proceed to N.Z. to do the same – but having once got involved in business – you cannot get out when you like.'[18] George was living in the Cottingham area of Hull with his wife and daughter. He had grain stock he could not sell on the corn market. After the repeal of the Corn Laws in June 1846 and a poor harvest the year before there had been a subsequent hike in the price of wheat, which peaked at the end of May 1847 then fell dramatically. The high prices led to increasing volumes of imports of grain but this forced prices downward, with bad results for speculators and merchants like George.[19]

The problem of how to tell his father and Aunt Mildred of the brothers' plans to emigrate was far more difficult. Early in the project George confessed to John:

[…] the task you gave me of *sounding* Father & Aunt on the subject I have long been endeavouring to perform. With respect to the latter I might […] have spared myself the trouble of going so carefully about it, hinting at possibilities, for Puggy [their sister Grace] had told her all she knew herself about it, which was of course as much as I knew myself. […] In consequence I get the character of wanting to *keep things from her, of being close*, etc. Father tho' I have attempted fifty times I have never been able to keep to the point, as he instantly gets off to something else – talking of *Clubs, high-living, living quiet in [the] country*, people doing as they like. However, my impression is with both – (Aunt has expressed it more openly) – that tho' it would grieve them they would consider health as of paramount consequence.[20]

As departure grew closer, John could no longer delay telling formidable Aunt Mildred why he wanted to leave England. We only have her reply to his letter, but can speculate on its contents. He was unsuited to office work and in November 1850 had described to his friend John Neall how it induced a state of 'morbidness' and an apprehensiveness of 'coming ill'. Neall had recommended change as the remedy. Aunt Mildred's response came in an emphatic letter from 'Scarbro' on 13 February 1852:

> To know that you are so miserable wounds me much [...] do not *launch* yourself into so much misery, it is not too late to change your mind [...] You are not aware of the *melancholy hardships* you will have to *endure*, on board of those Emigrant ships: and of the treachery you will meet with there in your new land, amongst the people you will have
>
> to deal with, and entrusting your property with; also in tracing the country *the risk of life* you are exposed to. Is all this my dear John desirable to undergo for a change. George I find has selected out all the bright side, to tell, but left out all the load. Oh my dear John, do not go even yet, your Uncle [William Fowler] justly remarks that you will ever repent it. Your request for some of your dear Mother['s] hair, as soon as ever I can find it, you shall have it.[21]

5.4 A lock of his mother's hair given to John by Aunt Mildred as a memento.

By late March Aunt Mildred was resigned to the great plan since it was going ahead at speed. Though grieved, she said she could only 'commit you into the hands of the Almighty'.[22]

Thomas W. Hall's contribution to the emigration decision

After purchasing his ship *Dauntless* in 1849 in Van Diemen's Land (now Tasmania), Thomas made at least three voyages to Buenos Aires. In July 1850, he set out from Cork for the Rio de la Plata ('river of silver', River Plate), with Sarah, already six months pregnant, and their first child, Tom. He had with him a list of enquiries for his contact, Henry Harratt, the cattle farmer living near Buenos Aires, but it was not until December 1851 that he was able to inform George and John of Harratt's reply.

> The information I could obtain was certainly satisfactory as to the results of the general investment of money in land, which could be obtained at a very low figure [...] for British subjects – as long as the present government holds good, but great [...] toil would be required to become thoroughly acquainted with the business, especially on a sheep farm to understand the different qualities of wool; two years would be about the time before a person would be sufficiently acquainted with it.[23]

Thomas's voyages were getting harder to justify in a time of economic downturn and increased competition. A month later, he had arrived in Cadiz and had received John's changed view about a suitable country for emigration. Thomas was pleased for religious and practical reasons, replying on 14 January 1852:

I was certainly surprised to hear that you had turned your views to New Zealand. I never liked or entered into the idea of your going to Buenos Ayres, amongst a set of B[rea]thless Unitarians or Savage Barbarians as the two parties elegantly denominate each other [...] New Zealand is a different tale & my first impression in perusing your letter was, that I was wishing myself in London to be off too, Brig & all. I hope, should you finally determine to go, that I may be back first – at all events write me all particulars as soon as possible.[24]

By the time he wrote again on 25 July 1852 warning that Argentina as a destination would be problematic, George and John had already decided on New Zealand as their preference. Thomas's letter was critical confirmation that their choice was the right one:

[...] you must take into consideration that the country [Argentina] is on the verge of a disturbance with the Brazils & some of the neighbouring provinces. British subjects have generally, as far as can be done, [had] their property respected in these disturbances.[25]

By March 1852, the month of his departure, John had already accumulated the necessary letters of introduction from influential colleagues and associates and had written his farewell letters. His colleague G. C. Cornwall from the General Post Office in Dublin wrote presciently, 'I doubt not that you will some day be a leading man in New Zealand, probably P.M.G. [postmaster general].'[26]

John, the first to leave

John sold his mare Bracelet at auction before leaving and bought a pup named Countess for £6 to take with him, since his friend

Henry Field, now living a bush life in Wanganui, New Zealand, had recommended, 'If you have a good retriever bring it with you as many birds are lost in the fern & bush after being shot.'[27] Field, a valuable informant, advised John to devote the first six months to a year just looking about and not arranging anything because there were many drawbacks to making sheep farming pay well. He warned that all the books about New Zealand seen in England were got up to induce people to emigrate and were therefore not reliable.

Field also gave advice on the state of land-leasing in the Middle [South] Island and in Canterbury:

> Now with respect to your own plans & views – you will find your idea of going on Maori land in the Middle Island prevented by a Government Ordinance passed some time since which forbids Europeans from renting land or living among the Maoris under a penalty of £100 per day. The Government found that the owners of Stations in the Wairarapa and Manawatu used their influence with the Maoris to prevent the land being sold to the Crown & therefore passed this law in order ultimately to acquire these other districts.[28]

He described a scene of some urgency in relation to licensing pastoral land. 'Great numbers of people' were on the lookout for runs. Whenever a new district was bought from the natives and given out by the government, 'it is all taken up in a few hours'.[29] Regarding staff and domestic arrangements Field cautioned:

> You will find it difficult to get a *good* shepherd as such persons soon get sheep entrusted to them on thirds as it is termed & thus become owners themselves [...] I am

of opinion that a bush life would not suit John Hall any more than myself particularly as I infer from your letter that you have come out without the help of a servant – you will soon find the want of this part of your household furniture and will feel it the more as I do not think you are a likely man to take up with a Maori woman as most bachelor settlers in the bush do before many months are over. The fact is that in theory it is very pleasant to be quite independent but in practice it seems very unnatural to a man to cook his own dinner & wash his own shirts at any rate after the novelty is worn off. [30]

Then George, Agnes and Aggie

George, meanwhile, was tidying up his grain business in Hull while his wife Agnes had gone up to London to consult a doctor. He wrote to John, who had already sailed from London on the *Samarang*, to say he hoped to clear out all his wheat as the market was rising (he realised about £1,000 before leaving). He was, however, anxious about the gold news from Australia, which he thought might cause a shortage of labour in New Zealand. 'We must hope for the best; let the worse come to the worst we are not bound to our plan.'[31] He took his sister Grace up to London to visit the Canterbury Rooms and to hear Sir Thomas Tancred, father of Henry Tancred who had emigrated to New Zealand in 1850, speaking about prospects and the latest accounts from Canterbury. Grace was feeling low. She might have considered accompanying her brothers but was torn by a strong sense of duty to those who had brought her up. A future without her brothers at a time when the country and Hull appeared to be in decline was depressing. 'These are sad times,' she wrote to John in May 1852, 'there seems no prospect for the future; my own heart sinks often when I think of my own prospects; it seems so dreary and it is so difficult to act up to what we know is right but it is wrong to doubt.' She remained in Hull and did not marry for another decade. Her future husband, John Sugden Neall, would become the brothers' faithful agent in England, helpful in sending equipment for their farms and notifying them of wool prices.

By August, George and Agnes had sold their furniture. They set off for New Zealand with little Aggie on 1 November 1852, travelling cabin class on the *Royal Albert* out of London. The ship was carrying 120 passengers, of whom 50 were bound for New Zealand.

Finally, Thomas and Sarah

Before they emigrated to New Zealand on the *Mohammed Shah*, the census records for Liverpool on 31 March 1851 show that Thomas (31), his wife Sarah (35) and the children – Thomas (2+) and George Buceo (1) – with Thomas's sister Grace (24) – presumably visiting to say her farewells – were all living in a boarding house in Dale Street, Liverpool. This was a central street running down to the George Basin and on to New Quay on the River Mersey, and the location for many coaching inns for travellers. Liverpool at the time was the second port in Great Britain, after London. Merchants and shipowners had profited from the demise of the monopolistic East India Company and the advent of free trade. The port was now a hub for emigration to the colonies.

Thomas may have had considerable second-hand knowledge of New Zealand already. The ship that had rescued him and his crew from the sinking *Andromeda* in the Bay of Biscay in January 1847, the *Bangalore* from Madras, was one of the ships that in 1844 had taken hapuka or rock cod from Auckland to a market in Valparaiso.[32] Thomas would have had ample time to talk with its current captain about New Zealand as a place of settlement on their passage back to England, providing its captain was still doing the same run. He had also had the chance to assess Australia as a prospective country for emigration when he purchased *Dauntless* in September 1849.[33]

In the two years before Thomas and Sarah and their sons emigrated, Liverpool was undergoing massive transformation as a port. By mid-century it had an unrivalled dock network of some 200 acres, with swing bridges which opened for ships and closed for horse-drawn traffic and pedestrians moving along the waterfront. The supporting warehouses, made from brick and iron, were fire-proofed. The great Albert Dock was opened in 1846 as an enclosed dock, with warehouses surrounding so that goods could be unloaded from ships moored at the quayside and taken directly into storage. This shortened the turn-around time for ships by two weeks and was a great advance. We must imagine Sarah, with her babies, and Grace, accompanying Thomas to and from his ship in this bustling port, a symbol of Britain's growing eminence and connection with a wider world, keeping in touch with George and John as the plans to leave Britain were evolving.

By 6 December 1851, when Thomas and *Dauntless* were again in Antwerp, he complained to John in a letter that 'times are so bad [...] it is impossible to make a vessel pay her Bills if allowed to stay still at all',[37] saying he was proceeding from Cadiz to the River Plate to load salt. While in Cadiz he heard that John would depart for New Zealand in March 1852. As he pushed his vessel rapidly on its way, Thomas's mind would have constantly been turning to better and safer ways of earning a living, knowing that his brothers were contemplating emigration. By the time he returned to Liverpool and had discharged his crew on 27 September 1852, his mind was made up. Three months later he had gathered his family, sold the *Dauntless* to release capital, and was heading to the antipodes for a new beginning. He wrote to John:

Geo leaves 1ˢᵗ or 2ⁿᵈ next month. [I] shall follow out by next vessel, the Mohammed Shah. I sold the Brig on my return, as my mind was made up long before [...] I got £1500 for the Brig, £400 less than she first cost after classing, but allowing for the depreciation in the property of shipping after three years' wear, I think it is a fair market price.[38]

A sum of £1,500 was ample resource to start life afresh in a new land, as Frederick Weld had indicated.

Before they left, Thomas and Sarah travelled to London to baptise their third child, John, named after his great-grandfather and uncle, at St George in the East, Wapping, the church where his mother Sarah had been baptised in August 1816. The journey also had another purpose, Sarah was saying farewell to her family in London.

5.5 Canterbury Association ships in the East India Dock, London, in May 1851. Two, the *Bangalore* (far left), which rescued Thomas in the Bay of Biscay, and *Lady Nugent* (third from right), on which George sailed to Calcutta, suggests that time on both ships may have linked the brothers' interests to New Zealand.

Notes and references

1. GWH to JH, 16 April 1851.

2. J. Greenwood, *Picture of Hull*, 1835: Hull, J. Greenwood, 5 Bowlalley Lane; London: Simpkin and Marshall.

3. Thomas Wilson, address to the 3rd AGM of the Hull Chamber of Commerce, February 1840 in Joyce M. Bellamy, *The Trade and Shipping of Nineteenth-Century Hull*, pp. 27–8.

4. ibid.

5. Thomas Allen, *A New & Complete History of the County of York*, 1828, vol. 1, p. 278.

6. British History Online, http://www.british-history.ac.uk.

7. John Hall, essay in the *Samarang Gazette*, vol. 5, written en route to New Zealand, 1852, TSA.

8. I. J. Holland to JH, Plymouth, 31 January 1850.

9. GWH to JH, 4 April 1850.

10. ibid., 16 April 1851.

11. ibid.

12. GWH to JH, 8 June 1851.

13. Weld's pamphlet with John Hall's inscription on it is in the Terrace Station Archive, Hororata.

14. GWH to JH, 16 April 1851.

15. Agnes Hall to JH, 22 April 1850.

16. ibid., 26 September 1850.

17. GWH to JH, June 1851 [unspecified day].

18. ibid., 13 January 1852.

19. Gareth Campbell, 2014, 'Government Policy during the British Railway Mania and the 1847 Commercial Crisis' in *British Financial Crises Since 1825*, Nicholas Dimsdale and Anthony Hotson (eds), Oxford University Press.

20. GWH to JH, 8 June 1851.

21. Mildred Fowler to JH, 13 February 1852.

22. ibid., 22 March 1852.

23. TWH to JH, 6 December 1851.

24. ibid., 14 January 1852.

25. ibid., 25 July 1852.

26. G. C. Cornwall to JH, 19 March 1852.

27. Henry Field to JH, 24 July 1852.

28. ibid., 20 June 1852.

29. ibid.

30. ibid.

31. GWH to JH, 28 and 29 April 1852.

32. Nicholas Twohill, 'The British World and its Role in the Relationship between New Zealand and the Southern Cone Countries of South America, 1820-1914' in

Historia, no 43, vol. 1, 2010, pp. 113–116.

33. Transcriptions and transactions for *Dauntless*, PRO/BT 107.101 show he bought the ship for £1,900.

34. Don Chambers, 'Timbers used for shipbuilding in the Tamar Valley in the 1830s and 1840s' in *Australian Journal of Maritime & Ocean Affairs*, vol. 3, issue 3, 2001.

35. GWH to JH, 6 November 1844: 'I did just happen to say a word about Father's taking a small share in a small vessel with me, but without the smallest success; he declaring he had been very liberal to me; he never would of course … it is the first time I ever named any thing of the kind, & of course the last.'

36. Crew list, Schedule C, Transcriptions and Transactions of the Dauntless, 1851, PRO/BT 98 2601.

37. TWH to JH, 6 December 1851.

38. TWH to JH, 29 October 1852.

6

EARLY YEARS IN NEW ZEALAND, 1852–1883

On his voyage out to New Zealand on the *Samarang*, one of the last vessels chartered by the Canterbury Association, John Hall edited the ship's weekly newspaper.[1] This gave him the opportunity to write about the aims of the Canterbury Association. It was clear to him that its purpose was to create a 'Britain in the South'.[2] In an overpopulated island like England, where competition for work and income was becoming more desperate, the emigration plan made perfect sense. But he was well aware of some of the prejudices held by those who remained against those emigrating:

> Time was, and that within the memory of most of us, when a person leaving England for one of her colonies, was looked upon by his friends and relations, as one who must be so devoid of industry or perseverance, that he was of no use at home; it seemed, in fact, to be a general opinion, that unless there was something wrong in such a person's previous conduct, or that everything else had failed him, he would never think of thus expatriating himself. [...][3]

Attitudes had changed with the success of settlements established in Australia. The native New Zealand Māori had been found to be 'the finest and most intelligent race of uncivilized men ever yet discovered', and their country, for the fertility of its soil and beauty of its climate, 'one of the most valuable dependencies of the British Crown'. Moreover, colonisation was now looked on as a promising, albeit a bold and adventurous undertaking, instead of 'the resort of a ruined ne'er do well'. John Hall approved of the principles of the Canterbury Association, to transplant a cross-section of English society and to retain its desirable features and institutions – particularly religion and education. He and his two brothers neatly fit into the category he describes below. He uses the word 'gentleman' in a looser sense not as the class description of someone whose unearned income allowed them to be a gentleman in their leisure time:

> [...] the gentleman whose capital has hitherto sufficed to bring up a family in a manner befitting his station, but who can see no prospect of being able to settle his children on the same footing; and to the *younger son* of such a family who prefers rural pursuits to the drudgery of an office, or honest exertion in a community where *labour is no disgrace*, to the really degrading situation of a dependent or hanger-on upon friends and relatives at home. Individuals of this class, not driven from home by the pressure of adverse circumstances, may reasonably look forward to occupying a prominent position in their adopted country, and to become, in the course of time, the founders of colonial families of importance.[4]

John's diary account of arrival

The *Samarang* came into Lyttelton Harbour on Saturday 31 July 1852 and for the next month John kept a journal of his observations. He found the harbour 'did not wear such a luxuriant wooded appearance as the views had led me to suppose, but reminded more of [a] Yorkshire Moor or a Sussex Down – however, altho' in winter season, it appeared by no means sterile, & was certainly picturesque'. There were many people on the jetty to see the first arrivals, eager for news. In spite of a splitting headache he went to the Mitre Hotel for a meal and arranged to get his dogs on shore.

> Saw a good many of the Aborigines; accosted one, but could get no English out of him. Others in stature & build [...] were fine & athletic but their features less handsome than had expected; broad noses & thick lips predominated very greatly. All wore European dress & were slovenly in their attire & 9/10ths of them tattooed. This however appears to be going out. Colour light copper as generally described. Altogether they give the impression of being the degraded portion of the race, as they are described to be. The clergyman [Revd D. Dudley] gave a good account of them – as being quaint, inoffensive people.[5]

Fortuitously, he met John Robert Godley, the chief agent of the Canterbury Association, and Captain Charles Simeon, an army officer and surveyor and presented his letters of introduction to them, thereby securing recognition based on his old-world connections. He welcomed an opportunity to give thanks to God for his safe passage and was surprised to find the Canterbury Association Barracks, where new arrivals stayed temporarily, fitted up as a temporary church and, the verité being chanted to a Gregorian tone; a sound that filled him with gratitude and wonder 'at this distant corner of the earth'.

John was surprised that there were more shops and hotels than in a large English village and the 'hillsides turned out to be covered with tufty grass or with moss knee deep'. He made some botanical and agricultural observations and checked the soils, noting that it was expensive to bring fern land into cultivation. The natives were 'willing to work in a number, but seem afraid to engage singly'. He trusted that 'this childish apprehension' would wear off in time. He was glad to hear that Māori pronunciation most resembled French and noted that the Māori were allowed to smoke tobacco but not take spirits; a publican giving them a glass would lose his licence. 'Excellent!' he wrote.

6.1 Pilgrims landing at Port Lyttelton.

On Tuesday 3 August, taking his dogs Countess in a basket and Emperor under his legs on the smaller boat to shore, John Hall began his preparations for going over the Bridle Track to Christchurch, leaving the dogs behind in temporary care. It was raining and the horses hired at £1 a day were 'very indifferent'.

> From summit of hill view of plain very limited [...] snowy mountains quite hid. Riccarton & Papanui woods most prominent objects on the immense flat. Cultivation

increasing as we approached Christchurch; rough as might have been expected; less wheat appearing than I had looked for, but quite as much water [...] From the ferry over the Heathcote, a road about 30 feet wide, ditch on each side partly metalled. At Christchurch went to the Land Office. Brittan [William Rolleston's father-in-law] impressed me as a consequential humbug: far inferior, & far more stuck up than Godley: he *is* a gentleman, other wants to play the great man.[6]

He headed towards Riccarton. Because it was raining and dark he could not return to Lyttelton so he stayed the night in the Golden Fleece and was disappointed in the hope of finding any person who could tell him much about the prospect of sheep farming.

By 9 August he was ready to go up country to explore south of the Rakaia River, accompanied by Arthur and Richard Knight, fellow immigrants from the *Samarang* who he thought 'a little wild'. The Knight brothers were the nephews of the novelist Jane Austen. They settled ultimately on Run 38 on the south bank of the upper Selwyn River on 7,000 acres which they leased, naming it Steventon, after their Aunt Jane's family vicarage in Hampshire.

James Edward Fitzgerald, who later became first superintendent of Canterbury, wanted to accompany John and the Knights but had to wait until the ship cleared. John engaged a Māori called Peter who was 'thoroughly acquainted with the country' and spoke some English though 'not sufficient to make his information of much use'.

In the following month, John reconnoitred potential pastoral land in the North Island leaving his servant and servant's wife, dogs and traps at Lyttelton. This expedition was exhausting, as he told his close friend and agent in England, John Sugden Neall:

I embarked in a little craft for Hawkes Bay and was caught in a gale, during which Master and Crew all turned in and went to sleep while the rudder was washed away, but arrived safely at last. I remained in the Ahuriri for about 3 weeks, at one time making an excursion on foot with a native to carry provisions and a white guide as interpreter, and at another getting on more quickly by the aid of horseflesh. On my return I had to trudge about 120 miles on foot, the only nag I could meet with being addicted to buck jumping. Thoroughly tired of 'camping out', i.e. sleeping under heaven's blue canopy and eating what you could carry, I got to Wellington two hours before the departure of a vessel for Lyttelton embarked, and arrived here 3 weeks since.[7]

By now he was reflecting on Canterbury and its advantages over other provinces in New Zealand. He told John Neall enthusiastically that there was hardly any circumstance which would tell a newcomer they had migrated to the Antipodes. The people did not have the rough, sharp, colonial ways met with in other settlements, he thought. Their conversation and reminiscences of England were as fresh as his own. Excepting that carts took the place of cabs and carriages, everything in society was 'exactly' as he had been accustomed to.

This seeming familiarity of the Canterbury settlement with what he had known in England partly reflected the prominent men he had so far met. Charles Simeon was an army officer, James Edward Fitzgerald had studied mathematics at Cambridge and John Robert Godley had been a co-founder of the Canterbury Association in London and formerly a poor law commissioner for County Leitrim during the Irish potato famine of the 1840s.

By December 1852, his fifth month in New Zealand, largely

because of the vagaries of postage, John was becoming terribly frustrated at not hearing news of his two brothers who were to follow him. He complained to John Neall:

It is utterly impossible for me to tell whether this letter will reach you in 3 months, 6 months, or at all and altho' we have accounts from home to the 2nd of June, more than six months ago, I am consequently in the greatest perplexity as [to] my brothers' movements. The steamers from Panama will remedy all this and will be the greatest boon New Zealand could possibly receive.[8]

With the help of Richard Harman, a civil engineer who later became his business manager, John secured a sheep run of 45,000 acres south of the Rakaia for his brothers George and Thomas. John thought the land very good, but it was situated unfortunately across a very difficult river, the braided and treacherous Rakaia. 'This like most of the rivers in the Middle Island is more of a torrent than a river, running in five or six channels of shingle which alter with every flood, rendering a ferry difficult, and fording being, from the force of the current, rather dangerous,'[9] he told John Neall, after a hopeless attempt to cross the river in a canoe. It was largely because of the difficulty of transferring stock and goods across the river that he cancelled this licence when Run 20, Rakaia Terrace Station, on its north side became available from Mark Pringle Stoddart whose licence was transferred by May 1853. It was the first sheep run selected within the Canterbury block and had the advantage of coming with house, improvements, stores and 1,800 sheep for the sum of £2,750. John later told John Neall that the brothers expected to shear 2,000 sheep by November 1853 and would like to use Neall as their English agent in selling it.

John Neall was an invaluable friend in sending John some essentials on request – six pairs of Merino drawers, both 'stout' and 'thin' (presumably for winter and summer wear), six pairs of white kid gloves, 12 pairs of strong gloves for rough work, a cork swimming belt (no doubt for the troublesome Rakaia River), three pairs of Blucher working boots and two pairs of button boots for town wear. He even sent dahlia seeds which were quickly planted. John told him that 'the greatest impediment to the propagation of European, or indeed any plants is *wind, wind, wind*' since it blew hard at least three days out of seven. Shelter from planted trees was gradually 'rising up' and though men, women and children thrived under wind, plants did not.

At the time of John's arrival in New Zealand, gold was discovered in Australia in Ballarat, near Melbourne. 'A mania appears to have seized the labouring population,' John told Neall, 'and most of those who have the means of leaving are off to the diggings.' Almost every craft in the waters was advertised for Port Philip. 'You may imagine the advisability of G & T Hall taking up their abode in Port Philip has more than once been pondered on', he wrote on September 1852, 'but I think digging would be folly when I have capital to employ' and after all, he thought 'sheep farming will pay best in the long run.' For John and Thomas, that was to prove the case.

The brothers, especially John, leased other properties on the south bank of the Rakaia (see map 6.5), but apart from Ashburton Forks (Ringwood) and Elloughton Station (Blackwood), they sold or abandoned these without ever stocking them.

The Hall brothers came to New Zealand with the expectation of becoming landowners. The idea behind the Canterbury Association initiative was that those men with capital, such as the Halls, would acquire large estates and become a land-owning aristocracy, operating with managers, while the poorer immigrants would be able to acquire smaller holdings and work their own land as yeoman farmers. Edward Gibbon Wakefield envisaged wage earners becoming landowners within three or four years of arrival, and the revenue derived from leasing land from the Crown would fund and promote further emigration to New Zealand.

John proved an effective manager and was able to secure the whole freehold of his Terrace Station run at Hororata, Canterbury, after his initial partnership with his brothers expired. By 1878 only 8,000 of his 23,000 sheep were on leasehold land. He managed to hold several runs without stocking them (a requirement of the Crown lease) and was able to profit from doing so because there was little or no inspection and only a challenge by another claimant before the Land Board could force a runholder to carry out his obligations to stock the land.

George, Agnes and Aggie arrive
The *Royal Albert*, with George, Agnes and little Aggie on board had arrived at the heads of Dunedin Harbour in early March 1853. Agnes's health after her recent childbirth had improved by the time they left England, but on arrival in New Zealand, John reported, 'Mrs George's health was so much worse that she cannot be removed to a distance of 47 miles from medical advice.'[10]

6.2 John Hall c.1856.

It is probable that her problem was endometritis (inflammation of the womb lining). 'An old internal complaint from which she suffered greatly at home' is how John discreetly described her illness to John Neall. It seemed to defy all attempts at alleviation. The family therefore lived for a time with the resident doctor for Kaiapoi, Samuel Beswick, brother of William Beswick, Thomas's friend. It is at this time that Agnes, probably out of boredom with her new colonial life without the amenities she had been accustomed to, a scarcity of friends and a husband away working with his brothers, apparently 'erred' with the man denoted in the letter below as 'Sam B'. News of Agnes's supposed sin, whatever it was and it may not have been much, was duly conveyed by letter to Aunt Mildred, whose outrage exploded in a letter to John, full of emphases:

> I cannot refrain sending you these lines to say how *grieved* and shocked *we all are* at the news which [h]as reached us relative to Agnes's *misconduct* and *insulting treatment*, which it appears almost breaks her Husband's heart, *after all* poor George's *kindness* and *affection* to *her* never having spared any expense however inconvenient to him. [...] 'Sam B we consider the *biggest villain* that ever stept this earth. I am astonished that George would *allow*

> *himself* to remain under the same roof of *such a fellow.* [...] she is a vain weak Woman [...] She has never been a good affectionate Wife to poor George.' [11]

6.3 Agnes Emma Hall, c.1870s, Canterbury Museum.

Aunt Mildred advised that George should bring Agnes back to England, then sent money to Thomas to be divided as a present, not knowing George's address. She wrote a new will while staying at Tunbridge Wells in July 1855, an extraordinary document in her own handwriting, John Neall told John Hall in January 1869, after Mildred and her husband had both died. Its purpose was to ensure that in the event of anything fatal happening to George or his daughter the money was to revert to the surviving brothers and sister, Thomas, John and Grace.[12] Mildred was anxious that if George died before Agnes she might benefit.

In letters to Grace in England, Agnes comes across as a strong, sensible and sensitive woman, much challenged by George's declining health and fortunes. Of the two Dryden sisters who settled with George and later John in New Zealand, she was the less fortunate, finding childbirth difficult. She had no further children after Aggie and then lost her only daughter from the age of ten to 18 to an eight-year-long education in England. She emotionally and practically supported a near invalided husband weakened by a digestive illness, and frequently assisted her often isolated and lonely sister Rose when John was away on government or provincial business. Of all the houses she lived in, she was most fond of Ashburton Forks, where she and George lived from 1857 to 1862, the 'happiest time of my colonial life', she told Grace. After 15 years in Canterbury she wrote, 'I am still "homesick". [...] I don't know how it might be, could we have remained in our home on The Ashburton, but since the losses that obliged us to leave it and other troubles since, I feel as

6.4 (a) George W. Hall, *c*.1867.

if we were never to know a settled place of abode again.'[13] But Agnes was stoic and though thinking of the station with regret, knew it was 'no use crying over spilt milk'.

Ashburton Forks Station (Run 97, later known as Ringwood) was situated between the north and south branches of the Ashburton River. George took over the run in February 1854. With the help of a manager he was apparently pasturing 3,900 sheep on 8,500 acres there in 1859, but a severe loss of sheep in the July 1861 snowstorm meant he and Agnes had to practise the strictest economy and dismiss their servant. When George was unable to manage his property holdings through ill health, John Hall sold Ashburton Forks for him in 1862 and George and Agnes moved to John's Selwyn Station homestead (Run 17), next to Rakaia Terrace Station, for a year. Their daughter Aggie had returned to England in 1861 to be educated under the guardianship of her Aunt Grace.

Thomas, Sarah and their three sons arrive July 1853

Thomas and Sarah would have preferred to come out with George and Agnes, but the birth of their baby John delayed their departure. They left Torbay in January 1853. Three months later their ship, the *Mohammed Shah*, caught fire south of Cape Leeuwin, 600 miles from the coast of Western Australia. Thomas, as probably the most experienced seafaring passenger, was commended for rescuing some passengers and, crucially, the ship's navigation equipment and specie, or passengers' money, as well as for removing the contents of the powder magazine near where the fire started. He remained on the ship, sending Sarah and the children to the brig *Ellen* which eventually landed all on board at Hobart. The family arrived at Lyttelton at the end of July. Relatives and friends in England learnt of this disaster through *The Times* and *Shipping Gazette* on 15 August 1853. It was not until then that they knew all hands had been saved.

In this setback, Thomas and Sarah lost all their belongings, including the letters of introduction so important to launch Thomas in the new colony. He described their situation to John Neall, in England, writing from Kaiapoi on 7 May 1854. The letter was received four months later. It was written without paragraphing and every margin was written over, to cut down the weight and therefore postage costs:

6.4 (b) Thomas W. Hall.

J.S. Neall Esq.

Dear Sir

I have to acknowledge the receipt of your favours dated Oct 31st and Nov 9th both of which came to hand together on the 4th inst. The case JH 3 came also a short time previous per Portland, but I only got it 10 days since.

Many thanks my dear Sir for your sympathy in regard to our disastrous passage and also for the trouble you have taken respecting the insurance etc. I was certainly very much surprised to find that any delay should have been incurred in the payment of insurance on effects as I have saved none, although I am aware some of the other cabin passengers did save a change or so.

When Mrs Hall left the *M.S.* for the *Ellen*, having 3 children with her, one an infant only 7 months old and also the specie [coins] which was rather heavy, I did not think it prudent, as the sea was high and coming on dark, for them to load themselves with anything further than what Mrs H had in a small reticule, viz half a dozen handkerchiefs for the children, nicks [knickers], and also about the same number of napkins for the baby, her watch (which has not gone since) and one or two miniatures of her mother, etc. I had previously requested her to avoid taking any of her trinkets with her, as before falling in with the brig it appeared most probable that if we did reach land with the boats we should have to travel some distance before reaching any settlement and in case of falling in with the natives, might have been a temptation to them.

I think I named before that I remained on board until the foremast went; the boat I then left in was half swamped by the sea, which was then tossing heavily, before we reached the brig, and were obliged to throw all loose things overboard, as well as to keep bailing with two buckets as fast as we could, the boat being nearly full up to the thwarts. Neither had I a chance of saving either chronometer instruments or even the plate which would naturally have been taken next to the specie. Indeed we had to borrow clothes at times for a change after we got on board the Ellen. The other cabin passengers who left in the evening, having only themselves to look after, had a better chance of saving a few things (few enough God knows), but any who could expect much to be saved in crowded boats, night coming on and a heaving sea can have little idea of the nice management required to board a ship in a gale of wind.

When I left I was fully convinced that we required the boats to show as bold a side to the sea as possible and the sequel proved the correctness of that opinion, for had we been much deeper, our boat could not have recovered herself from the sea that broke into her.

I have been until last week, at our Sheep Station which lies about due west from Christchurch and 8 miles from the foot of Mount Hutt. Our term of partnership which was altered to 9 months from the 1st August, having elapsed, I have come down to Kaiapoi with my family. It is a rising place, about 12 miles north of Christchurch and the principal site of the massacre of the Southern natives [Ngai Tahu tribe] which took place between 30–40 years ago under Raupara [Te Rauparaha] and Rangahaeta [Te Rangihaeata.]

Beswicks have taken up part land here for agricultural purposes and I have done the same; Geo [brother George] and I having our runs south of the Rakaia, do not think it advisable to go there as yet. John has gone up to the old Station which is situated on his run and where until now we have been working the sheep together. We have just been busy lambing and had a very fair one so far. When I came down last week we had saved 95% on the lambs dropped. As soon as it is over and the lambs are strong enough to travel, Geo and I intend placing ours on a run near here.

The province is rather in an excited state with the cheap land question. A great quantity has been bought up outside the block and if cheap land is introduced within the same, the sooner we sell the better.

I intend going into town tomorrow and shall have a declaration drawn up by a notary and forward in duplicate.

Respecting the Ellen's claim for salvage, I always considered they had very little. The specie was not saved by any extra efforts of theirs. Most undoubtedly had mine been on freight it would not have been saved, being too weighty to have brought down the tacklefall which was the way we had to take to the boats at last and the small apology for a lifeboat in which Captain Martin came was as full of water as she could be when we got alongside the Ellen.

Mrs H joins me in kind regards to yourself and Mrs Neall and family. Geo and John are both up the country at present so I must pass on their respects for them. Again thanking you for your kind services and offers

I am Dear Sir

Yours truly

T.W. Hall[14]

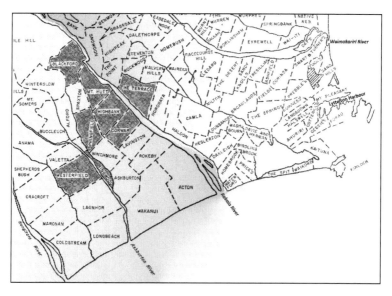

6.5 Map showing by shading land leased on either side of the Rakaia River by George, Thomas and John Hall.

The Terrace (Run 20, 20K) JH, GWH and TWH initially. Bought from M.P. Stoddart April 1853 for £2750 with 1870 sheep, lambs, horses, stores and sundries. Extended 1858 to include Run 17 (10K) from John, Paul and Michael Studholme.
Ashburton Forks (Ringwood, Run 97, 8.5K) GWH Feb. 1854. Pastured 3900 sheep in 1859. Sold 1863 to C.H. Greenstreet.
Highbank GWH and TWH (Runs 112 & 113, 20K) Oct. & Dec. 1852. Sold 1859 to Brown & Allen.
Springfield (Runs 54, 10K and 106 10K). JH and GWH 1852 but then abandoned.
Mount Hutt. JH obtained licences for Run 115 Aug. 1853 and Run 148 in 1855; did not stock and sold to Alexander Lean Feb 1857, unstocked and unimproved, for £1400.
Westerfield. JH secured Run 15 (later Run 451) Oct. 1854 and sold it to Charles Reed for £2000 before 1864.
Lendon (Corwar, Run 116. Taken up with Run 117 (part of Lavington) by Hall brothers c. end of 1852.
Blackford (Elloughton, Runs 291, 264 June 1858, Run 329 July 1857).Sold to Henry & Alfred Gray 1859.

Table 6.1: Hall brothers' holdings in the Rakaia area

A combined effort

The original plan was that the Hall brothers would work Rakaia Terrace Station for nine months to see how they pulled together, and then would be at liberty to continue or dissolve their partnership. However, because 'Mrs George's health' required George and Agnes to live with the doctor in Kaiapoi, Thomas only was permanently located at the station and John, after securing a seat on the Provincial Council, could not leave Christchurch easily. John and George would 'go up to assist [Thomas] whenever practicable'.[15] John was very satisfied with this arrangement. Thomas was in charge at the station, and managed with a good deal of energy, ensuring that 15 bales of wool of about 300 lbs each was the first wool to appear in Christchurch that year. Once the partnership was dissolved in 1855 and John became more embroiled in provincial politics from his base in Christchurch, he sublet to T. H. Potts and Henry Phillips until 1862, then bought neighbouring property, Run 17, the Selwyn Station, where George and Agnes resided for a year after getting into debt.

A daily 'Station Journal' was kept by the three brothers and covered the period from June 1853 to June 1854. It shows the extraordinary conditions they faced when none of them had any experience in farming. They began on the windiest place in Canterbury, Windwhistle, where their 20,000 acres ran from the Rakaia River almost to the foothills. Their modest dwelling was apparently near the river and down the terrace. In 1953, John's grandson, John Williamson Dryden Hall, described this time in a newspaper article:

> The runholders who took up land were obliged to stock it with one sheep to every twenty acres within nine months; failing this they forfeited their lease [...] The first consideration for a new runholder was to build up his flock as quickly as possible. There were no precedents for the work they were starting; mostly they learned from experience. There were a few English and Scottish shepherds well acquainted with a certain type of sheep work, but even they must have felt themselves at a loss when confronted with thousands of sheep running on vast areas of land. Where they came from a man shepherded a hundred or so sheep on land securely fenced and provided with good shelter. The ewes got individual maternity care, and new-born lambs were not exposed to the elements until some time after birth.[16]

The brothers' own accounts from 'The Station Journal'[17] bear out the conditions they laboured under:

[Lambing in midwinter:]

2 July. Very cold, hard frost, clear sky. Nine lambs in the night, of which four are dead. 6 July. Thick raining weather and blowing strongly from the S.W. all day.

[Sheep pens were constructed from beech timber cut from the nearby hills:]

Self busy all day after assisting to cut out lambs and ewes, in shifting ewe pen, cutting off the wild Irishman [weed] which was very thick in the new yard and putting up shelter. Nine lambs today of which two were dead.

[The timber was hauled from the bush by bullocks and horses pulling drays:]

Went on the woolshed spur to look for the drays, and saw the bullocks coming in but without the dray. On joining the men they informed me they had been bogged with the bullock dray, and had been obliged to unload, and that on getting the dray out of the bog, the bullocks made a start with the wood, and capsized it wheels up. Having left one of the chains behind in the morning, they were unable to right the dray, not being able to get all the bullocks on after several attempts were obliged to come without it. They got in with the bullocks about 6 p.m.

[Horses and cows went missing: 10 October, Thomas reported:]

The boy Jack looking for the cow all the morning, but not able to find her.

1 October: Rode down as far as Sanderson's on the river flat to look for Boxer and Picton, which had taken off yesterday or last night, but did not find them.

[Bullocks broke out and rampaged through the newly established vegetable garden, trampling the peas, turnips, potatoes, onions, and the cucumber and strawberry beds:]

28 September: Found the bullocks, which had been camped in the upper paddock last night to have broken into the garden, having partly knocked down the wall in three places and devoured the whole of the cabbages, besides treading down many plants and severely defacing the garden.

Stores came by horse-drawn dray from Christchurch some forty miles away and included on one occasion, eight bags of flour, two chests of tea, one bag of sugar, one wheelbarrow wheel, one iron pot, and sundries from town for the station. Neighbours often called to borrow provisions when they ran out of them, and travellers called on their way through to another destination. Runholders were endangered by others bringing scabby sheep into their area. Sheep with the skin disease scab were treated with tobacco water as a preventive measure. Thomas and John, having received information that a Mr P. had purchased diseased sheep which he intended to bring to pasture near their run, procured letters from other runholders to present to him as a protest against him crossing their runs or bringing scabby sheep into the vicinity.

The combined arrangement between the three Hall brothers expired on 1 May 1854. It is not surprising that two men used to independent lives at sea, commanding a crew of men, and their younger brother, used to office life, found the close inter-relationships needed to run a difficult new venture uncongenial. John was pragmatic:

Sheep farming above all other things requires between partners a perfect similarity of habits and ideas, and this, from the different course of training we have gone thro' does not exist. Our joining together at first has however been a great assistance to us, especially to my brother [Thomas].[18]

In 1854 Thomas sold his share of Run 20 in the Rakaia to John and was living in Kaiapoi on 50 acres, engaged in crop farming. Perhaps the motivation to move there was the presence of Thomas's old Scarborough friend, William Beswick.

Four Beswick brothers had emigrated to New Zealand – William, John, Joseph and Samuel. William began a diary in London in 1850 before leaving in which he recounts visiting the newly opened London zoo and witnessing surgeons in a London medical school performing an operation. His New Zealand entries were brief and filled with weather reports, a useful guide for future predictions in planting and stock movements, with brief mentions of Thomas Hall and his family, though they are not wildly illuminating. He and 'Tom' rode to the Phillips homestead to dine on 21 November 1853, and on 7 December they delivered wool by dray to the quay at Kaiapoi on the Waimakariri River, the main transport artery for the embryonic town. On 21 January he entertained Tom and his brother George to tea. He let Tom have a hat (no doubt he and Sarah were missing many essential items from the shipwreck) and William's wife Liz gave George further clothes. On a fine sunny day William, Tom and George 'went up to Kaiapoi', probably to inspect the newly leased land

6.6 St Bartholomew's, Cass Street, Kaiapoi.

William Beswick and Thomas Hall shared. They had taken out a lease for 21 years on 50 acres of rural land[19] and presumably built a homestead there because Kaiapoi was where Will, the fourth son of Thomas and Sarah, was born and christened, on 15 September 1854, the sponsors being William and Liz Beswick and Sam Beswick.[20]

William Beswick was keen to establish a school for his and other settlers' growing families in Kaiapoi. On 17 November 1854 he wrote to John Hall, who now represented the Country District on the Canterbury Provincial Council, to say he had heard of a man who wanted to be headmaster and wanted to go ahead with the school.[21] By January 1855, the Halls and Beswicks were resolved to build a suitable church for Kaiapoi to satisfy the community's spiritual needs. William recorded that he with George and Thomas Hall were on the committee for building St Bartholomew's, which claims to be the earliest church in Canterbury.[22] As their mother's Williamson forebears had done in Gothenburg, the Halls were establishing an Anglican church in another country. As Thomas mentioned in his letter to John Neall above, as recently as 1830–1831 the Māori chief, Te Rauparaha, had besieged the Kaiapoi *pā* and killed members of the Ngai Tahu tribe living there. This was not a land grab but a revenge attack on another tribe, but still it would have been reassuring for the Halls to have their old Scarborough friends, William and Sam Beswick, living close by for moral support and friendship.

Old Yorkshire ties

The Beswicks, like the Halls, were a Yorkshire shipowning and merchant family, well embedded in the maritime and social life which the Hall brothers had enjoyed between Hull and Scarborough. William Beswick visited Thomas's father before sailing for New Zealand, to say farewell and to carry news to the Halls. They shared books as well as land and expertise. Beswick family letters show how closely interconnected these seafaring families were over generations. A letter of 5 November 1836 written from Odessa by William to his father Sam in Scarborough mentions that he has known a George King who 'used to work in Mr Geo Fowler's sail loft' (a relative of shipowner William Fowler who Thomas's Aunt Mildred married). Aunt Mildred's love is forwarded to Thomas by William's father, Sam Beswick, when William and Thomas were both in Odessa. These family alliances support recent historical theories that regional affiliations among emigrants to New Zealand were unsurprisingly stronger than any allegiance to their mother country.[24] Thomas Hall and William Beswick eventually moved to Timaru with their families and both helped to establish the early facilities of that town. According to the historian, Oliver A. Gillespie, another Beswick brother, Joseph, in 1860 provided an early ferry service in the Mackenzie Country, probably across the Pukaki River, with an old whaler (the smaller boat used to approach whales) he had taken with him to New Zealand. He had grazed his sheep with the Hall brothers in 1854 in mid-Canterbury and in 1858 owned Gristhorpe station, between Balmoral, where George Hall grazed cattle, and the Mistake, owned by Thomas Hall. They worked the stations together. In 1864 when he ran into financial difficulty, Joseph sold half of Gristhorpe and 4,000 sheep to John Hall.[25]

After a year of growing crops in Kaiapoi, Thomas found that agricultural farming suited him less than sheep farming, and therefore resumed working his Elloughton Station near the foothills of Mount Hutt, on land between the Rakaia and the north branch of the Ashburton River. An expedition to reconnoitre land by Potts, Phillips and Leach in mid-1857 'made Blackford, where the Tom Halls entertained them hospitably'.[26] Elloughton Station, which I think is the Blackford mentioned in this quote, was named after the Hall family's summer cottage in Elloughton, Yorkshire, to please Thomas's father. My grandfather, Richard Williamson Hall, the fifth and last son of Thomas and Sarah, was born there on 9 December 1856 and baptised in Kaiapoi.

By 1856 George was corresponding with John over the acquisition of land, paying rent on the Mount Hutt run and applying for a licence on John's behalf. Thomas had also given him authority to act in the matter of his Kaiapoi section, leased jointly with William Beswick.[27] John had in this year been appointed Colonial Secretary in the Fox Ministry and was Resident Magistrate in Christchurch, a job that combined the offices of Commissioner of Police and Sheriff.

Wellington had experienced an earthquake in January 1855 which some locals tried to hush up so as not to deter settlers from arriving, because runholders were desperate for cooks, nursemaids and labourers to assist them. Young women tended to marry shortly after arrival, so turnover of staff was frequent. The bed of the Wellington Harbour had been permanently raised four feet. In the Wairarapa the sea rose 27 feet and washed away some wool sheds. Some Māori were drowned. Though Canterbury people were very much alarmed, the only damage done there was some falling books and smashed crockery. It had proved to be out of harm's way.[28]

In England, the family the brothers left was slowly adjusting to their absence. Mrs Sarah Holmes, who had acted as matchmaker in George Hall's second marriage, wrote to say young Grace was 'remarkably well, and [...] as kind and amiable as ever' though 'she seldom speaks of any of you without tears in her eyes' and even their father 'drops a few tears' at the thought that all three sons are in New Zealand and 'gone and left him in his old age', though once the idea has passed 'he is all right again'.[29]

Expansion into the Mackenzie Country

After the brothers abandoned their original business contract in 1854–1855 they began to lease enormous holdings in the Mackenzie Country near Timaru. William Vance described the majestic landscape and its perils as, 'a vast unrelieved plain of billowing tussock that merges through the shimmering heat into an array of snow-capped mountains. Masses of black clouds pout through the passes only to melt into clear sky. Glacial rivers flow into lakes of azure blue. Windless mornings give way to afternoons of howling nor'westers. Sahara summers recede to Arctic winters.'[30]

In the early to mid-1860s the Halls' combined holdings in the Mackenzie Country, mainly below Mount Cook between Lakes Pukaki and Tekapo, were 130,000 acres, comprising The Wolds, Balmoral, Braemar, Castle Hall (formerly Gristhorpe, now Glenmore) and The Mistake (so named because of an error as to its boundaries, now named Godley Peaks). They retained managers and shepherds to do the hands-on work such as overseeing sheep, acquiring and building timber and wire fences, lambing, shearing, supervising bullock drays for carrying wool and supplies, and building outhouses for shelter and living quarters. For men with no farming background, the licensing of such vast tracts of land now seems to us ambitious or greedy beyond belief, though the large size of the Hall's acquisitions was not atypical.

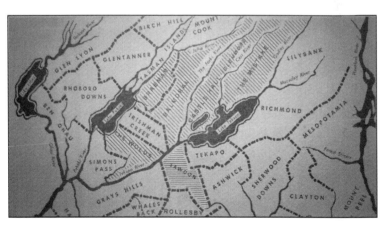

6.7 Map showing by cross-hatching runs in the Mackenzie Country in which the Hall brothers had a leasehold interest.

Balmoral (Run 251, 40K) GWH May 1858 with Edward Stericker; solo GWH from 1862; taken over by JH late 1866 and sold (with Glenmore) to Alfred Cox April 1869 (registered 1872) for £13,500 with 20,000 sheep. Part east of the Forks River was split off and taken up by Joseph Beswick who named it Gristhorpe.

Glenmore (initially Gristhorpe, then Castle Station, then Castle Hall), JH Dec. 1866 from Beswick; sold with Balmoral by JH to Alfred Cox Mar. 1869.

Braemar (Run 274, 10K) TWH Sept. 1858 and Run 325, 10K in 1859; sold to Alfred Cox 1867 for £1000.

The Wolds (Run 275, 20K, then 30K acres) TWH Sept. 1858 to 1867. Part managed by William Ostler who left in 1863. Sold to Smith & Saunders Aug. 1867. West of Lake Tekapo near Mary Range.

The Mistake (Hall's Mistake, Run 273 ± 379; 16K to 64K including 10K 1860). TWH 1858. Sold Aug. 1867 to Smith & Saunders; became Godley Peaks in 1921.

Sawdon (Run 252) GWH bought 1857 with Stericker; taken over solely by Stericker 1861. Initially 20K acres, extended Aug. 1858 to include part of Whalesback Flat (20K), then part of Grampions (JH) May 1859 and Sawdon Hill (Run 320) Nov. 1859. Sold to Packerson Bros. 1863.

Whalesback: Vance says '2 runs of Whalesback flat' were 'owned by Halls' but leased to Packerson and sold to Goulds 1869.

Grampions Hill Homestead (Run 296) JH 1859; transferred to John Tucker Ford 1860. Probably not lived in by the Halls but run together with the Whalesback Flat and Sawdon (Vance).

Table 6.2 Hall brothers' holdings in the Mackenzie Country

In 1858, George began the process of acquiring the Hall brothers' holdings in the Mackenize Country when he leased Runs 251 and 269, the Balmoral Station of 60,000 acres, extending to the Forks River and bounded on the south by Irishman Creek and on the north by the Jollie River. John took this station over in 1867 and sold it in 1869 to his friend, Alfred Cox. The Halls leased other properties in the Mackenzie Country, some with other squatters and sometimes for only short periods.

While some of this land would be seen today as uneconomic to farm and was later given up by the Hall brothers, it gave them prestige as colonists and landholders and capital from wool obtained from their holdings. John Hall corresponded regularly with his brothers about station affairs but he never lived on any of the Mackenzie Country stations. He did, however, represent the Cook district in the Provincial Council.

Runholders had to start from scratch once their land had been licensed. They made fences, mainly about their dwellings, built sod huts, arranged drainage, drove and managed stock, planted shelter belts, burned off tussock to create green pastureland for sheep who would not eat tussock, forded rivers and streams at great danger to themselves, and operated under primitive conditions.

Thomas worked hard to maintain his 64,000 acres – The Mistake, Braemar and The Wolds (named after the Yorkshire Wolds). He put his sons Tom and George Buceo to work as soon as they were old enough, and employed other men, shepherds and managers as required. Tom relieved John Evans, the manager at John's Castle Hall station (later Glenmore) in 1868. This land extended on the south-east shore of Lake Tekapo to the Leibig Range, and from the Cass River on the west to the Forks River, an area of 53,000 acres.

Young Tom Hall's 26 letters to his Uncle John from August 1867 to July 1869 record life in the harsh Mackenzie Country – the damage to horse drays and equipment for fencing or building through heavy flooding and the heavy losses after the extreme snowfall of winter 1867 when thousands of sheep were never recovered. Shearing might be completed successfully but then the wool was lost in transit because of heavy rain. Two tons of wool on two drays with 80

6. 8(a). Side view of Elloughton Grange, showing Thomas in overcoat and hat with Sarah, receiving visitors arriving in a horse-drawn buggy.

bundles of wooden standards for fencing and other supplies were washed away in March 1868 after heavy rainfall when a creek overran its banks. By June that year Tom wanted to begin mustering but unfortunately 'we have been unable to do nothing with the sheep owing to bad weather. At the early part of the week it was foggy & rained, and on Friday it came on to snow and yesterday we had between 17 & 18 inches. [...] The men fencing on the Burn will have to give it up [...] as the ground is so thoroughly frozen [...] it is impossible for them to do the work.' By July, Evans had 'shorn 6,800 sheep but [...] the young horses broke down the paddock fence and let mainly all the unshorn sheep out'. By September Tom was putting wire around the newly constructed cob house 'to keep the horses from pulling off the thatch & licking the cob away'. They had made quite a hollow all round the hut, almost three inches deep, and he was afraid that if they continued in this way the whole thing would come down. Lambing was going well by late October but he was sorry to say 'the paddock won't keep the rams in even now, for they jump out and get into the wether flock and only the day before yesterday [he] saw some jump in again'. Poor Tom's dog had run away and his bullock, Turpin, had strayed. It was hard and sometimes very dispiriting work.

The sheep were driven into the hill country through passes, sometimes 4,000 in a mob. Thomas W. Hall held small holdings on the way to his Mackenzie Country runs (one at Fairlie) in order to pasture sheep when mustering them along the way. The sheep were mainly merinos and adapted to the dry climate and tussockland, grazing on young green growth after the scrubland had

6. 8(b). Sarah and Thomas farewell visitors to Elloughton Grange.

been burned off. The greatest danger was snow, which could lie over pastureland for months and trap sheep. These early high country pastoralists did not know how to sustain vegetation, lacking fertiliser, so once the land was over-grazed, their leases were simply sold.

A move to Timaru

Thomas W. Hall sold his runs in the Mackenzie Country in the late 1860s. The decade had been one of economic recession induced by financial uncertainty in Britain which resulted in reduced prices for wool. He bought land below the Opihi River in Timaru, and called his station and home Elloughton Grange, after the village his father retired to in the 1840s. Bought piecemeal between January 1861 and October 1867 it comprised 1,010 acres for grazing and crops. His wool was exported to England from the Port of Timaru. 'The wool season is just commencing. The first load of wool came in last week. A vessel is just coming here [Timaru] direct from London,' wrote Sarah Hall to her sister-in-law Grace in November 1864.

An early photo of the Hall's Elloughton Grange homestead shows a two-storeyed verandahed wooden house alone in almost prairie conditions, the landscape without afforestation except for shelter belts of macrocarpa trees on the boundaries, and a few native trees. By 1881, when Thomas sold to William Grant, there was an avenue of oak leading to the homestead frontage and an avenue of silver birch to one side.

Life was far from dull in Timaru which was growing at an alarming pace. My grandfather, Richard, wrote to his Uncle John, about the kind of entertainments young men could enjoy in 1876, give or take a few class restrictions. It was written in February, 11 days after the Main South Line was opened, the rail link which connected the port of Lyttelton with Christchurch and Timaru along the east coast, enabling Thomas and Sarah and their children to visit their relatives at Hororata more easily.

The races came off on Thursday and Friday but I don't know whether they will be of much account. The most interesting events in Timaru are the Athletics Club Sports, which are confined to gentlemen, & which will take place in May; after the Sports, the Show in October. I expect Father will be coming up to see you when the harvest is over. It is very convenient being able to go up & down by train now, the time is so much less. The Railway has had the effect of reducing the fares to Lyttelton by sea, to £1; it was £2 before. It [goods carriage] also used to be 35/- per Ton, now it is 25/-.[31]

It was also the first time in nine years, Richard told his uncle, that the family had been able to meet together. Schooling and work had kept them apart. At the time of writing, George Buceo and Will were at their friends the Le Cren's for the evening. Tom, working as an accountant in the Timaru branch of the National Bank of New Zealand, and Jack, at the *Timaru Herald*, only came out occasionally to visit, so Richard, the youngest son, was mostly home alone with his parents. They were all expecting a weekend visit from Jack's employer, Edward Wakefield and cousin Aggie who were now married.

In mid-July 1881 a fire broke out at Elloughton Grange, between the fowl-house and the stable in an open space. It consumed the stable which was some distance from the house. Thomas and his sons managed, with the help of two other men, to salvage a buggy, several ploughs and other agricultural machinery but, tragically, three horses were burnt to death, one a prized chestnut who had broken free of its halter and was found lying close against the door. It had been with the family for 16 years. The premises were uninsured, according to a report in the *Timaru Herald* of 12 July 1881. The fire must have been devastating to the family and by the following month Elloughton Grange had been put up for sale and purchased by Mr William Grant.

Following Thomas's lead, John and George sold their Mackenzie holdings in the early 1870s because they presented difficulties of size and risk. Thomas was 'very glad as the country was most risky in winter and neither of them were able to attend to it'.[32] Young Tom's time at Castle Hall had not been entirely beneficial and, from the correspondence above, obviously quite stressful. His Uncle George reported to John in 1874, in Tom's first year as a bank accountant, that he had been suffering from sciatica in his left side from hip to foot and was being 'galvanized' for the condition, under a doctor's direction. It was 'a sad look for a young man' and George feared it was a legacy of the Mackenzie Country. John Hall had used his influence to secure Tom his job and Thomas had also supported him in the form of a financial guarantee to the bank presumably so that work as a Commission Agent would come Tom's way. By December 1877 he had made such a good impression in his new work that John was soon endorsing him to the family agent, John Neall, in England. He wrote: 'You can safely recommend young Tom to any individual would-be investors in New Zealand; he is shrewd, business-like and trustworthy.'

Notes and references

1. John's editorial in volume 5 of the *Samarang Gazette*, the ship's newspaper. John Hall changed its title when he became editor from the *Sootee Samee*, TSA.
2. ibid.
3. ibid., vol. 7, TSA.
4. ibid.
5. John Hall diary July–August 1852, MS 2663, TSA.
6. W. Rolleston was Canterbury's last superintendent.
7. JH to John Sugden Neall (JSN), 12 December 1852.
8. ibid.
9. John Hall, 'Sheep-driving in the early days' from *Canterbury Old and New 1850–1900*, Whitcombe & Tombs 1900, p. 1.
10. JH to JSN, 30 January 1854.
11. Aunt Mildred to JH, 18 January 1854.
12. John Neall who married Grace Williamson Hall, wrote to John Hall on 1 January 1869, after Aunt Mildred's death, about her legacy to her surrogate children. He said, 'You and Thomas get £833.6.8. each, Grace the same under trust – and truly sorry am I to say that George's will again cause him disappointment. In July 1855 when at Tonbridge Wells [*sic*] your Aunt made a will – an extraordinary document in her own handwriting the purpose of which is that in the event of anything to George or his daughter the money is to revert to the surviving Brothers and sister … it will be a great blow to George.'
13. Agnes Emma Hall to GN, 5 June 1868, TSA.
14. TWH to JSN, 7 May 1854.
15. JH to JSN, 24 September 1853.
16. John Williamson Dryden Hall, 'The Station Log', TSA.
17. 'The Station Journal' written by the Hall brothers, 30 June 1853–14 June 1854, the source of J.W.D. Hall's article, TSA.
18. JH to JSN, 30 January 1854.
19. William Beswick diary, 14 February 1854, courtesy of Jill Grenfell, Oamaru.
20. William Beswick diary, 15 September 1854.
21. William Beswick to JH, 17 November 1854, John Hall Papers.
22. William Beswick diary, 1 January 1855 ('WCB, TWH and GWH were on the committee for building St Bartholomew's church at Kaiapoi.').
23. Extracts from the Beswick letters, courtesy of Jill Grenfell, Oamaru.
24. Lyndon Fraser and Angela McCarthy, eds, *Far From Home*, Otago University Press, 2012, p. 10.
25. Robert Pinney, *Early South Canterbury Runs*, A.H. & A.W. Reed, 1971, p. 88.
26. L. G. D. Acland, *The Early Canterbury Runs*, Whitcoulls Ltd, fourth edn, 1975.
27. TWH to GWH, Kaiapoi, 22 August 1856.
28. William Beswick diary, 1 Jan 1855, courtesy of Jill Grenfell, Oamaru. A 7.1

magnitude earthquake struck Canterbury in September 2010, damaging St. John's Church, Hororata

29. Sarah Holmes to JH, 16 October 1856.

30. William Vance, *High Endeavour*, publisher *Timaru Herald*, 1965, p. 1.

31. RWH to JH, 15 February 1876.

32. TWH to JSN, 14 March 1872.

7

GEORGE BUCEO HALL (1850–1880): DISGRACE AND DEATH IN BATTLE

'George has been guilty of great extravagance and culpable irregularity. His Supervisors urge his resignation. All liabilities which might entail criminal consequences have been settled [...] but he is heavily in debt and his Father declares he must get out of the way as best he can.'[1]

Thomas and Sarah Hall lost their second son when he was killed in the First Boer War in 1880. He had left New Zealand in disgrace after running away from huge debts incurred during a surveying job on the west coast of the South Island. He was carrying guilt about his behaviour and had left the country to avoid disgrace. The split-second decision which preceded his death may have been motivated by a desire to show the kind of heroism that expiates other debts.

George was probably born on his father's brig *Dauntless* on 4 October 1850 at Buceo, Montevideo, during a voyage to South America, hence his unusual middle name. He was a toddler when the family emigrated to New Zealand and had already experienced shipwreck by the time they arrived, when the ship carrying them to New Zealand caught fire off Hobart.

7.1 The young George Buceo. 'George […] is naturally […] quiet and very fond of reading.'

Schooldays and station life
In July 1859, George Buceo was admitted to New Zealand's Eton, Christ's College in Christchurch, on the same day as his older brother Tom, who was then 11. George was eight. He had been schooled at home and on arrival records show he could read tolerably, had done a little arithmetic and was placed in the first form. At Christmas that year he won the class prize. He had only six months' education at Christ's and was not re-enrolled at the half year beginning 26 July 1860. Instead, he continued his schooling for five further years at the Pigeon Bay Academy on Banks Peninsula with his brothers William (Will) and John (Jack). The school was accessible by sea from Timaru and had an excellent reputation for scholarship. It took boarders and older boys. When George was 15, his Aunt Agnes wrote to her sister-in-law Grace in England, 'The boys are expected home from school in 7 weeks' time. George is to leave these holidays, he will be a great help to his father.'[2] Will was a prize-winning student at the school and Jack had started there in April 1864, leaving Richard (Dick) the only son at home.[3]

7.2 Christ's College, Christchurch. This photo was taken a decade after George and Tom's attendance.

George Buceo then assisted his brother Tom, who was managing their father's sheep station in the Mackenzie Country. This was most likely the Wolds Station (30,000 acres) south-east of Lake Pukaki, so named because the hills surrounding it resembled the Yorkshire Wolds. The station was about 60 miles from Timaru where their parents were then living. Sarah Hall describes her two older sons at this time:

> Tom junior is Manager for his Papa now at the Station. He was at home for a few days in March. He seems to be settling down into a sedate man. I suppose he feels his responsibility now that he has charge, but he is the same dear considerate boy he always was, so loving and gentle in his manner. He is a favourite with all who know him. George who is with him is naturally more quiet and very fond of reading.[4]

Aunt Agnes and Uncle George who were in Timaru in August 1866 reported that they had met the two older boys when they had come down from the station and were surprised at how tall they now were, Tom nearly 5ft 8 and George 5ft 6¾. They thought them 'nice boys' and 'a great comfort to their father' since they 'managed the station so well'.[5]

Thomas and Sarah and their family had been in Timaru since 1859 after the sale of their South Canterbury station. They were well settled in Elloughton Grange, set in rolling farmland below the Opihi River and overlooking the east coast of the South Island. From here the former sea captain could see any incoming and departing sailing ships in Timaru Bay. Thomas gradually expanded his leaseholding to 1,010 acres during the years 1861–1867, planting shelter belts of macrocarpa for his grazing sheep and oaks and silver birch trees in avenues closer to the homestead and stables.

The arrival at Timaru of the immigrant ship *Strathallan* in 1859, with a hundred British settlers, had stimulated the growth of the emerging town. Houses were springing up around the landing stage and support businesses growing up to serve the burgeoning population – a smithy, butcher, tailor, two hotels, two stores and further houses. From 1862, a steamer service connected Timaru with Lyttelton and therefore Christchurch, a voyage of four days. A carriage service between Timaru and Christchurch, established in 1864 by Cobb & Co, gave passengers a bumpy and sometimes dangerous ride since passengers crossed rivers by dray or punt and if the rivers were in flood passage was impossible, rendering the town somewhat isolated. Nevertheless, by 1866, Timaru had a population of a thousand people and this number doubled over the next decade.

Rose Hall mentioned to her sister-in-law Grace in January 1865 that she hoped to take her two children Mildred (2) and Wilfred (1) to visit their cousins in Timaru, but the journey from the Rakaia would take 17 hours, beginning at 5 a.m. and 'this for two young children is very fatiguing'. Mildred had not been seen by her aunts Sarah and Agnes since she was six months old. Only her Uncle Thomas had seen Mildred. Besides the rivers to be crossed 'were so raised' that the length of the excursion was quite uncertain.

This was the environment in which Thomas and Sarah raised their five boys. What was achieved came about through cooperation in hard pioneering work. Thomas was directly involved in the development of the town, as a commissioner able to transact business for Timaru and Waitaki North on behalf of the Canterbury Provincial Council. Some of the early settlers in Timaru were experienced intelligent people who worked together to establish the essentials of what would become one of the most important ports in the South Island. Some men had multiple roles. Lieutenant Belfield Woolcombe, a former naval officer, was magistrate, pilot to ships, sub-collector of customs, returning officer for elections, coroner and sub-treasurer. 'Belfield' is often mentioned in Thomas's letters, particularly in relation to the *Timaru Herald* newspaper, when Thomas was a board member. Henry Le Cren, another friend, and commissioner, established a store and landing stage in the town, enabling ships going between the ports of Dunedin and Lyttelton to call in at Timaru. He employed Captain Henry Cain to run the shipping service. Thomas was appointed Warden of the Canterbury Marine Board in Timaru in 1863 and in 1877 was a member of the first Timaru Harbour Board, remaining so until 1883. He was one of four commissioners who undertook to supervise the rebuilding of the government-erected Timaru Hospital, which had partly burnt down in 1868 and a ward was named after him. He wrote to John, 'we have the Hospital extension finished & a very great success it is, especially as we are now in a position to thoroughly isolate this part for a fever ward whenever necessary.'[6]

Thomas's sons had a role model in their father who was a valued and responsible member of Timaru society. Their uncle, John, a significant participant in provincial and national politics, was able to use his influence to persuade and cajole favours for the family, deserving individuals, or the town.

As one of five boys, George Buceo must have been pleased when his cousin Aggie returned in July 1868

7.3 Timaru *c.***1872 from the tower of Carr's windmill on the corner of Elizabeth and Theodosia Streets.**

from her eight years of schooling in England. It was an opportunity to get to know her and to show off his physical prowess, honed on the sheep station. She wrote excitedly to Aunt Grace in England, that when George was 'up in Ch Ch on business for a day or two' he 'took me for a jolly ride [...] we went about 30 miles. Uncle John lent me a horse.'[7] But a year later when George and Tom spent Christmas at her parents' home in Addington she provided a sharp portrait of the differences between the two brothers and made her preference clear:

> We shall only have cousin George to dine with us on Xmas day so shall be very quiet. George is not nearly so nice as Tom, he is much quieter and does not like noise and will sit for hours without talking, I think [he] rather prefers it. One advantage of that is you need never be afraid he is dull if you do not talk to him. Tom is full of fun and has always plenty to say and amuses one immensely with the nonsense he talks, he can however be both quiet and sensible which is a great advantage.[8]

In the spring of 1868 the London sharemarket crash and a severe winter drove Thomas W. Hall to sell his three stations in the Mackenzie Country – Braemar, The Mistake and the Wolds – and George Buceo, now 18, turned to surveying work to make a living.

George Buceo Hall's misdemeanour

An early survey of the west coast of the South Island had been done by Thomas Brunner and Charles Heaphy in 1846 with the help of Māori guides. It was John Hall, as the member for Mount Cook on the Canterbury Provincial Council, who accompanied in 1865 the talented surveyor and provincial engineer, Arthur Dudley Dobson, to examine possible routes across the mountain range separating Westland from Canterbury. He authorised Dobson to widen the satisfactory Arthur's Pass to allow better access to the newly discovered goldfields on the west coast. Dobson described John Hall as a close friend. He worked on his Hororata property and stayed with John in London during one of his lengthy periods abroad. During the years 1862–1864, Dobson had already surveyed a block on the Canterbury west coast from the Grey River southwards to Abut Head, about 75 miles. With increasing development in the region, more in-depth surveying was required. Arthur Dobson again began an intensive surveying project of 'roads to be made in the Grey Valley and on the coast from Westport to Charleston, country to be explored for a line of road up the Buller to Lyell, and buildings to be erected at Reefton'.[9] He brought his family to live in Westport as his base. It is likely that in 1874 George Buceo was working on Arthur Dobson's west coast survey and then one close to Motueka in the Nelson region, since letters written by his Uncle George to John Hall mention both Greymouth and Motueka in relation to his work and Dobson is described as his 'superior' or employer. At the time, Nelson Province was larger than at present and included the Grey

District north of the Grey River. It is possible that George Buceo had obtained his job through his uncle's connection with Arthur Dobson. He may even have been privately funded because he is not listed in the roll of civil servant employees for New Zealand in 1874.

In his reminiscences of this period, Dobson recalls that he was in the saddle 'from morning till night'. He had taken charge of the Public Works staff of surveyors who were setting out the railway line to the Mokihinui and had constructed a dray road from Wesport to Charleston, and another dray road from the Arnold, the south boundary of the Nelson Province, to Reefton and Black's Point, down the Inangahua Valley to the junction with the Buller. This was arduous and skilled work. Dobson had in the past used Māori guides, lured to work with 'flour and bacon and tobacco and pay', essential to maintaining the flood supply, catching birds and eels and knowing where to find mussels on the beach. They could light fires under any conditions, had canoes on every river, including the Grey, and were adept at taking stores up river when necessary. The surveying gangs carried their own blankets and theodolite, 'taking observations and booking the chains [distances] as we travelled,' wrote Dobson, who usually planned his provisions to last three weeks. Bad weather could be the death of men in this work if heavy rain came on, rivers were flooded and food consumed already. The conditions were uncomfortable, particularly in heavy rain. One surveyor in South Westland, Robert Bain, described taking off his jacket to find he was covered from head to foot with live maggots.

Uncle George reported George Buceo in his surveying work to be 'somewhere in Nelson' – likely to be Motueka – in a letter to John written on 31 July 1874. Though a hard worker George B., by now 24, was casual with money and not able to manage it well, with a tendency to spend it wildly in his leisure time. Perhaps this was a habit which came naturally to the son of a prosperous landholder and member of the Canterbury gentry who had grown used to feeling entitled to whatever pleasures life threw at him and had little sense of responsibility. The family were becoming worried about him. Tom told his Uncle John:

> Since my last letter to you, George's affairs have again cropped up, but as we have in any way refused to assist him – and as nothing has been heard of him for the last fortnight or three weeks I conclude he has managed to settle these himself. People who know him tell me he is the most tremendous worker when out in the field, doing about two men's work and getting more than any other Surveyor out of his men, but yet withal so careless, that what he does is often almost useless – in town he is only what I can call, 'an utter fool', spending his money on hiring horses, buggies, going to balls, getting up shooting parties, etc. quite regardless of the cost; he neither drinks nor gambles but gets rid of his money in the way I have mentioned.[10]

Young George had caused concern when surveying on the west coast, by leaving the office with an enormous debt. The location is likely to have been near Greymouth, since that is where his father went to investigate after being alerted to the problem. George's misdemeanour was relayed by a telegram from William Ostler, the red-haired Yorkshireman and manager of Benmore Station and, at the time, owner of Ben Ohau Station in the Mackenzie Country. Receiving the news via young Tom Hall, who was working as accountant for the Timaru National Bank of New Zealand, Uncle George immediately took action to remit monies to cover the debt crisis to George's employers and to stave off enquiries in his absence.

George Buceo's father came to stay with George and Agnes in their home in Addington near Christchurch to discuss the problem and investigate further.

This crisis obliged young George to leave New Zealand. George senior even suggested a little paid intelligence work to find out who 'GB' had been associating with. Family letters do not disclose anything other than the 'horses', 'buggies', 'balls' and 'shooting parties' described by Tom above, but none of these expenses at the time could have accounted for the £400 debt owing (multiply by 50 for an estimate of today's value). A list of 'New Claims' in the gold fields of the Ahaura River, a tributary of the Grey River near Greymouth, offers a clue. On 7 May 1874, the *Grey River Argus* lists 'Hall, George Buceo' as a householder having a claim on the 'Ahaura River' which was 'not in occupation'. Perhaps gold fever had struck George and he had asked friends to invest in a claim, then when it came to nothing, could not pay them back and had simply scarpered. There was often a lot of work and investment needed to bring a claim into working order, particularly if a water race had to be constructed. From newspaper reports of the time a sum of £400–£500, depending on the size of the claim, would not be unusual. The gravels in the Grey Valley had concentrations of gold, but in low quantities.

The children of the early settlers did not have the same skills or experience as their fathers and were operating in a less developed and more lawless society, probably with far too much money for their own good in the case of Thomas Hall's sons. With more cash at their disposal than their contemporaries, and certainly more connections with men of power and influence in New Zealand, this could often backfire in the context of their immediate working situation. In a reversal of the usual British practice of sending sons to the colonies if they misbehaved, Thomas Williamson Hall exported his sons, George Buceo and later his younger brother Jack *from* the new colony. A sequence of letters from George senior to John Hall, then on a visit to England, explained young George's trouble:

> I at once gave my guarantee to the bank to enable Tom [junior] to remit, until he could communicate with his Father. There was no time to lose. The teleg [from Ostler] said distinctly – enquiry might be *disastrous if not worse*. Whatever it was, George had in a most inconceivable manner, and leaving the office to explode at any moment behind him, gone off on survey to the Motueka, difficult to communicate with, and in spite of several telegrams has not yet been heard from. Dobson his superior advises (equal to order) his instant resignation. Meanwhile debts are already known to [be] more than £400 – and says one of the last telegrams significantly – some *worse*. His Father is waiting further news, to decide about going over to Greymouth. He has resolved to leave George to fight out anything amounting only to simple debt, so far as this can be done without other risk. We cannot imagine what he can have done with all his money – his income has been good. Only a few days before this burst on them at Timaru, a gentleman from the W[est] coast had been at Tom's house speaking of G in the most flattering terms, as generally liked and respected, and clever in his profession. It has been a sad blow for young Tom too; he of course was obliged to confide it (partly) to his principal. We can only hope it may not turn out so bad as we have feared. If Tom pere has not said anything to you on the subject, I think it would be better for you not to mention it to him until he does. Ostler has behaved like a true friend apparently in this affair throughout. [11]

George senior continued his report to John in a later letter:

The news from the West Coast, by Ostler's letter, leads us to understand that George has been guilty of great extravagance and culpable irregularity. His Superiors urge his resignation. All liabilities which might entail criminal consequences have been settled so far as is known – but he is heavily in debt and this his Father declares he must get out of the best way he can – yet is still inclined to hope and think that on getting G's full explanations, he may not have [been]so culpable as it would seem, and I hope sincerely such may be the case.[12]

To the Halls, exile was the only way to deflect public interest. George senior was able to manage the repayment of monies before George's father arrived from Timaru, but the tension over his profligate son caused Thomas embarrassment and pain in both the public and personal spheres, revealing a little of the family dynamic between George W. and Thomas W. Hall. On hearing rumours of his son's misbehaviour, Thomas senior had set out for Christchurch to join Sarah and young Tom who were staying with Agnes and George in Addington, but he had to return to Timaru, ill. George senior believed his brother's illness to be a result of 'the violent excitement he works himself into – to which doubtless [young] George's conduct has contributed'. Thomas was also angry with young Tom for detaining Sarah at Addington to give his mother a well-earned rest when Thomas had already telegraphed for her to return and tend to him in his anxious and ill state. Feeling somewhat responsible in the 'collusion' with young Tom to persuade his mother to remain behind in Addington and finish her vacation, Agnes wrote one of her 'oiliest letters' to him, and Tom wrote to his father, too, but 'no replies [had] been vouchsafed'. In fact, Tom's letter was returned to him unopened.

Even a local newspaper was getting mileage out of the scandal at Thomas W. Hall's expense, implying that it was his strict or bullying fathering of George Buceo that had caused the problem. Thomas W. Hall had a reputation for wanting his own way in his dealings with others and was prone to passionate outbursts of anger. George senior explained to John:

> [...] in connection with Tom senior's well known reputation for ebullitions [exuberant outbursts], I cannot refrain from retailing a squib communicated, I was told the other day, to one of the Timaru papers, by a correspondent who professes to relate a singular dream, to the effect that a gentleman from the immediate vicinity of Timaru (indicating unmistakably whom) presented himself for admission below, and in the absence of his – Majesty, was received and questioned by his Lieutenant as follows: Ah! You come from the immediate neighbourhood of Timaru? Yes.
>
> You were a member of Timaru and Gladstone Board of Works? Yes.
>
> A gentleman of much nautical experience?
>
> Yes.
>
> It is all right I see – we have been expecting you for some time. His majesty is from home, but has left orders with me to say, there is no room for you here, but that you are to have *one ton of brimstone given you and to set up for yourself.*
>
> This yarn has almost sent Mother and daughter into a Hysterics! You may suppose I have nothing fresh to tell

you but in the absence of news and of yourself I must
fancy I am having a quiet chat.[13]

There is a whiff of sanctimony in this letter to John, and
schadenfreude, too, in the recounting of the newspaper jibe.
Thomas, just a year younger than George, was an active member
of civic society, a more effective runholder, considerably wealthier
than his older brother, and had five sons, whereas George was by
this stage effectively prematurely retired, comparatively inactive and
relatively poor. Ostler, who had fallen out with Thomas W. Hall,
while apparently mismanaging his sheep during a winter snowfall
thus leading to many losses, had spent a Sunday in Christchurch
with George senior, relating the details of the George Buceo disaster.
'I was desirous of showing him attention on account of his kindness
in George [B,]'s last affair, and that we appreciated the generous
manner in which he had waived all old sores,' George senior reported
to John Hall in his next letter. Ostler could not think that George
B. was addicted to any 'vicious habits' but felt he ought to leave
the country having disgraced himself financially. 'All such debts had
been paid so far as they are known,' wrote George, 'but his Father
rightly refuses to go further.'[14]

Free of debt but needing means to escape, George B. had
borrowed more money from his brothers before disappearing.

Reputation and social position in the new colony were vital to
progress in a career, mainly advanced by patronage. Two years later
in 1876, George B.'s brother Will, who sought his Uncle John's advice
and help in securing a place in a legal firm in either Christchurch
or (his preference) Dunedin, feared the behaviour of his two older
brothers, George and Jack, would blight his own prospects. George
B., though he left New Zealand after the scandal, had returned by
February 1876 and was living in Timaru. Will wrote:

In any case I want to leave Timaru as soon as I possibly can. Everyone of our family is here at present, a circumstance which considering what has occurred in connection with two of the family is, or rather will be, anything but conducive to my future career. You will be so sorry as I am to hear that George thinks of remaining here for a time at least, and obtaining work as a Surveyor. I am much afraid that he will injure our name here as he has already done on the Coast, by getting into debt and then going away without paying. It was so far as I can see a very great mistake to allow him to come home again, and one which will sooner or later be much repented.

J[ack] is weak, but may be guided for good or ill; but what in [his] case is weakness, is I believe in George's, absolutely bad principles.[15]

The upstanding Will had a dim view of his two older brothers. The exception, for the moment, was his youngest brother, Richard (my grandfather), who left his job with the National Bank of New Zealand to be articled to Will in Invercargill in June 1884 and later became Will's partner in the firm of solicitors, Hall Bros. Despite this auspicious professional beginning, the reputational blight reached Richard too (see Chapter 11).

George Buceo's arrival in Pretoria

By 1880, George Buceo was in South Africa, as his father reported to John:

We have letters from George, who apparently has made many friends, & on the closing of the railway extension in the Cape Colony, has after saving a pretty sum, pushed on to the Transvaal, with letters of Introduction from the Attorney General of the Cape Colony to men in high positions in the Transvaal & in Griqua Land West, where he, George had arrived. This is pleasing, but the recollection of the past is still more than I can bear.[16]

7.4 Standerton before 1881.

It appeared that George B. had found work as a surveyor in Pretoria. His mother had last heard from him on 6 December 1880, in which he had said he was under instructions directly after Christmas to proceed to the goldfields. His father had hoped he would not be detained in the interior by the Boers. No doubt he was caught up in the excitement of impending war in the Transvaal because he opted to fight as a volunteer with the imperial forces in the First Boer War. Letters received by his parents showed him to be very popular with English society in Pretoria. Winston Churchill's father Randolph was touring the Transvaal at the time and George had dined with him amid other members of the Pretoria elite. Having an uncle (John) who was premier of New Zealand at a time when the previous Governor of New Zealand, Sir George Grey, was now governor in Pretoria, would have helped him socially. It is doubtful whether the social elite in Pretoria knew of George's financially reckless behaviour in New Zealand. Though he was effectively exiled, he remained in close contact with his parents. His father reported that 'every Orient mail inevitably brought his Mother or myself, some times both, letters until his last of December 9th [1880]'.[17]

Death in action

When George arrived in the Transvaal after its annexation as a British colony there were seven small British garrisons defending it, including one in Standerton on the Vaal River north of the Natal border. In command was Major William Montague, who led 350 regulars drawn from the 94th and 58th regiments of Her Majesty's troops, including 70 local and mostly mounted men.[16] George joined the Standerton Volunteers on 20 December 1880 after the 94th regiment had been ambushed by the Boers, resulting in many casualties. According to the official report written on 2 July 1881 by J. C. Krogh and sent to the family:

> He was sent out together with 22 volunteers to scout on the south side of the Vaal River. On arriving on that side of the river, Hall was sent, alone, to scout along the river some distance away from the main body of volunteers or mounted-men; and after having proceeded some three miles, he suddenly came upon a body of mounted Boers. Instead of returning as he came he rode past the Boers, towards the volunteers, who seeing him then pursued by the Boers, turned and made their way into Town by the best way they could. Hall in trying to carry out his intention to warn the volunteers was shot; it is reported that he might have saved his life by returning to Town direct.[18]

In charge of the mounted volunteers was Commandant Frank Cassell. He wrote on 4 July 1881 to Lieutenant Colonel Brown, 94th

Regiment, Commanding Troops, Standerton, describing riding out with George Buceo, his rear vidette, to do reconnaissance duty east of the Vaal River:

> My orders were to feel the enemy who were supposed to be near Beshof Farm [...] Mr Hall['s] orders were to search a krantz [a cliff-faced rocky crag] capable of concealing a great number of men, and so situated as to call off our retreat after advancing beyond it. Had Mr Hall thought only of his own safe retreat at the moment he found the enemy he could have secured it by making for the Vaal Drift; instead of which his sense of duty led him to ride away from the Drift back to the Troop, giving us such timely warning as enabled us to secure our retreat with comparatively small loss; as had Mr Hall not performed this gallant deed, we must have been shot down or cut off to a man.
>
> The Boers did their best to cut off our retreat but finding that they could not do this they swung around to their left and opened fire at the same time were cleared right flank, and I saw Mr Hall active for the last time, his horse appeared quite done up, and he was riding between the Boer ranks, their front rank had passed him, but, when last seen by me, he was still urging on his horse. Seeing that he did not fall when they opened fire, I thought they had made him prisoner. The morning after peace was declared however (27th March), I found his remains within 300 yards of the spot where I last saw him alive.
>
> I examined his coat carefully and found he had been shot through the chest in three different places, one bullet in particular must have passed through his heart. With the sanction of the Officer Commanding (Major Montague) I had

a coffin made, in which I carefully placed the remains, which were interred in the cemetery with military honors attended by all the Troops in garrison and most of the townspeople.

Major Montague informed me that had Mr Hall lived he would have recommended him for the Victoria Cross.

I have the honor, etc.

Frank Cassell, Commandant[19]

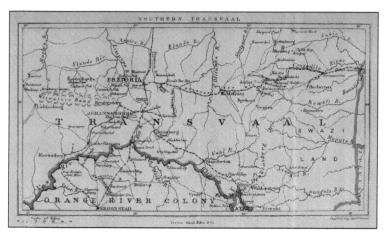

7.5 Map of the Southern Transvaal showing Standerton and the Vaal River.

Thomas and Sarah Hall learned of George's death from Mrs Melville, wife of the Surveyor General of Pretoria, and a notice was posted in the New Zealand newspapers. He was 30 years old and was regarded as the first New Zealander to be killed in action outside New Zealand.[20] His father wired immediately to his brother John, asking for all particulars 'respecting George and his death'. He was worried that 'changes might otherwise occur out there so that we could have no further information about him'. He wished John to ask 'our late Governor', Grey, to make enquiries.[21]

A diagram of George B.'s fatal ride was sent by Sir Evelyn Wood from Government House, Transvaal, to John Hall on 9 July 1881 along with the official report. An envelope from one of his brothers was said to be found among his effects. Evelyn Wood had defeated the Zulus at Kambula and in the final battle at Ulundi. Made a Knight Commander of the Order of the Bath, he was sent back to South Africa in the first Boer War with the rank of major general. He wrote of George:

> He behaved with such marked gallantry, as to interest me in his fate, and I rode out to see the scene of his death when I passed through Standerton. Major Montague and the Troops in garrison were much impressed by the devoted courage of their comrade and had he survived I should have had the pleasing duty to recommend him for some mark of distinction.[22]

In addition to the official report of the incident by Krogh, Cassell and Wood sent to John Hall was another electrifying and later account of the incident by Lieutenant Colonel W. E. Montague in his book, *Beseiged in the Transvaal*. He describes hearing at luncheon on 29 December that hundreds of Boers had collected in a valley three miles away from the encampment, and showed signs of coming on. He sent out mounted men to reconnoitre, of which George was one:

> They looked a serviceable little knot of men as they crossed the "drift" and rode along the road towards Newcastle, their centre led by a fine soldier, not many years before a sergeant-major in the 16th Lancers; ahead a couple riding slowly; on either flank "look-out" men, perhaps 400 yards

away. The small party rode steadily along, keeping their distances as on parade, slanting up the sward towards the sky-line, nothing right or left of them, all open veldt for miles and miles, till they were mere dots against the green. In camp all was still; the men had finished their work, and were lying down; of the officers a couple had ridden to the town, two more were a mile away picking peaches in a deserted garden – when of a sudden – and my heart gave a great beat – out of a fold of ground that lay behind them, and on their left, grew out all at once a great cloud of horsemen, galloping, coming towards us it seemed. Then they caught sight of the scout on the left, not far away, and changed their course a little, making for him, he galloping for dear life, not towards the "drift", where were friends and safety, but right ahead, slanting towards his right, waving his carbine and shouting – we could hear it faintly – to warn them of their danger. Another minute and they heard him and turned, and with backs bent, and faces towards the "drift", galloped their hardest, just a race for life. It was touch and go. The Boers were nearer to the river, but their mass told against them, and our men gained a trifle, a few well mounted of the Dutch showing ahead, and threatening to cut them off. Then those puffs of smoke we got to know so well and distant shots, and shouts growing more and more distinct – that awful race for life seemed to last for hours, when indeed it was all over within ten minutes, and I was almost powerless to help.

We got our men into a koppie, the point nearest to the "drift" which they were making for, and cleared a space of half a mile round it with our rifles – once within that circle and they were safe. The Boers held back when they heard our bullets; and our fellows rode in, heads drooping, horses done up completely, and five of their number on the ground. [...]

The noble fellow who had gone to warn the troop lay dead beyond. For months we hoped that he had been taken prisoner; but when the ground was cleared and we got out across that fatal field, we found a skeleton in a shallow grave on the hillside, a skull at one end, two stockinged feet protruding from the other; a horse beside the grave shot through the head, and another facing it a hundred yards farther on; and close to the turfs that covered up the bones, a coat, edged with red, faded now, the badge of our volunteers, and one we knew was his – all that was left of a brave soldier.

We buried him in the churchyard among the rest lying in that poor spot, a fort frowning close above, and half-a-dozen mounds to mark where others lay – his bones followed by every man, soldier or civilian, in the place – and fired our volleys over them, presenting arms, and sounding one last salute upon the bugles.[23]

A headstone in the Garden of Remembrance in Standerton commemorates George's short life. The siege at Standerton had lasted 88 days and brought four deaths – two privates of the 58th, one of the 94th, and George Hall, trooper with the mounted volunteers.[24]

The loss was particularly brutal for Thomas and Sarah Hall knowing that they had urged their son to leave home. Thomas reported to John that 'Sarah is pretty well, naturally low spirited at times'. He was preoccupied with the new breakwater at Timaru harbour which had withstood a fierce gale without the slightest injury being made to it and on his farm at Elloughton Grange, he and helpers had just finished loading the tenth grain of the season. Thomas comforted himself by reading George's last letters at night 'when alone it is solace to me, although so sad'. He wrote to John on 8 June 1881:

> My heart is very full, although I know I have no right to complain, as all our families have hitherto been preserved. I cannot but think sometimes this may have been for the best, I mean his falling in all honour, for if the success which seems to promise for him had been so, he would no doubt have been brought more prominently before the world, when at any time his antecedents [previous actions] would have been sufficient to crush him, if brought up.[25]

And a month later:

> His letters were always so full of life & hope & pleasure in being able to let me see that he was redeeming the promise made to redeem the past. How bitter G felt his disgrace & [...] his error. His earlier letters to me fully showed & he seemed to feel as much the sorrow he had caused as his own loss of position through his misconduct.

In one of his last letters to his brother Jack he had sent his parents a photograph of himself taken at Cape Town on 1 October, just before beginning his surveying job in Pretoria. Thomas was getting a few copied to send to John and Rose, George and Agnes and other family members.[26]

Always a dutiful uncle and brother, on his return to New Zealand from a visit to England in 1886, Sir John came via Cape

Town and took a hansom cab to Government House to make enquiries there about George, then drove to the house of the Assistant Surveyor-General, Melville, 'young George's friends'. He recorded in his diary, 'Young G seems to have been a great favourite here.'[27] He enquired of his nephew's grave in Standerton to ensure that it be kept in order, enclosing the newspaper cutting which outlined his nephew's act of bravery.

7.6 Last photo of George Buceo Hall taken in Pretoria for his parents. In the re-framing I discovered it had belonged to George Williamson Hall.

Notes and references

1. GWH to JH 16 March 1874.
2. Agnes Emma Hall to Grace Neall 14 October 1865.
3. Sarah Hall to Grace Hall, 6 April 1864.
4. Sarah Hall to Grace Neall, 14 May 1866.
5. Agnes Emma Hall to Grace Neall, 16 August 1866.
6. TWH to JH, 4 November 1880.
7. Aggie Hall to Grace Neall, 4 December 1868.
8. ibid., 23 December 1869.
9. Arthur Dudley Dobson, *Reminiscences of A. Dudley Dobson*, Whitcombe & Tombes Limited, 1930, second edn.
10. TH to JH 22, November 1874.
11. GWH to JH, 10 March 74, Addington.
12. GWH to JH, 16 March 1874, Christchurch.
13. GWH to JH, 10 April 74, Addington.
14. ibid., 7 April 1874.
15. WYH to JH, 29 February 1876.
16. TWH to JH, 15 November 1880. Griqualand is in central South Africa and was made a British colony in 1873 with a capital at Kimberley. The Griqua people were semi-nomadic, mixed race and Afrikaans-speaking.

17. TWH to JH, 1 July 1880.

18. J. Bryant Haigh, 'A Casualty of the First Boer War, 1880' in *Volunteers*, vol. 28. no 2: 81.

19. J. C. Krogh, Landdrost (a Boer magistrate), Standerton, 2 July 1881, official account in John Hall Papers, TSA.

20. Commandant Frank Cassell to Lieutenant Colonel Brown, 94th Regiment, Commanding Troops, Standerton, 4 July 1881, TSA.

21. J. Bryant Haigh, *Volunteers*, vol. 28, no 2.

22. Telegram TWH to JH, 22 June 1881.

23. Evelyn Wood, Government House, Transvaal, to Sir John Hall, 9 July 1881 (with enclosed diagram, too faint to reproduce here).

24. Lieutenant Colonel, W.E. Montague, *Beseiged in the Transvaal*, William Blackwood & Sons, 1881.

25. M. Gough Palmer, 'The Beseiged Town of the First Boer War, 1880-1881' in *Military History Journal*, vol.5, no 2, South African Military Society.

26. TWH to JH, 8 June 1881.

27. ibid., 1 July 1881.

8

THE YEAR OF TROUBLES, 1886

'[…] Other sins only speak; murder shrieks out'[1] – *The Duchess of Malfi*, John Webster, Act 1V, Sc II

'It is almost too bad to be credible; but it seems almost impossible to believe that he is innocent.'[2]

The year 1886 brought a cataclysmic change to the North Island of New Zealand when the Pink and White Terraces, an area of natural beauty near Rotorua, were swept away in the volcanic eruption of Mount Tarawera. For the extended Hall family it was the year when events were similarly cataclysmic, wrecking the security and happiness they had achieved so far in the new colony.

Sir John and Rose, Lady Hall, left New Zealand in January 1885 for Britain via South America. He had resigned from the premiership in 1882, due to ill health from overwork, and been knighted in the Queen's Birthday Honours that year. The route via South America allowed him to inspect the sheep-farming industry in the Rio de la Plata of Argentina, which was fast becoming a rival to New Zealand's wool and frozen meat markets. The cheap labour and high carrying capacity of the large estates there provided good opportunities for young men. John wrote in his diary after a dinner party he attended in England in January 1886: 'someone enquired about openings for young men in New Zealand. I recommended South America.'

On a late March evening Rose had read aloud to him from Robert Louis Stevenson's *The Strange Case of Dr Jekyll & Mr. Hyde*, which had just been published. He found it 'very thrilling & sensational', though he recorded in his diary that 'the chief explanation of duality done by drugs – outrageously improbable'; Rose, on the other hand, was so excited by the tale, 'she could hardly sleep'.

On 17 July, John had taken his daughter Mary by train from King's Cross, London, to Hull to visit some of the old family haunts. 'The country looking very green and beautiful', he wrote in his diary. They stayed at the Railway Hotel in Hull, sat in Holy Trinity Church in the Trinity House seats, walked 'thro High Street to Wilberforce House & other old places, then thro' Savile Street to Prospect Street, my birthplace in Moira Buildings'.

This holiday idyll ended drastically on their return to New Zealand, where a catalogue of horrors concerning the extended family awaited them. Charges of attempted murder and forgery had been made against their nephew Tom; there were rumours of further bad behaviour concerning another nephew, Jack; they learnt also of the extreme illness of Grace's son, John Neall, who was visiting from England and had been bedridden for 14 weeks; and finally, the adultery of their niece Aggie. Thomas's son Will summed up this ill-starred state of affairs:

> You have come back to a lot of trouble, what with Tom, Jack, Agnes and John Neall & can have little thought of politics yet, but the wish that you should take part in them again is so general throughout the Colony that I hope you will decide to do so.[3]

Tom Hall's trial was due to start in Christchurch soon after Sir John's ship, the *Kaikoura*, docked at Lyttelton. John skilfully managed to avoid press attention by removing his name from the ship's passenger list and having Rose and the children disembark at Dunedin, and travel by coach to their Hororata home in Canterbury. He then continued by sea to Lyttelton and overland to Christchurch to visit John Neall on his deathbed.

8.1 Tom Hall. 'He talked well, dressed well, shot well, danced well, was ready for any amusing enterprise, always had a good horse and knew how to sit it.'

The *New Zealand Herald* reported Sir John was in the country, remaining in comparative seclusion on his Canterbury estate, prompting his business manager, Richard Harman, to state that the story was being disseminated by his rival Vogel who was 'trying to worry you out of public life'. Harman's advice was to fight back by re-entering politics.[4]

Despite the disturbing events in his extended family life, to John's surprise, a leader in the *Lyttelton Times* congratulated the colony on his return, and patted him on the back.[5] It must have been a relief to know his achievements of the past were not to be cancelled out by the behaviour of his nephews and niece. John announced his intention in the Christchurch *Press* 'to offer services to a Constituency' and return to politics.

John's diary displays no shock or horror at the events that were unfolding in Timaru. He was busy 'consigning my poor nephew's remains to their last earthly resting place'. Grace's son, John Neall, was only 23. 'Several of my men & a good many neighbours came up to follow the coffin from Coalgate.'[6] His brother Thomas also attended the funeral and John's diary records that on 25 October, 'Self drove Tom in dog cart for a round about Hororata' and on 27 October, 'Had a good walk with Tom around fields & plantation'. Their discussions would have been exhaustive on the latest family crises and notably took place outside, where privacy was guaranteed. On the evening of the 25th John attended a local meeting about the appointment of a medical practitioner for the district. By 29 November he took a train to Rolleston and from there the express to Timaru where he met Thomas and Sarah, who took him for a drive on their estate at the back of Timaru where he found the country hilly, very pretty, all enclosed and cultivated. He was, not surprisingly, 'suffering a good deal from headache'. He also met with Will Hall, Thomas's solicitor son, who had married Archdeacon Edwards's daughter, Ruth. Will impressed Sir John very much by his clearness and shrewdness, but he also found him to be 'the most taciturn man I have met with, & utterly devoid of sentiment'. Will proved very capable in the coming months over the family's various crises.

Tom Hall and his two criminal trials
The aberration in character which caused Thomas Hall junior to attempt to poison his wife Kitty in mid-1886, shortly after the birth of their first and only child, was a surprise to all his family. His motivation seemed to be that disposing of his wife and becoming sole trustee of her estate before their son's maturity meant he could inherit her life insurances and thereby wipe out his imminent bankruptcy caused by fraudulent business practices. He was well loved and respected by his two uncles and considered a mainstay and support to his parents and brothers. Socially he was popular and in demand at parties and gatherings. He had received the best available schooling,

first at the Pigeon Bay Audsley Academy under Mr Knowles, a school heavily imbued with Christian values and priniciples of conduct, and subsequently at Christ's College in Christchurch (modelled on the English Eton and Harrow), where he had won the Class Prize in 1859, the Mid-Winter Prize for History in 1862 and jointly the Christmas Prize for Mathematics that year.[7] His health was not always perfect, as was well known. He suffered from sciatica, brought on, it is thought, by heavy lifting while managing his Uncle John's sheep station, Castle Hall, near Lake Tekapo in the Mackenzie Country. He had helped to manage the station during the years 1867–1868. For his sciatica he took doses of morphine. Though the effects of morphine as a painkiller wore off after months of intensive use, it also depressed the central nervous system, relieving anxiety and fear. He also suffered from asthma, for which he smoked cigarettes made from a mixture of tobacco and antimony, which at the time was thought to relieve the condition. Antimony was the substance found in the analysed contents of his wife's stomach by doctors in Dunedin. Within weeks of being charged with poisoning his wife, he was also charged with the murder of his father-in-law, Captain Henry Cain (1816–1886) in January that year. Formerly a mayor of Timaru. Cain ran the Surf Boat Landing Service in the town with Henry Le Cren, who also had a store close to the service supplying essential goods to arriving settlers. Symptoms at the time of Cain's death seemed to stem from natural causes, but in the light of the poisoning charge against Tom Hall, that diagnosis began to seem questionable.

The prosecution for the trial of Tom Hall for attempted poisoning of his wife was conducted by the Attorney General, Sir Robert Stout, a Liberal who had been prime minister of New Zealand during 1884–1885 and who became chief justice in 1899. His half-brother, William A. Stout, later practised law with Will Hall, Tom Hall's brother, in Invercargill in the firm of Hall, Stout and

Lillicrap. Peter Graham, the author of *Vile Crimes*, on the Tom Hall prosecution case, maintained that it was convention in England for the attorney general to lead for the prosecution in poisoning trials but this convention had not taken root in New Zealand. He explained Stout's interest as being partly political: 'No politician could resist the opportunity to put himself in the limelight, and how better to do that than by personally prosecuting Thomas Hall and Margaret Houston in the most sensational case in New Zealand history?'[8]

Margaret had been engaged as a nurse for Captain Cain and though she was eventually exonerated from any complicity in both trials, it is Peter Graham's belief that she was probably complicit in the attempted murder of Kitty, having access to Tom's bedroom as a housekeeper and knowing he kept poisons in his room and a book he consulted on their use. Tom had also been witnessed adjusting her stays, a too-intimate act with a family retainer.

Tom Hall's first trial over his wife's poisoning was held in Christchurch, beginning on 11 October 1886. The medical evidence was found to prove conclusively that Kitty Hall had been poisoned by antimony. Hall had a motive to murder his wife, since he stood to receive £6,000 in insurances on her death. He had purchased poisons and a book on poisons into which he had written a false date and place of purchase. He was found to have given a false explanation for the purchase of antimony (for his asthma cigarettes), and he was convicted of the attempted murder charge. In the second trial concerning the death of Captain Cain, held in Dunedin on 24 January 1887, Tom faced a charge of murder, the killing of Cain by poison. The defence argued that Cain died of kidney disease and brought evidence to show the antimony found in his body was not sufficient to cause his death. In the first trial Tom had been sentenced to penal servitude for the rest of his life. In the second trial he was also found guilty by a jury but Mr Justice Williams who presided referred a point of law in the case to the Court of Appeal, of which he was a member, and Tom escaped hanging. His wife Kitty and his father had instructed solicitors to petition the governor to commute the death sentence as an act of mercy, but Tom had escaped hanging on technical grounds. After Justice Williams had admitted evidence of the poisoning of Kitty Hall and directed the jury that they could take that into account in considering whether antimony had been administered to Cain by Hall, the Court of Appeal quashed the conviction of Tom Hall for the murder of Henry Cain on the grounds that evidence of the commission of one crime could not be used to prove the commission of another.

A lengthy discussion of the reasons is given in Peter Graham's book, which suggests this was a volte-face on Mr Justice Williams' part, and wrong as a matter of law. Tom Hall served his sentence of over 20 years in Mount Eden Gaol, a longer sentence than was usual for attempted murder, but its length reflected the seriousness of his case. He had knowingly married his wife to lay hands on her fortune to extricate himself from his self-inflicted financial predicament, having first established that if she had a child he would have certain control of her income before their child reached the age of majority, 21.

When John Hall had found the 'chief explanation of duality done by drugs' in Robert Louis Stevenson's novel *The Strange Case of Dr Jekyll and Mr Hyde* 'outrageously improbable' from his reading in March 1886, he could not have anticipated that his nephew Tom, who had been so useful to him in managing his Tekapo station and passing on local gossip helpful to his political career during Tom's years in the National Bank of New Zealand, would come to resemble such an implausibly dual character in the same year. That Tom's financial difficulties would lead him to attempt to poison his wife defied belief. An act of desperation, certainly, but from someone who had until this time acted as a morally upright, rational man, protective of his

younger brothers when they got into trouble with money. He helped
George Buceo when he ran out on debt by sending a friend to talk up
his character to his father, helped young Jack when he appeared to
be in trouble and was solicitous of his cousin Aggie's future security
when her husband Edward Wakefield looked as though he might turn
into a neglectful husband. It seemed likely, as his brothers and father
thought, that the morphine Tom took to relieve his sciatica was most
likely the trigger for this evil bout of irrationality, which was so contrary
to the character his family knew and loved.

One account of Tom's character is given by Helen Wilson in
her memoir *My First Eighty Years* (1959). Her description helps to
explain his family's initial incredulity towards Tom's crimes. Wilson's
father, William Ostler, had managed Thomas W. Hall's station, The
Wolds, and had agreed to take over half of it from Thomas. Bad feeling
prevailed between the two men after a heavy snowfall had resulted in
a huge loss of sheep, and Thomas blamed Ostler for incompetence
in not clearing ice and snow so the flock could feed. He then stalled
on transferring Ostler's share of the run to him. Wilson was probably
recalling her mother's impressions, since she was only a girl of 15 at
the time of Tom's trials:

> Tom's manner was cordial and most attractive. It was
> said [...] that when he came into a room everyone in it
> seemed the happier for his coming. He soon became a
> star in the social firmament, for he was everything that
> Timaru admired. He talked well, dressed well, shot
> well, danced well, was ready for any amusing enterprise,
> always had a good horse and knew how to sit it. [9]

An unusual aspect of the days during and after Tom's trials,
and even in the years afterwards, was that his wife Kitty seemed to

continue to respect and love him, or at least to pity him, despite being the victim of his attempts to poison her slowly and inflict the most vile suffering on her as a young mother. She took their baby to visit him in Lyttelton Gaol when he was under sentence and argued fiercely for his innocence among friends and family. She petitioned for mercy with his father after the second trial when he was sentenced to hang, subject to the examination of a part of the evidence in the appeal case. Both his father and Kitty were in denial about charming Tom Hall.

A decade earlier, Tom had been manager and accountant of the Timaru branch of the National Bank of New Zealand. Following an economic boom period, largely as a result of high prices for wool, he left the bank and joined Edward Tate in a land-broking business in Timaru. That business was dissolved in 1882 after Tate was found to be forging agreements and Tom then joined Gilbert Laing-Meason, a civil engineer and licensed surveyor, in a stock and station business which made loans and arranged mortgages and insurances. Tom married Kate Emily Espie, the step-daughter of Captain Cain, in 1885 but in June 1886, when a long economic depression and a worldwide credit crisis was affecting everybody, the knock-on effects to his clients who had over-extended themselves and subsequent pressures from banker and creditors led to his firm getting severely into debt. His business finances were in a mess. He was using his recent client's money to pay off debts and was dependent on a stream of new money coming into the business to keep it solvent. To retain his elevated social position and to conceal the extent of his losses, he began to commit forgery. He also insured his wife's life with two policies of £3,000 each and insured the property they lived in for £1,175. He then requested his wife to make out her will in his favour. When her health deteriorated over weeks with symptoms that would normally suggest poisoning – ulcerated mouth, trembling legs, skin irritation, blue-rimmed gums – and the family doctor eventually had her stomach contents analysed, it became obvious that she was being slowly poisoned by the administration of antimony in Tom's possession. Tom seemed to be nursing his sick wife with caring attention, but at the same time was administering poison in her iced drinking water. This calculated and watchful process over time was what convinced the judge in his summation that Tom was by far the vilest criminal in New Zealand history so far.

Much has been written about the case, which was an enormous scandal, both locally in Timaru and nationally in the whole of New Zealand, particularly as the family was so highly respectable. Timaru people were concerned that because of his connections Tom's trial would not be a fair one. The reluctance of local professionals to condemn Tom Hall was obvious when they came to give evidence at court, as Peter Graham has pointed out. Two doctors involved, Kitty's family doctor, Pat McIntyre, and Hedley Drew, the surgeon in charge at Timaru Hospital, were both slow in moving Kitty from her home

at Woodlands to hospital even though they were almost certain she was being poisoned. Drew thought Kitty was taking something she should not be taking. They eventually informed the police after a sample of her drinking water they analysed was found to contain antimony.

8.2 Scene in the Christchurch supreme court during Tom Hall's trial for the attempted murder of his wife. Dr McIntyre, his friend, is in the witness box, and the attorney general, Sir Robert Stout, is to the left. Lithograph from the time of his trial.

When the police arrived at Woodlands to arrest Tom they also had a warrant to arrest Margaret Houston, Kitty's lady companion and help. Meg, an attractive Scottish girl, had held nursing jobs at Wellington and Timaru hospitals before being employed by Captain Cain and, after his death, Tom and Kitty Hall. Tom never confessed to the crime. The nearest Tom came to confession was when he described using antimony for cigarettes he smoked for his asthma, adding tartar emetic to the mix. He told Inspector Broham, 'Whatever I did in this matter I did alone. There was no other second person involved in it. Miss Houston has nothing whatever to do with this.'

To his parents, uncles and brothers Tom had seemed a hard-working, loving husband. The first charge of attempted murder at first seemed bizarre and ludicrous, and impossible to believe. The second suspicion that he might have also attempted to poison his father-in-law, Captain Cain was equally incredible. Cain was a family friend.

Tom Hall was removed from Timaru to Lyttelton Gaol 'because the number of his visitors in the former establishment was interfering with the ordinary discipline of the prison', according to the *Timaru Herald* of 17 September 1886. A spirited defence of his rights as a prisoner on remand on the charge of attempted murder was made to determine who he needed to see, especially his creditors. His firm had gone bankrupt shortly after his arrest and since he was the partner responsible for most of the conduct of the business, his creditors had been deprived by his removal to another prison.

Tom's father, Thomas, was relieved to be able to discuss these events with John:

Timaru, 10 October 1886

My Dear Brother

I can scarcely say how welcome your letter was. I only got it yesterday evening & I replied shortly as you requested. I heard yesterday that Rose and the young folks had gone through the day before although I should much have liked to have met them, it was better not as it would have been too painful to do so in public. How much I should have liked to have come at once to Hororata, you may be sure, unfortunately I cannot possibly get away at present. On Tuesday there is to be a meeting of Hall & Meason executors & as I believe I am, I feel sure, the principal & Perry & Kinerney being both in Christchurch I must see Arthur Perry [Timaru solicitor] and may have to attend the meeting myself. Further I am in correspondence with Harper & L [unknown] & Willie [his solicitor son] re arrangements about mortgages, which will I fear be almost a total loss. I have no one here except my lawyers to advise with & the strain is very heavy with all other fearful troubles. With Willie the correspondence exacts time. [He] believes one letter from him has been opened & another not come to hand. As these both contained matters referring to Tom, business I fear may have been tampered with by the prosecution. Another thing is, I scarcely like leaving Kitty at present. She dear girl is as true as can be to her husband and gives no more evidence to the fearful accusations against him in regard to herself than we do. Still such efforts have been made by the prosecution's testimony to her from him, that it might not be advisable for me to leave her. Cecil Perry also told me before leaving, that they (the defence) might possibly want Sarah and myself, but would not call us if they could avoid it. Some of this evidence brought forward so far is so utterly false that it looks like some deep lewd and devilish plot.

Since commencing this and wiring you to Port Chalmers, I got Goff's [Godfrey, John's youngest son] telegram sent at 10 h[our] saying you were leaving directly. [...]

Willie came up and stayed a week & Dick after he left came for two & then George [Thomas W. Hall's brother] kindly was with us twice & this was a great relief. Still the time is very fearful. I scarcely like to say more my dear John, but when I see you I shall have much more to tell you.

I do not think I have written to anyone (except short [...] notes), for more than a month, but to our brother George, our Willie & this to yourself. The nervous strain is so great, that although I am obliged to be out with the lawyers & others, I am only too glad to be quiet by myself.

I will let you know as soon as I can get away. With very kind love to you all & from Sarah also I will close. Kitty & her baby are here now, I generally get them here on Sunday & see them almost every day.

Yours very affectionately
T. W. Hall

Meanwhile Richard, young Tom's youngest brother, pressed his Uncle George to persuade his parents to leave Timaru while the trial was under way and go to John Hall's home at Hororata, which they did. Richard wrote from Invercargill on 1 October 1886:

It is I think absolutely necessary they should not be alone if the worst comes – as there is little doubt it will. Here we are so terribly busy that it is very doubtful if either of us [he and Will] could get away for some little time [...] I don't wish them to know that I take a very gloomy view of our prospects in NZ. Indeed I did all I could to divert their minds as far as possible – at the risk of appearing callous – but the fact remains – there are so many unhappy associations connected with NZ – that my own inclinations if nothing else stood in the way would be to leave the Colony for good.

I wish yourself, Aunt, Father and Mother could travel together somewhere – you all want constant changes for a time to lighten the terrible troubles of the last year or so.

Uncle George was also concerned about the probable effect of the trial's outcome on the accused's parents and wrote to John, 'You will no doubt have heard from Tom [snr] – I think truly your being with him when the end comes, will be a very great comfort – for

truly I fear the end will be a *blow* he is hardly prepared for – We but hope for the best – but every thing looks very black.'[10]

Kitty Hall had been invited with her baby Nigel to Hororata, partly to keep her away from the prosecution lawyers and local interest. Richard warned Rose 'of one or two of Kitty's peculiarities before you see her'.

8.3 Kitty and Nigel Hall, *c.*1890.

Timaru, 26 October 1886

My dear Aunt

[…] Don't be surprised if you find her apparently in such high spirits than one would expect under the circumstances – but the fact is that she is up and down half-a-dozen times a day – one moment expressing herself bitterly about her husband and the next one taking his part. On the whole she is a queer compound though when you know her I feel sure you will like her & she you.

Kitty, who had been bedridden and vomiting during the time of the poisonings, was free of symptoms now that her husband had been removed. She was working at renting her house and getting it ready to leave so that she could go to John and Rose in Hororata. Baby Nigel was teething.

On 4 December John Hall wrote to Dr Courtney Nedwill, the Irish physician who had treated the family's tubercular nephew John Neall, and asked a critical question that all three brothers were concerned about:

Is it your opinion on the evidence that Captain Cain may have died simply from diseases from which he is thought to have suffered? I should feel much obliged if you would let me know through my brother George your impressions on the points I have made. Anything you say will be treated as confidential, to be communicated to the Solicitors for the defence.[11]

The preliminary inquiry into Cain's death, which began on 29 November 1886, was held at Timaru before Joseph Beswick, resident magistrate and brother of Thomas senior's friend William.

Thomas was concerned that the Coroner continually stopped Perry, representing Tom Hall, especially in reference to Cain being cheerful at the end of his life. Perry thought the administration of antimony produced very great depression. Cain's body was exhumed and re-examined and a top pathologist, Dr Francis Ogston, was the key witness for the prosecution. He had undertaken the post-mortem, the main objective being to find antimony rather than the cause of death, though he found Cain's heart enlarged and the arteries and aortic valves diseased. He found antimony in the body and concluded that the samples showed a little over two grains of antimony, enough to kill. Cain's doctor accepted that this could have accelerated the death of Cain but he found the original cause of death to be kidney disease and dropsy.

Thomas reported to John on 13 December 1886 that Kitty was showing volatility in her attitude to her husband, being easily influenced by her visitors and their opinions. She and her sister, Ellis Newton, were 'all they should be or that I could wish in their feelings towards Tom' but during a later visit 'she could not possibly be more bitter against her husband'. She said she knew he had given her father antimony and that he had told numbers of persons that it was Kitty who had proposed to him. Presumably Tom was doing this to allay the rumour circulating in Timaru that he had married Kitty rapidly for her money when he got into financial difficulty. His father was in turmoil:

> I cannot, my dear brother, get rid of my first impression
> which subsequent events seem to strengthen & that is
> that McIntyre [Tom's friend and the local doctor who
> first obtained analysis on Kitty's stomach contents] wants
> Tom out of the way, that he may get his wife. However
> horrible this may seem, the cold blooded & bloodthirsty
> way in which this prosecution is followed up speaks

strong. Further it has been dinned into Kitty's ears that he (McIntyre) had saved her life, when by the evidence of others he seems to have been aware some time previous to this evidence being laid, that her life was tampered with, & he ought to have put a stop to this before. He a rejected suitor, & dismissed both by Tom & myself for negligence this would show an envious & a malicious intent. No doubt my judgement in this respect is biased [...] I want to get away. My head seems to get less & less under control.

Many thanks for all your sympathy. With kind love to all

Yours affectionately

T. W. Hall

While Kitty was safe at Hororata, away from the prosecution and prying friends, John and Thomas Hall continued to correspond on details of the case. Thomas senior was beginning to believe his son's crime. He wrote:

I fear my dear John I must accept as you say the fact that the verdict is true. But I feel certain that nothing but insanity could have led to this conduct. This is also his brother Willie's opinion, as he says he (Tom) was as thoroughly unselfish & kind-hearted & always willing to assist others, that nothing but aberration of mind would have caused it.[12]

Both Jean Garner, John Hall's biographer, and Peter Graham found that John Hall did not use his influence officially to intervene in his nephew's case once he was committed to gaol, which is true. However, during the trials he was predisposed to find out what the likely natural cause of death was in the Cain affair. He offered unconditional support and succour to Tom's parents and went to Dunedin to be present at this second trial concerning the death of Cain, held in the supreme court before a jury. He was present for the verdict and was active in supporting his brother Thomas and his two nephews, Will and Richard Hall, in the lead-up to it. He and Rose also took in Kitty Hall and her baby Nigel during these anxious days. As Will wrote to Sir John, 'Without you and Aunt as general comforters to the family I don't know what we should have done.'[13]

8.4 Tom's parents, (a) Thomas W. Hall and (b) Sarah Hall, at the time of the trial, c.1886

Will Hall was very concerned about his parents during the awful weeks of Thomas's trials, and he and Richard persuaded them to leave Timaru for Invercargill where the brothers were in partnership as solicitors. He feared that his father's losses would be heavy over Tom's affairs and that the best thing he could do would be to sell his fixed property and invest the capital so that he and Richard could manage it in his absence, if he and Sarah chose to leave permanently. He reported to his Uncle John that his father and mother were visiting him in Invercargill, the weather was fine and Richard and he were on holiday so spending all their time with them. Will's wife Ruth had taken the children to her parents in Dunedin. Thomas and Sarah had experienced some relief from the Cain trial and its attendant anxieties thanks to the arrival of an old sailor. 'One of the Provicks of Hull who lives here called to see us the other evening & to talk of old sailor days with Father, & for several hours the air was thick with "foretops", "mizzenstays", "main decks" & "port & helms" so that it was almost dangerous to move – but it brightened our parents up.'

Tom's second trial was to take place in Dunedin. Will would go up to Dunedin that week to look up medical evidence and thought that Brian Haggitt, the Dunedin crown prosecutor, was 'fortunately a man who recognizes his duty to be to ascertain the truth & not to ensure a conviction so the trial will at least be fair; & the press will be unbiased'.[14]

The shocking news of his cousin Tom's trials had reached John's son Wilfred at Oxford University. Wilfred wrote from Keble College to his father that he had read the news of Tom's deed in a newspaper. Everyone he met knew of it but the New Zealanders there were discreet about it. It was a burden on his mind. Even if his father left New Zealand, he would himself at some time return and felt 'bound to do my utmost to uphold the honourable name which you, my dear Father, have made for yourself and for us in New Zealand'. He was 'truly sorry for Tom' for he could quite understand that 'without any religious principles, and without any trust in God to support him, he gradually became incapable of resisting temptation which a little while ago would have had no power over him'. He was glad he was not allowed to complete so terrible a deed and given an opportunity to repent and turn to God.[15]

Some conservatives were afraid of losing John Hall from politics over the scandal, and on 29 November 1886 he was requested to stand for the Heathcote Seat by H. Augustus Bamford.

What is astonishing throughout the trial of Tom Hall is that his wife, the victim of the alleged poisoning, continued to visit her husband and continued to act as a devoted wife. It seems clear from the letter quoted below that she attributed his actions to the influence of the pain-killing drug morphine, which he took for his sciatica, and that she, with John and Rose Hall, was urging that Tom be persuaded to repent through Christian faith. It was of course by no means certain at the time that he would not hang for his alleged crimes. During the second trial concerning the death of Captain Cain, of which he was at first convicted, Kitty Hall was able to visit her husband in Lyttelton Gaol and told Rose Hall: 'He says it is a great comfort to him & I like to do the little I can to lighten his gloom.' The clergyman who was attending him told her that Tom had been difficult to bring to the right way but,

> he has great hopes of his soul's salvation. He says he has had to study his character & has tried to convince his reason that he has succeeded. He's getting him to read the bible & attend services. I know you will be glad to hear Mr Fitzroy thinks as we do that Morphine had so much to do with it. I do think there was not sufficient proof that poor Daddie's [her step-father] life was shortened by poison. I think honestly he is not guilty of this last crime [...] Tom dreamt last night that we were all together at Hororata! [...] He seems quite resigned but broken down terribly on Saturday. He was better today. The wretched Warden keeps me from being able to talk freely. [...] He is very pleased with baby but he thought with me & Mr Southerby also, that it would be unwise to take baby there anymore.[16]

Death of John Neall

While the family in Timaru was struggling with the revelations about Tom, George Williamson Hall had his hands full in Christchurch visiting John Neall as he slowly died of tuberculosis. Uncle John had found his nephew on arrival in New Zealand arrogant, exasperating, lacking in will power, and generally in poor health. No one in the family at first realised that John Neall was suffering from tuberculosis, and his attempts to avoid hard work ('going in for colds')[17] were taken to be proof of his dilatory nature.

Thomas senior had met his nephew on arrival at Port Chalmers at the end of April 1886, since George and Agnes Hall were 'in no condition to receive him', and he stayed for a time in Timaru. 'He looks fairly well, but very thin & stoops & has also occasionally a very nasty cough. He tells me he caught it about fourteen days since, that it is much better at present,'[18] Thomas

8.5 Grace Neall with her children, c.1886 John Neall is centre back.

wrote to John. John Neall stayed with his Uncle Tom and Aunt Sarah in Timaru where he was courteous and drove his aunt about in the family gig. He took to going on long bicycle rides to alleviate his chest symptoms. Doctors could do little for tuberculosis at the time and fresh air was a favoured treatment. Two months after arrival he was invalided in Christchurch. George employed a nurse to look after him ('the poor woman [...] never spared herself, but nursed John with the tenderness & love of a mother')[19] and visited him daily in his lodgings, but John died on 17 October 1886. George wrote from his Papanui house:

Bligh's Road, Christchurch, 17 October 1886

My dear John

Our poor nephew breathed his last at 6.30 this morning. [...] It is now nearly 15 weeks the poor boy has been more or less confined to his bed. During all that time, with few exceptions, I have seen him every day. At one time we all thought he had a fair chance of pulling through. Against it was clearly a want of stamina, & also a total lack of will force. But I am strongly of opinion that the disease that carried him off, has been at work for a very long time & probably nothing could have saved him. I shall be very glad to see you as soon as you can manage.[20]

Grace, on receiving news of her son's death, wrote to John and Rose: 'Did you and dear Rose see my boy again? I have been thinking so much that you might – he did love you very much. His faults were on the surface but he was true and conscientious and very tender and loving to his mother.'[21]

Young Jack Hall's fall from grace

These two crises would be enough for any family to endure, but Thomas and Sarah Hall's third son, John ('Jack'), also became an intolerable burden during October of this painful year, having been suspected of misbehaviour. It is not at all clear from available correspondence what his current sin was. There was a positive description of the 15-year-old Jack from his Aunt Rose to Grace Neall in 1867 when she wrote, 'Young John seems a very nice lad [...] he is tall for his age and will be very good looking.' Intimations that his character was not all it might be surfaced in a letter from George to John as early as May 1875 when Jack was 'committed to trial on a charge of larceny, or something of the kind', in Greytown, in the

Wairarapa, though he 'stoutly declared his innocence' and was in due course 'honourably dismissed'. His brother Tom was planning to take leave and go north to get to the bottom of the case. If Jack was convicted, his father declared, he could shift for himself; he would have no more to do with him since he was 'shamefully endangering [his] brothers' prospects'.

Colonial life, particularly for the sons of wealthy men, could be dangerous since the temptations towards profligate behaviour if single could be numerous — pubs, gambling, the races, and the availability of male and female prostitutes, could easily undo the best of them. In 1886, Jack had been married for 12 years and had children. His wife, Lizzie, was the sister of Edward Withers (see Chapter 9). They had settled in Timaru and Jack was working on the *Timaru Herald*. Marriage for him was not apparently the panacea as described in a letter written by E. Jerningham Wakefield, the only son of Edward Gibbon Wakefield, to Richard Harman, the English land agent and friend of John Hall:

> A new colony is a bad place for a young single man [...]
> The hospitality is so great that a young man who can make
> himself agreeable, may live in idleness ... till he becomes
> unfit for marriage by becoming wedded to his pipe and
> his bottle, not to mention the billiard-table. Whereas if he
> is nicely married, he has a sweet home to go to after his
> day's work, and his mind is kept tranquil enough to bear
> without injury the intense excitement of sharing in the
> creation of society [...] The success of a young colonist
> who remains single is a rare exception [...] the same
> capital goes further with a wife than without one. It is her
> moral influence that both saves the money, and stimulates
> her husband's energy and prudence.[22]

In the winter of 1884, Jack's father Thomas, was taking no chances. Knowing Jack's potential waywardness, he had bought a cottage adjoining his own home, according to Uncle George.[23] He had it repaired and intended to move his son and daughter-in-law and their children into it. Sarah thought it unwise because Jack and Lizzie did not want to come but 'none of them dare say a word'. She added: 'I think the risk is great & I fear the children will put him out. He will however have his way.'[24] Perhaps Jack had gone AWOL under paternal pressure.

At this troubled time Jack seemed to be a liability to the family and they made hasty plans to deport him as they had George Buceo earlier. The sensitivity of the family to their public profile may have partly been the result of all three brothers' deep involvement in the upkeep of the law. Both Thomas W. and George W. Hall had served as Justices of the Peace in Timaru during the 1860s (they sat together for one hearing in September 1865 in the Timaru Magistrate's Court) and John Hall had been appointed a Justice of the Peace for Canterbury in 1854 and from 1856 to 1860 served as resident magistrate in Lyttelton, an office combining that of commissioner of police and sheriff. He occupied a similar position in Christchurch until political duties called him to Auckland in 1860.

The younger generation were very dependent on the goodwill and influence their father and Uncle John had exercised on their behalf in securing jobs and security in their lives. Tom and Richard wrote freely to John about themselves or their brothers when in need of his help or influence and in return for his support, updated him on local news and political life in Timaru and later Invercargill, helpful in a country where distances were great. Sir John found Will more taciturn and wished he had more colonial chat, but thought perhaps his brothers had depleted the family allowance.

Thomas's sons had benefitted from John Hall's patronage in

seeking positions – Tom at the Bank of New Zealand in Timaru, Jack in the telegraph office in Wellington, Will in seeking who should employ him to study law. Thomas, as a board member on the *Timaru Herald*, had probably also used his influence to secure Jack a job on the paper. The men who had been pressured to give these young men jobs might be alienated from the senior Halls when those they had helped had so obviously failed.

In 1867 John had found Jack a job in the Wellington Telegraph Office where, according to his mother, he was a postmaster. From there he had been promoted to the office at Wanganui in November 1869. His brother Tom, who otherwise had been confined to station life, wanted to see more of life and Uncle John had been introducing him well in Auckland. Tom accompanied Jack to meet the Wanganui postmaster, Mr McDonagh, and Jack liked the place better than Wellington. His mother was anxious about this last appointment because rebel Māori under Te Kooti were said to be mustering horsemen and fighting men to attack Wanganui.

By 1873 Jack had moved further north to the Napier telegraph office, receiving an annual salary of £160. He had now been in the service nearly six years. He wanted a salary rise but his superior said it could not be granted. Foolishly, using his connections, Jack then wrote to the superintendent of Hawkes Bay Province, the Honourable Donald McLean, to see if he could speak on his behalf to ensure a rise. His boss, he wrote to McLean, 'goes on the principle that as long as you have enough to live on you must be content with that [...] and though I have some money of my own, I do not think that should be in any way taken into consideration'. He had offended Mr Barry Rupell very much. 'I'm not sure of the reason,' he told McClean, 'but have a good idea; & it was simply through doing my duty.' He reminded McLean of his kind promise that if [Jack] wanted anything, to take notice of it. Jack loved the climate in Napier, and the people very much too, 'as they are all so kind and sociable and free, as a rule, from the cliques, etc. which exist in most small places'. Napier was growing at a wonderful rate, new buildings were going up in all directions. The Napier telegraph office was just starting the third wire to Auckland from the town and as well the line to Poverty Bay.[25]

Jack's letter illustrates the dilemma for the children of well-connected men. They were used to having a charmed life, probably a parental allowance, and access to jobs that others would be denied on merit. It was the old patronage system imported from England. John Hall had suffered from it himself in being passed over to become chief postmaster in Brighton by a candidate favoured by Queen Victoria. In New Zealand, as part of the ruling class, these memories had faded with success. John could not refrain from helping his relatives. Jack clearly had a sense of entitlement in writing to the superintendent of the province over his boss's head. He probably received a rebuff because he left Napier and took up a job on the *Timaru Herald* under the editorship of Edward Wakefield. It was now 1886 and he was in fresh trouble.

Will updated Sir John from Invercargill on Jack, and Tom:

My dear Uncle

Dick has written to me saying [Jack] is leaving the Colony, a fact which can only be for our good as he most certainly would have got us all into such serious trouble before long. You must have thought a good deal over the matter & probably have good reasons for preferring San Francisco – but speaking offhand it seems to me that Rio would be a better place. There are so many Colonists about California – probably many of Jack's acquaintance – that *if he gets into trouble again, as he assuredly will*, the fact is certain to get into our papers & make things as bad as ever for the rest of his relatives. But in Rio though he may be at a disadvantage on the score of language yet whatever he does is not likely to reach our ears except through himself. There ought to be employment there for an English pressman.[26]

It was clear that Jack was out of control, possibly suffering from some addictive behaviour, either drink, or sex, or gambling, though there is absolutely no clue as to what it was in any of the letters remaining. Thomas and Sir John had decided that Jack should go to California, leaving behind his wife Lizzie and the children in Timaru while he looked for work. He was dispatched with due efficiency, with testimonials obtained from his employer Edward Wakefield, editor of the *Timaru Herald*, and another colleague. The testimonials attested to Jack's ability as a reporter and desk editor and also said that he had at times been left in full charge of the editorial department of the paper. His wife Lizzie was reconciled with him before he left and was anxious to join him as soon as possible.

Jack's passage was paid for, it seems, by Sir John, while Thomas Hall had the burden of untangling his son Tom's financial affairs. His money was fast dwindling under the strain of lawyers' fees and Tom's creditors' demands and Sarah, now desperate, wrote directly to John to ask if 'something might be planned to keep us away from here' because although some friends were doing their utmost to persuade her and Thomas to remain in Timaru she felt it was a mistake and she would rather not live there again. Thomas was taking chloral to help him sleep but was waking up more depressed than ever and felt so terrible it was impossible to sooth him. His troubles relating to his son Tom's affairs were increasing rather than diminishing.[27]

Jack's younger brother, Richard, was to act as his escort out of the country. In other words, Jack could not even be trusted to avert trouble even on a boat up the coast to Auckland, or perhaps his family thought he would abscond if unaccompanied.

Richard wrote to Sir John assuring him: 'I will as you wish send a telegram directly [Jack] has left the Colony – also give him clearly to understand that if he ventures to return he will not be assisted in any way.' The return fare to Auckland with a one-day stopover came in total to £14. Their father Thomas arranged through Richard that money be given to Jack on board the steamer to Auckland and sent a bill of exchange 'in his favour for £10 on his arrival at San Francisco with a note to say that the same amount would be forwarded again in two months' time'.[28]

Throughout these trials, Richard, the youngest son of Thomas and Sarah, seemed to carry on cheerfully, regardless, reporting to his Uncle John on the logistical problems that beset his parents – where they should live, what to do with Tom's wife Kitty and their child, and what Lizzie should do after her husband went into exile: 'Lizzie has heard of a house which will suit them very well & the rent 8/- per week – added to this it is quite removed from here & in case Father & Mother should not move at once – will remove one source of irritation.'[28] Even the carriage horses were a worry with all the toing and froing for Tom's trials, but a solution was at hand:

> The horses I hope would reach Hororata safely today & the only trouble you are likely to have is to keep "Vic" (the mare) in any paddock if she wants to be elsewhere as her jumping capabilities are simply marvelous though I don't suppose she will try it on as long as she is either in foal or has one cut foot.[30]

After dispatching Jack to Auckland, Richard wrote a very cheerful letter to Sir John. His *joie de vivre* is unmistakable in spite of the prospect of three of his older brothers – George Buceo, Tom the poisoner and Jack – falling like ninepins before him over the previous four years:

> The trip up the West Coast [North Island] was rough in the extreme & turned [Jack] upside down [...] though it set me up for the trip down the East Coast which was the most enjoyable I ever had in my life. Beautiful weather the whole way down and a very steady & well ventilated boat (the Te Anau) made everything very pleasant. Added to this [...] I found some Southland friends on board & they came the whole way down.
>
> [...] Coming down the Coast we went out of our course to have a look at White Island [...] In Auckland I had beautiful weather & found one or two men I had known in various places & saw rather more of the place than I expected I should.
>
> Altogether I may say I thought it far ahead of the rest of NZ taken as a whole – though the climate is rather trying [...] [Jack] gave me no trouble whatever on the road up & I gave him pretty plainly to understand that he was not wanted back.
>
> With best love to yourself, Aunt, cousins & Kitty
>
> I remain dear Uncle
>
> Your affectionate nephew
>
> RW Hall[31]

Two years later, Jack, now in exile, wanted to return to Sydney for work but was discouraged by the family response and remained in North America. The atmosphere greeting his overtures to return was decidedly chilly. His Uncle John wrote: 'Willie declares that if Jack returns, he shall leave at once & I shall do my best to follow him.'[32] Whether this is a serious statement is unclear. What had Jack done to make two of his family want to leave the country if he were in it? Sir John made his views on the subject of Jack clear but in doing so also revealed an all-too-human double standard as regards the failings of his third son Dryden, an Oxford undergraduate at the time. He told his brother George, now living in England, that Dryden only ever wrote when he wanted something and had 'got into serious difficulties' through imprudence and extravagance in Oxford. John had agreed to extricate him this time but was uneasy about his future.[33] Meanwhile, as John reported to George, Jack had left San Francisco for Oregon in May 1888: 'for which God be thanked.'[34]

Thomas's will went through various codicils as he struggled to decide how to dispose of his estate between his surviving sons, Tom, Jack, Will and Richard, which he did fairly and equally. It also offers a clue to the problem with Jack since he subtracted the debt that had led to Jack's hurried exit from New Zealand and which he had himself cleared at the time, leaving money in trust for Jack's benefit and that of his issue 'lawfully begotten' to divide equally among them. Jack's sin was probably extra-marital sex, but without direct evidence there is only speculation. Perhaps his sin was magnified in the hysteria surrounding his brother Tom's actions. In his father's will there was also provision made for Tom after his release from prison, and after his death for Tom's son Nigel.

Thomas never reconciled himself to the actions of his sons. His efforts to discuss the agonising problem and mystery of Tom's crime with George W. Hall was met with stonewalling. Whenever Thomas broached the matter, the lengthy interval of time in replies to letters reaching New Zealand from England, where George lived for much of the next decade, meant George could ignore whatever was raised which he found difficult to answer. Besides, the embarrassment of the crime had forced George and Agnes to leave New Zealand, and even in St Leonard's, where they stayed temporarily on the Sussex coast, George had bumped into a gentleman at the local club who had known of the horrible events. No one in the family could comprehend how a seemingly loving and helpful son and nephew had turned into a calculating criminal.

Thomas and Sarah had received heartfelt sympathy and support from John and Rose over the events of this terrible year and were grateful, though Thomas wrote that his heart was generally 'too full & too stricken to reply to all [their] offers and consolations'.[35] He and Sarah moved to Invercargill to be near to Will and Richard, taking lodgings 'well out of town', according to John's diary of April 1887, with 'rooms very handsomely furnished'. Thomas felt very much the loss of Timaru. For the last 27 years he had poured his energies into the town's development. He and Henry Le Cren had been appointed by the Canterbury Provincial Council to transact council business in Timaru and Waitaki North in 1862; he had served on the Canterbury Board of Education the same year. In 1863 he was made chairman of the Timaru Hospital Board and warden of the Canterbury Marine Board. He had led the charge for separating the southern districts from Christchurch in provincial government. He was one of four commissioners who undertook to supervise the rebuilding of the government-erected Timaru hospital when it partly burnt down in 1868 (the hospital extension was completed by November 1880, he told John), and he was a member of the Timaru Harbour Board from 1877 to 1883, involved in choosing plans for the breakwater construction. He had also been on the board of the *Timaru Herald*. Despite these achievements, after his oldest son's appalling behaviour and trials which had drawn attention to Timaru, the powers-that-be in the town over time renamed Halls Road, named after Thomas, Pages Road. It was too difficult to return.

In the midst of her own grief at the death of her son John Neall, Grace, having received the news of all these terrible events wrote: 'How are poor Tom and Sarah? Are they able to bear up? My tender love to them.'[36]

Meanwhile, another drama had been unfolding, part of the reason why George and Agnes Hall were in no condition to receive John Neall when he arrived in New Zealand. It concerned their daughter Aggie who had married Edward Wakefield, young Jack Hall's former employer. She was living in Timaru at the time her cousin Tom was accused and convicted of poisoning his wife.

Notes and references

1. *The Duchess of Malfi*, John Webster, Act 1V, Sc II.
2. RJS Harman to JH 5 October 1886.
3. WYH to JH, 26 October 1886.
4. RJS Harman to JH 1 November 1886.
5. John Hall diary, 6 November 1886.
6. ibid., 20 October 1886.
7. Christ's College school records.
8. Peter Graham, *Vile Crimes*, 2007, p. 87.
9. Helen Wilson, *My First Eighty Years*, Paul's Book Arcade, Hamilton, p. 40.
10. GWH to JH, 15 October 1886.
11. JH to Dr Courtney Nedwill, Hororata, 4 December 1886.
12. TWH to JH 21 January 1886.
13. WYH to JH, 30 March 1887.
14. WYH to JH, 27 December 1886, Invercargill.
15. Wilfred Hall to JH, 1 December 1886.
16. Kitty Hall to Rose Hall, 21 February 1887.
17. JH to John Fountaine, 10 February 1886.
18. TWH to JH, 29 April 1886.
19. GWH to JH, 15 October 1886.
20. GWH to JH, 17 October 1886.
21. Grace Neall to JH 4 November 1886.
22. Jerningham Wakefield to RJS Harman, 12 April 1850, EJW *Founders*, pp 255-6.
23. GWH to JH, 14 August 1884.
24. ibid.
25. John [Jack] Hall to Hon. Donald McLean, 2 April 1873, ATL, MS-Papers-0032-0310.

26. WYH Hall to JH, 26 October,1886.
27. SH to JH, 15 November 1886.
28. TWH to JH, 29 October 1886.
29. RWH to JH, 2 November 1886.
30. ibid.
31. RWH to JH, 17 November 1886.
32. JH to GWH, 31 May 1888.
33. JH to GWH, 31 May 1888.
34. JH to GWH, no date but *c*.May 1888; filed with JH's 1888 correspondence.
35. TWH to JH, 29 October 1886.
36. Grace Neall to JH, 4 November 1886.

9

THE WAKEFIELD–WITHERS SCANDAL

'I always feel for Aggie as one of my own.'[1]

The heartfelt comment above from her uncle, Thomas Williamson Hall, came from someone who had only sons. He had known Aggie as a tiny girl growing up initially on Ashburton Forks station, then as a young woman, following her schooling in England and, finally, as a married woman when she came to live in Timaru with her first husband, Edward Wakefield.

George and Agnes Hall's only child, Agnes Mildred (known as Aggie and sometimes 'Adie') was born on 7 January 1851 in Spring Street, Hull, and emigrated to New Zealand with her parents on the *Royal Albert* in 1853. Schooling for girls was not readily available in Christchurch until the mid-1870s. When she was ten, therefore, knowing 'little or nothing', according to her mother who had taught her at home, she was sent back to England for eight years to a boarding school run by a Miss Siffken in Snaresbrook, near Wanstead, Essex. It had been recommended by Rose Hall, her mother's sister. While there she was a ward of her father's sister Grace, who had inherited a family of five boys when she married John Sugden Neall in 1862. Unsurprisingly over eight years, with no return visit to New Zealand

and her parents, she became closer to her aunt than her mother. This caused friction when Aggie eventually returned in 1868. Her passionate letters to Grace, 'my own Darling Auntie', some of which are published,[2] were an outlet for her disappointment on finding her parents comparatively impoverished.

Aggie returned from schooling in England by steamer at a time when New Zealand was in severe depression. Her parents arranged through Grace that Mrs Emily Harper, the wife of Bishop Henry Harper, Christchurch's first Anglican bishop, would be her chaperone on the return voyage. She wrote to Aunt Grace en route to say that 'Wherever I may be I shall look upon the happy time spent with you as amongst the *happiest* in my life.'[3] Her father's financial affairs were in decline and her parents were living in a tiny house in Addington near Christchurch, rented from John Hall. She disparagingly called it 'the Nutshell'. Aggie was disappointed. Her school

9.1 Aggie Hall, aged 18, after her return from schooling in England. 'I have been here [NZ] a month. It seems more like a year! I am not at all reconciled to the place […]'

holidays had been spent living in a grand house in Croydon with Grace's large boisterous family of five boys and many servants. It was a far cry from her parents' reduced circumstances. She was pleased to have cousins in Hororata (John and Rose Hall's family) and in Timaru (Thomas and Sarah's five boys) but she could not understand her relatives' constant habit of doing without things or wearing clothes when they were shabby. Thomas was sympathetic to her needs, splashing out on a dress so she could attend a Christchurch ball when her father could not because money was tight. She recorded, 'I wore a white grenadine skirt over a white silk slip, and a white silk body trimmed with tulle and blonde [...] Uncle Tom gave me the white silk when he was in town last. He had it made for me, was not it kind of him?'[4]

Aggie's romance and marriage

Aggie's romance with Edward Wakefield (1845–1924), the son of Felix Wakefield, and nephew of New Zealand's founder, Edward Gibbon Wakefield, began in the early 1870s. Edward was born in Launceston, Tasmania, in 1845, the eighth child in a large family of nine. He spent his childhood in Christchurch and Nelson, New Zealand, then, with the financial assistance of his Uncle Edward was educated in France and at King's College, London, returning to New Zealand in 1863. Very gifted, at 21 he became private secretary to the

9.2 Aggie's mother, Agnes Emma Hall (left) with her Aunt Rose, sisters and wives to George W. Hall and John Hall, c.1870s.

premier, Edward Stafford, in the second year of Stafford's ministry, 1866, and was secretary to the Cabinet for four years.

His background was colourful. Felix Wakefield (1807–1875) had joined his father in a silk business in Blois, in France, and while living there had married a French maidservant, Marie Félice Bailley. He had then moved to Launceston, Van Diemen's Land, to farm and work as a land agent and surveyor until he was unfairly struck off the list of authorised surveyors by the surveyor-general for errors of measurement, later winning his appeal with the Lieutenant Governor, Sir John Franklin. He had tried, unsuccessfully, to get his beleaguered wife Marie Félice committed to an asylum when she left home after bearing nine children. Three doctors found her not of unsound mind, implying that Felix and her large family had driven her to distraction and hysteria. He had arrived in Canterbury in 1851 to a hostile reception after publishing a pamphlet entitled *Mutual Relations*, which attacked the conditions and management of Canterbury.

George W. Hall would no doubt have known some of Edward's family history from Christchurch gossip when he described in a letter to John Hall the burgeoning relationship between Edward and Aggie. John and George thought Edward Wakefield was not the right suitor for her, despite his extremely promising career progress. Did they know that Edward Gibbon Wakefield had devised his dream

of the planned colony of New Zealand while he was in Newgate Prison on a charge of abducting a 15-year-old girl from her school and marrying her for her fortune at Gretna Green? Perhaps they knew that this talented, visionary and ambitious man had imported books and papers into Newgate and written a newspaper column, 'Letter from Sydney',[5] as if he was a resident of the city, using a pseudonym. It was in Newgate that he formed the idea of Canada, New Zealand

9.3 Edward Gibbon Wakefield, founder of New Zealand and uncle to Aggie's beau.

and Australia becoming the suppliers of raw materials for England's growing industrialisation.[5]

George wrote waspishly to John on 11 June 1873 from Leeston: 'They [his wife Agnes and Aggie] have struck up a wonderful intimacy with the Wakefields of Fendal Town [now Fendalton] – who as far as I know are very unexceptional people – but whose connections I take to be the main attraction.'[6] As the relationship deepened with letters flowing between Edward and Aggie, and photographs as well, George's despair at the liaison deepened. In a private note to John on blue paper fixed with a red seal, he wrote [his emphasis]:

> Thanks for yours on Wakefield. I do not think as you say that anything I can tell them would do more than confirm both mother and daughter in their determination to go on. Since you left I have never heard a word about him (although I know, and this of course is not concealed, constant correspondence goes on). Until a day ago, when the mother told me that "Edward" had an offer of advance [...] to edit the Timaru Herald at £300 a year. [...] I at once said to her that although I would receive him in a friendly manner, she must understand at once I would *not have him ask to stay in the house.* This gave her great umbrage, for it was just this she wanted to do. She does all she can to make it distinctly understood her daughter is engaged. So what can I do? If women will go to the dead they must. My life has been made wretched long enough, and I will not always endure it. They will bitterly rue it some day. You may as well reckon with your dog as with a woman, *against her inclinations.*[7]

By early February 1874, Wakefield had become editor of the *Timaru Herald*, a bi-weekly newspaper which under his management would become a daily newspaper with a national reputation. George's initial resistance to a probable marriage was waning. He was even acknowledging Edward's professional abilities when writing to John. The *Timaru Herald* had improved considerably under his management, a fact corroborated by Thomas who was to become chairman of its board and who was quite 'taken with him'. Wakefield had begged George to write to him and Agnes entreated him to do the same but, as he told John, 'I have not done so, for I hardly

9.4 Edward Wakefield, politician, newspaper editor and author, Aggie Hall's first husband, 'a man of undoubted ability, and considerable energy and determination'.

know what to say.' Within the month, George became resigned to the romance in the face of Wakefield's job success and confessed to John: 'I am bound to say I think he has got more nearly in the right place, as a journalist, than he was before and with application there is no reason he should not succeed in his new line.'[8]

By April George's standoff had collapsed:

I was forced to acknowledge to myself that it was useless keeping up a farce, so transparent a pretence. I therefore [...] gave my consent and as he was coming up to Ch.Ch. the Mother begged me to ask him to stay with us. If the thing were to be done it might as well be done graciously and I consented to that too. [...] I have fairly told him already more than once that they cannot look to me, who have but a bare maintenance for myself. Before he leaves, which will be in a day or two, we shall discuss the matter more fully and I shall not fail to let you know any decision that may be come to. I know you sympathise with me and you know how I value that sympathy. It is a difficult task for one placed as I am to guide a daughter – with so many adverse influences to contend with and feeling the impossibility of placing confidence when I ought to be able to do so most fully. I will say no more at present for really there is no more to be said.[9]

In June 1874 George finally gave his consent to the marriage. Belfield Woolcombe, Wakefield's employer on the *Timaru Herald*, had raised his salary to £400 a year, a very handsome salary even in today's terms. Wakefield, for his part, assured George he would insure his life with the Mutual Provident for £500 and had enough money to furnish a small house in Timaru, which he planned to have built. The marriage date was set for 15 July. Her father gave Agnes £70 for her outfit and promised a further £100 'to make them comfortable'. George wrote to John on 1 June 1874:

E. Wakefield has ability and since he has entered this new line has I believed worked hard and lived economically with an object in view. I hope he will continue to do so, his object gained. I tell the old woman – she has been incessantly plotting, ever since we came into this house to *get her daughter out of it*. You may fancy her wrath at such an accusation. She is writing as usual to Rose and will be sure to tell her all the details.

Nevertheless, George felt he must now let Edward know of weaknesses on Aggies's part. He was worried that her strong will might come into collision with her prospective husband's considerable energy and determination. He told Edward that her temper was not all that bad, that she had remarkable decision and self-control, but that it was marked with a determination to have her own way, fostered by her mother, who never 'had a will of her own where her daughter chose to assert hers'.[10] He added that he had taught Aggie the value of money, a reminder of her former disappointments on returning to New Zealand and finding her parents in straitened circumstances.

The wedding took place in St Michael's Church, Christchurch, on 15 July 1874. The wedding party was small, wrote George to John, with only one other couple attending beyond the bridesmaids and their parents. Thomas and Sarah with Tom junior attended and George felt the cousins were 'better friends than ever' as a result. He added the pungent comment:

> If the child is happy that is all I can desire. Like all women she is a born slave when she meets her master (and those who scream for women's right's *only want a master.* The most wretched are those who have *no* master). Aunt Rose told her that.[11]

Since he had fallen on hard times himself, George was keen that the young couple were sensible about managing their own finances: 'Almost my last exhortation to Edward Wakefield was never to let his wife be in ignorance of the exact extent of his means, for I said rely on it she is the woman to help you by making her expenditure square with it.'[12]

Aggie's wedding was vividly described to his absent Uncle John by young Tom Hall, a friend of Wakefield's and his best man:

The chief event on the Colonial branch of the Hall family during the last month is Aggie's wedding – which needless for one to say much about as you are sure to have full particulars from Addington – Aggie and her husband left for Dunedin yesterday to stay with my Father and Mother until their own home is ready for them. It was the first wedding I ever took an active part in – and must admit that in spite of the solemnity of the ceremony, to me from various circumstances it savoured a good deal of the ridiculous. First the bride & bridegroom were as cool as if they were performing a duet at the Piano – while Uncle who stood close beside them, looked so unmistakeably fierce that his hair almost stood straight on end while in a pew just behind was Aunt [Agnes, Aggie's mother] in a flood of tears – then again neither Agnes nor Wakefield had prayer books – and apparently had not studied what they had to do beforehand, so they were both in the most happy ignorance, Mr Edward telling them in a stage whisper which was heard all over the Church.[13]

Her father, buoyed by the proceedings, was relieved and satisfied with the wedding and match, despite his initial misgivings. He wrote to John that a large party went to Lyttelton to see off Aggie and Edward on the steamer to Timaru. George had provided for them as best he could in the marriage settlement, settling on Aggie 'all property in which she may have a reversionary interest, or to which *she is or may become entitled* by will or deed'. George felt that it would be Wakefield's own fault if he did not advance. 'Already he has made himself a name amongst the Journalists of NZ.'[14] Belfield, Wakefield's employer, had shown his appreciation in a handsome manner by sending with Thomas senior a £20 cheque to present on the wedding morning. George hoped for the best and believed the couple had begun married life with as fair a prospect as most. Aggie had been quite overwhelmed with presents.

Thomas and George Hall had frequent cause to discuss George's son-in-law. In November 1874, young Tom Hall was reporting to Uncle John about a narrowly avoided libel suit by the geologist Julius von Haast against the *Timaru Herald* after

9.5 The *Timaru Herald* building on Stafford Street where Edward Wakefield was editor, Thomas W. Hall, board member and one-time chairman and Jack Hall, a desk editor and proofreader.

a 'very scurrilous article' had appeared in the paper critical of Haast, who sought legal advice then decided against it:

> Uncle [George] wrote two letters to Wakefield, the first telling him what Haast proposed doing, the second telling him to take no further notice of it unless it [the article] was republished.[15]

George asked Thomas to mention the matter to Wakefield, which he refused to do but subsequently changed his mind and Wakefield agreed not to republish. Aggie, exasperated with her father and uncle, wrote to her mother, 'I wish Papa would leave Edward alone, for he is quite able to manage his Editorial duties himself.' Young Tom thought that 'annoyances of this kind' seemed to 'prey' on his Uncle George 'until he loses command over himself' but he 'was very well today, and shortly purposes going to stay with father at Timaru – which will do good'. Haast, who had been provisional geologist to Canterbury from 1861 to 1868 and had discovered and named several South Island glaciers, had been appointed curator of the Canterbury Museum in 1870 and by 1876 was appointed professor of geology at the newly established Canterbury College. George's concern was understandable.

Perhaps Edward's escape from a charge of libel prompted George to visit Timaru and his offspring. He travelled by train from Dunsandel to Ashburton 'by narrow gauge at the splitting pace of 15 miles an hour', marvelling at the changes to country he had not crossed for nine years, finding Timaru greatly improved and enlarged with stone buildings (grey with white facings) going up all over, streets widened and leaded and new ones laid out. A fire in 1868 had destroyed the original wooden Bank of New Zealand on the corner of Stafford and George streets and the *Timaru Herald*

building on Stafford Street South, among others, and these had been rebuilt in stone to the great pride of the town's residents. A building act had legislated for there to be no more wooden buildings in the main streets of their town.

9.6 The refurbished, stone-clad Bank of New Zealand in Timaru, a competitor to the National Bank of New Zealand where Tom Hall was an accountant.

After his December visit to Aggie and Wakefield, George wrote to John:

They seem to be living in a very quiet unostentatious way [...] They are diligent with the garden, both for vegetables and flowers, in which Wakefield seems to take much pleasure, and Mrs W certainly gives herself infinitely more pains than I ever would have thought she would. But improving *her own property* is a great stimulus.[16]

George's son-in-law, however, was a continuing concern to the family. Wakefield combined qualities of brilliance with the inability to moderate his ambition and particularly his desire to perform and shine publicly. He seemed to make enemies effortlessly. In 1876, as the Member for Geraldine, he was summoned to appear before the House of Representatives, charged with breach of privilege after an anonymous article in the *Timaru Herald* concerning the rabbit nuisance, over which he and a fellow Member had different views, boiled over into hubris. Wakefield had disgraced himself by describing his fellow MP, a Mr Joyce, as 'one of the very lowest members of the House', 'an ignorant prejudiced ruffian' and 'a coarse boor'. He was forced to acknowledge his authorship of these insults when the printer and publisher of the *Herald* were called to parliament to account for them. The charges were dropped after he apologised to the House. 'Surely, never was a hectoring, literary swaggerer made to abase himself more completely than Mr Edward Wakefield', opined the *Evening Post*, which actually supported his argument on the rabbit question but not his cowardice in insulting another member anonymously in a newspaper. Yet Wakefield's later newspaper campaigns on behalf of Timaru gaining a port and waterworks were instrumental in their success and a speech he made in August 1879 was described by William Rolleston as 'the finest speech ever made in the House'.

There were other ways in which Wakefield was a continuing concern to the wider family. In the year of the breach of privilege issue, young Tom and Uncle John, while waiting for Uncle George at Addington, had been discussing the intricacies of George W. Hall's will, thinking it advisable that the trustees be given a discretionary power to prevent Aggie willing her property unconditionally to Wakefield at her death in case he married again and her estate would then be divided among the children of a second wife. Tom warned her father: 'Wakefield is hardly as steady as he ought to be. There is no reason to be alarmed but we think it is a contingency which should be provided against. Wakefield is an amazingly free liver [...]'[17]

Edward Wakefield, politician, editor, father and author

In 1875, the year after his marriage, Edward Wakefield had become the Member of Parliament for Geraldine, South Canterbury, and held the position until 1881, his political and newspaper careers fuelling each other. As a fellow politician and by 1879 premier, John Hall was in a unique position to assess Wakefield as a public figure as well as a relative. His view was severe. He saw Wakefield's undoubted abilities but did not admire his character. To his brother-in-law John Neall, who had married Grace Hall, he wrote in August 1876:

> Edward Wakefield has not become a favorite: he is admittedly talented, but conceited in conduct and intemperate in language. He made a brilliant speech the other evening but composed chiefly of vituperation. Of course this line of conduct makes him many enemies and no friends.[18]

Wakefield had been defeated in the 1881 election but the following year was elected a governor of Canterbury College (the initial 23 founding governors – John Hall and Joshua Williams included – were initially allowed to fill their own vacancies) and in February 1884 was elected unopposed for Selwyn, Sir John's former seat, apparently by renouncing further government borrowing and immigration. In these turbulent political times, his penchant for intemperate language was perhaps better under control, for the *North Otago Times* at the time of his election to the Selwyn seat reported enthusiastically:

> As a journalist and as a politician, Mr Wakefield has a reputation which, if not one of the enviable, is at least one of the most emphatic in New Zealand. [...] Apart from his other characteristics [he] is one of the most fascinating public speakers in New Zealand. In that respect [he] is believed by competent judges to surpass Sir George Grey himself – the Grand Turk of New Zealand oratory, the man who, as a public speaker, bears no brother on his throne.

Wakefield did not receive a ministerial position in the new Stout-Vogel ministry (1884–1887) so changed sides becoming colonial secretary in Harry Atkinson's ministry, which only lasted a week. His Selwyn constituents sent him a dead rat for fleeing the sinking ship.

In May 1884, Aggie's uncle, Thomas W. Hall, was elected chairman of the board of the *Timaru Herald*. A letter he wrote in April 1882, shows how an earlier Board of which he was part had attempted to muzzle Wakefield's editorial control. Thomas considered that the newspaper should support John Hall's ministry (1879–1882) and in return gain the premier's support for Timaru's affairs in which he himself was heavily involved:

My dear John

For your information the Timaru Herald changed hands yesterday. The Company [again] installed Wakefield as Editor as I named was intended; but for a time this was rather dubious, as the terms he asked & also the tone assumed were inadmissible. He asked for the full control of the paper & staff, full liberty to write in his leisure time for other papers. [...] All these demands were considered excessive by the Director. However sooner than lose him without a trial we came to terms for six months on the understanding that he shall take a political line pointed out by the Director, & have control of staff within certain limits. I trust by this arrangement we shall secure your ministry & true support. We have given in to Wakefield on almost all other points, but made it a sine qua non that he should follow the practical line pointed out to him. *His ability is undoubted, but his stability we consider requires watching* [my emphasis].

Yours affectionately TW Hall[19]

Wakefield was accustomed to being commissioned to write leaders for the *Otago Daily Times*, the *New Zealand Times* and the Christchurch *Press*, so his request to write for other papers in his leisure time would not have seemed unusual to him. He also wrote for the *Australasian*, the *Melbourne Argus* and *Sydney Daily Telegraph* under a pseudonym 'Taniwha'. George commented, 'how he [Thomas] and Wakefield will get on is more than I can say. The latter has, with regard to the bad times, voluntary submitted [to a] reduction of £100 in his salary, receiving £400.' Wakefield was able to move his wife and five children into his brother Oliver's house in Timaru, retaining the housekeeper. Oliver, Edward's greatest friend, had been killed by unwittingly walking in front of a tram in Christchurch. Wakefield, wrote George, 'is going to take Aggie and Queenie [their daughter] to Wellington for the winter. Altho' the former has not had a return of her cough, she is looking very thin, & Edward is anxious about her.'[20]

By October 1884, the relationship between the directors of the *Timaru Herald* and their politically volatile editor had taken a turn for the worse, which George duly reported by letter to John on 9 October:

> Last evening I had a telegram from Tom, saying, that at yesterday's meeting of Directors of T Herald, a motion, which had taken him quite unawares, had been carried, to give Wakefield *3 months notice* to appoint another Editor. Tom said he would write particulars & I am expecting a letter from him this afternoon. I can hardly say I am surprised, for the relations between Wakefield & many of the Directors have too often been what you politically call *strained*.[21]

The Wakefields were back in Timaru by December and John Hall, always anxious about family affairs when they went wrong, visited them by rail. (The train service which was opened in 1867 had reached Timaru by 1876, passing near to Rakaia Terrace Station, at Selwyn.) On 16 December 1884, John's diary entry records that he took 'presents for the children' and found 'Aggie looking better than yesterday & children bonny'. Aggie's first son, Edward ['Chunky'], had returned from T. S. Baker's school at French Farm in Akaroa. 'Chunk [...] came in morning by Akaroa steamer [...]'. After dinner with Thomas and Sarah on the 18th, John sent his luggage to the Wakefield's house and that evening 'went to Amateur Dramatic performance of Sorcerer at Theatre', staying with Edward and Aggie. 'Aggie's children very nice. Youngest, Grace very like Chunk, Mildred black eyes. Oliver strong & very pleasant. Chunk much improved by Akaroa, browned & stronger & less self-asserting.'

Edward Wakefield took John and Chunky to Bruce's Flour Mill which John found 'a most perfect establishment South of the line'. That night: 'at Wakefield's a small dinner party. Mr & Mrs Hannah, Dr McIntyre, Tom junr. Passed off pleasantly. Shewed my American photos. Children very good.' (John Hall had spent 1884 in Europe and England, returning via South America.) He left the next morning to return to Christchurch. 'Raining. Wakefield & Aggie both up & breakfasted. He came with me to Station. Left 7.30 a.m.'[22]

This sanguine account of happy family relations was not to last long. Edward moved to Wellington in 1885, leaving Aggie behind in Timaru, and became co-owner and editor of the *Evening Press*. Aggie, like many a political wife, was beginning to find her husband's long absences from home on parliamentary and newspaper business wearing and lonely.

Aggie's fall from grace

The year 1886 was a tumultuous one for the extended Hall family in Timaru. The Thomas Hall trials concerning his charge of attempting to poison his wife and possibly also her step-father, Captain Cain, were being conducted amidst public clamour. Aggie's father George was at the same time arranging for the nursing of Grace's son John Neall, who had developed tuberculosis after his arrival in New Zealand for work experience. He was now in Christchurch and required constant visiting. John Hall had just returned from a trip to England, arriving back at the height of the Thomas Hall trial period.

Aggie, lonely in Timaru while her husband was busy in Wellington, became close to his friend Edward Withers, formerly an officer in the Irish Guards. Withers, after a banking job in Napier, had become manager of the Bank of New Zealand in Timaru. Wakefield's rival to his wife's affections is first mentioned in the correspondence between George and John Hall three years before, in a letter of 13 July 1883, from George's Bligh's Road house, Christchurch:

> You will remember perhaps poor old Major Withers died lately. Edward Withers, his son whom we know so well, has been promoted to the Managership of the Bank at Napier, whither his father's widow and 3 young children have returned to dwell.[23]

In Edward's absence, Withers began to look in on Aggie. Their affair began in December 1885 and when discovered, led automatically to Aggie's divorce from Edward Wakefield on 28 April 1886. Divorce was then comparatively rare in New Zealand, but necessary in this case because of Aggie's pregnancy to Withers. Their child Aimée (meaning 'loved one') was born on 10 September 1886. Until the New Zealand Divorce

9.7 Edward Withers, son of Major Edward Withers.

Law of 1894 made the grounds of divorce virtually equal for men and women, neglect of household duties was a sufficient reason for a man to divorce a woman, while adultery on a wife's part was sufficient reason for her to lose her children. A newspaper report of the divorce proceeding describes what happened in the supreme court, Dunedin, presided over by the esteemed Mr Justice Williams,[24] who that year also presided over the Thomas Hall trial concerning the alleged poisoning of Captain Cain.

> During the month of December the respondent's [Aggie's] letters became short and constrained, and she complained bitterly of having to go to Wellington, and when the family met at Christmas her manner caused them great uneasiness in consequence of her resistance to the proposed change of residence. The petitioner [E. Wakefield] took only a furnished house in Wellington for just long enough to tide over the session, a member of the family agreeing to occupy his house at Timaru during that term. He then returned to Wellington on the understanding that the respondent would follow with her children in a fortnight or three weeks. She delayed her coming till the beginning of March. On arriving at Wellington she complained bitterly of the change, and displayed no disposition to settle down happily. Her manner caused the petitioner great distress and alarm, but he was unable to get any explanation of it or obtain her confidence. Weeks passed in almost total silence. At length the petitioner being compelled to go to Dunedin as defendant in a law suit, and fearing to leave his wife in the despondent state of mind she was in, implored her to relieve his anxiety and enable the estrangement to be removed. At first she would say nothing except that she was unhappy at Wellington, but subsequently she told petitioner that she had been unfaithful to him at Timaru in December, and had formed an intimacy with the co-respondent. She then made a full confession. [...] The evidence of the respondent's

father, taken on commission in Christchurch, was put in. It corroborated the petitioner's evidence in every particular, and stated in addition that the co-respondent had made a full confession to the witness at Timaru. In answer to his Honor Mr Cook said he had nothing to say. His Honor pronounced a decree nisi, with costs, against the co-respondent [Withers], the petitioner [Wakefield] to have the custody of the children.[25]

Aggie's Uncle Thomas wrote an account of the affair to John from Timaru and gave some indication of Aggie's standing among her women friends before her affair, but also indicated the disruption to his son John's family, since Aggie's lover was the brother of young John [Jack] Hall's wife Lizzie (née Withers), and she defended his behaviour. Regardless of her fall from social grace, Aggie was much loved by her uncles, aunts and parents, who rallied around her. Though not exonerating her behaviour, they saw her adultery as partly the result of neglect and sympathised with the unbearable predicament she found herself in with the loss of all her children in the divorce proceedings. George – extraordinarily – was made to give evidence and it supported Wakefield's case, an intolerable position for a father, particularly, as young Tom Hall had suggested, Wakefield was a 'free liver' and controversial if not universally unpopular, but George was a conventional man and one who felt at times defeated by the women in his family, and himself. Aggie says in her letter below that Edward had made her father do things he should not have had to do, so presumably the pressure to give evidence against Aggie came from her husband.

Thomas wrote to John, showing how the affair and divorce were causing disruption to his family in Timaru, too:

I do not know if George would have the heart to tell you much of this miserable affair. Probably not & I believe it was only the necessity of taking action & keeping his mind fully employed that enabled him to bear up at first as well. At present by his letters he is very low & I shall try to get up & see him again next week. The first trial in this case for decree nisi comes on the day after tomorrow before Judge Williams (alone) at Dunedin. Considerately George's evidence has been taken by Commission in Christchurch. Society both here & in Christchurch was completely I may say stunned when this affair was divulged. [...] Just before Aggie left Timaru for Wellington, her friends here made up a picnic on her account & had it by Elworthy's. About seventy were there. This shows how highly she was thought of & she was considered the last lady in the country who could be guilty of such a thing. It is one of those unaccountable anomalies that take place at times. The fellow himself with nothing to recommend him, & having by what we now hear, been removed from Napier & blackballed at the Club there for a similar affair. Numerous cases of his low loose life are now coming out & my dear John what has hurt us more is that John's (our son) wife spared no means to exonerate her brother, at the expense of his victim & stated more than once that her brother had been entrapped to enable Mrs Wakefield to get a divorce from her husband. This has caused me to forbid her (Lizzie) the house & both Tom & Willie, who was here, have done the same & forbid their wives to see her. In return, although I told John it would make no difference with him or the children, he (John) is imbecile enough to join her in forbidding the children to come to see their grandmother or myself, although he or rather they have been living free in my places & a great part of the children's things have been supplied by myself & Sarah.

The whole of this is very very sad. Wakefield with his sister Josephine & little Oliver called here on the evening of the 27th, they [are] leaving for Christchurch & Wellington in the morning. What a mercy it is that Josephine Wakefield is out here to take charge of the children; but what answer can be given to them when they ask for their mother? The eldest boy is too old & too acute to be put off with any subterfuge. All George's friends have been most kind to him & the Mother, but it has been very very hard to bear & I always feel for Aggie the same as one of my own. After being some time with George in Christchurch, I saw her & my great offer kept up [we don't know what this was, possibly financial]. She looked very ill. Sarah & John Neall [Grace's son, staying with Thomas and Sarah] join in best love to you, Rose & all your family. I will now close this painful letter.

Your affectionate brother
TW Hall.[26]

The toll on all parties of Aggie's affair with Withers is apparent in her father's letter to John Hall two months later. Edward Wakefield's unmarried sister, Josephine, had stepped in to look after his children. George was under tremendous stress. The 'dread calamity' that was Aggie's predicament had prevented him taking in poor dying John Neall, since there was only one spare bedroom in the house, now occupied by his distraught daughter. Judge Joshua Williams, ever-present it seemed during this family's extreme events, had pronounced the decree nisi on 3 May with three months' notice to petition to apply for the rule absolute when the divorce would be finalised. George wrote:

> There was positively no defence whatever. Custody of all the children adjudged to the Father – I instantly made a temporary codicil to my will [...] To prevent my being dragged into the witness box, my evidence was taken on commission.

> Dear Josephine has been an indefatigable comfort to us all – There is no doubt that Edward has suffered most terribly. The condition of our poor child has been hard to describe. Sometimes stony – sometimes [...] violent, hysterical & doubtless at moments mad, which it took all my determinations, strength, firmness, & forced calmness to subdue. At other times softer grief, all hinging on the loss of her children. It was a bitter task to have to prove to her against her will that her husband could not possibly hand over her children to the man who had wrought all this ill.

> During the last week she has been calmer & more resigned & I hope will keep up so. The consequences in a money point of view to her are disastrous beyond everything. *Withers* has lost his situation & has nothing & MacKenzie, the head manager, says he will give him recommendations to assist him on condition he makes the prompted atonement by marrying his victim so soon as the law permits (which is not before Aug. 8) – it follows that *all the costs* will fall on me & in addition I should

have to support them until he can earn enough. I have been down to see him where he is awaiting [...] the time when he can make her his wife & when that comes I have to send for him in requisite time & they must be quietly as possible married at the Registry, Ch.Ch. There is no help for it. He must then leave her with us (being unfit to travel) & go over to Australia & seek work, which by recommendations he may secure. When he has done that, and she is fit for the journey I shall take her to him. Then I can do no more. He has promised solemnly everything. I hope poor thing the news may soften her suffering – which I cannot for a moment deny she has brought entirely on herself. But there was fault on both sides. Nothing I could learn from her (for she *would say nothing*) or others could enable me to help her. [27]

George acknowledged that he and Agnes had no inkling that Edward and Aggie were not living happily together. Her friend Maude, who had stayed with Aggie in Timaru, had told them of 'the supercilious, contemptuous manner with which [Edward] treated her – galling beyond all to a woman of proud spirit & I am forced to add extremely high temper'. George had consulted with Edward's friend, young Tom Hall, who had at first objected to the remarriage but learning of Aggie's pregnancy had to acknowledge it was necessary for her to marry because of 'the solemn duty she owed to her coming child – to give it a name to which it could claim a right'. The feeling against Wakefield in Canterbury was very bitter, wrote George, and all Aggie's friends had been kindness itself and were coming to see her. George was trying to save 'a little of poor Aggie's [marriage] settlements' which Wakefield's lawyers were claiming to have altered. John Hall, soon to return earlier to New Zealand than formerly planned, had offered Terrace Station as a retreat but George felt the isolation would be disastrous for Aggie's state of mind. He was trying to keep Aggie cheerful but he had experienced too much lately of what it was to keep an unruffled face 'with sorrow, shame & anxiety gnawing' at his heart. Aggie herself felt 'great terror' at the prospect of meeting her Uncle John again, but his letter 'brimful of love & pity' would remove that fear.

Aggie was close to her Uncle John and Aunt Rose and confided in them her agony of mind, indicating how friends and family had rallied to her, with the exception of Aunt Sarah who was compromised because her son Jack was married to Withers' sister Lizzie. Aggie found relief through her religion and her children continued to write to her. She poured out her anguish and remorse to Uncle John and Aunt Rose:

> I know you would be heart-broken & be good to my dear parents. But I hardly dared sometimes to [wonder] how you could think of me who has brought this terrible shame & trouble on all my dear ones. No words can tell the hard punishment it is losing my darlings. None but [God] could have made me bear it – many times I felt so utterly overwhelmed that I hardly dare trust myself. The love and kindness I have had shown *me* on all sides perfectly astounds me. People I hardly know make a point of coming to see me or writing to me & I cannot help feeling it is a sign of His sorrow for me & forgiveness & that He moves people to act as they do one & all. How many poor creatures who are in the same way are just cut & kept down – but I have not had one hard word said to me.

> You must not think any of my friends do not feel the wrong done. They do & openly say so; only try through their love & kindness to make me feel tho I have suffered so much I shall be forgiven if I really try to atone.

Such splendid letters I have had from our Archdeacon Harper, so good & great trying to lighten my sorrow by his wise counsel. Indeed, dear Auntie, I have sought His forgiveness & turned to Him for strength & help – otherwise I feel I could not have gone through all I have had to bear.

You need no telling about my good parents, I am sure no others could have behaved as they have & are doing & nothing I can ever do will in any degree repay their good deeds & mercy.

Edward has I consider treated my poor Father most selfishly & made him do things he should never have had to do. It hurts me sorely, but I can do nothing & can only help him by being quite quiet. I cannot think how Edward can tell the stories he does. He seems to have no knowledge of truth & says anything to aid his cause.

There is no excuse to be made for me I know if I shall *ever* get over the sin & shame but I do feel for all of us: children, my parents, all relations. Edward might have shown mercy. The past as far as I was concerned never once entered his head & I dare to say he does not even now realize how hard he was to put up with. For the last two years or so, especially the last he has been quite altered & plainly showed he cared more for others than for me. I used to speak to him sometimes but he always laughed or [illegible] but to be snubbed & neglected when he did come home made me wretched. However it is all over now, & only the future to look to.[28]

George had made enquiries about his daughter's future second husband, Edward (Ted) Withers. He told John that he had been 'a good servant at the [Colonial] Bank, sober & trustworthy', his temper was good and he was fond of children and had been kind and generous to his relations. His father, Major Edward Withers, had told George that his son was a man who did not break his word. Nevertheless, as a father, George found Withers' conduct in the Aggie affair, 'base' but was concealing his feelings and hoping for the best.

Aggie was an only child and fiercely independent, particularly when it came to be told how to live and what to do by her somewhat overbearing father and two uncles, as well as their wives. Before she left for her education in England at the age of ten, she had grown up on a sheep station, mixing with station hands and managers, and learning to ride a horse. She possessed a 'very determined manner' and had, according to her mother, exhibited 'proud, disobedient tempers'.[29] During her English schooling, her urban Neall cousins, with whom she stayed during vacations, were all boys and she probably enjoyed quite a lot of rough and tumble with them, leading their father, John Neall, to describe her as 'a thorough wild one'.[30] Her father confessed to John Hall, in his anguished letter of 18 June above, that since her return to New Zealand from schooling in England, she had shown no confidence in him or confided in him. If she had he thought he might have been able to help her better.

Earlier, in April 1883, Aggie had been staying with her father in Christchurch at Bligh's Road suffering from bronchitis together with her sick daughter, Queenie. George wrote to John saying, Aggie was 'not easy to manage, and resents anything she thinks looks like interference'. She was angry with her father for suggesting to her husband that she be sent to Tauranga for the winter if her symptoms did not abate, on doctors' orders. 'I was forced to tell her that I considered it my duty to do so and should do it. Whereat she was much displeased.'[31]

During the decade after their marriage, Edward and Aggie had produced five children: Edward Howard St George (Eddie/Chunky), Gerald Seymour, who died as a baby, Oliver, Grace Josephine (Queenie), and Mildred. Chunky, Queenie and Mildred all married, but only Queenie had children.

Aggie's affair with Withers had tragic results for herself, dire consequences for the children of her first marriage, separated from their mother thereafter, and brought prolonged sorrow for her parents who subsequently spent much of their time in England, moving between different lodgings. Their flight from New Zealand was partially provoked by the ignominy of their relationship to the by now notorious Tom Hall, serving his sentence in Mount Eden Gaol. Aggie had lost custody of her children, Withers had lost his job; Wakefield, who obtained custody, had the added burden of supporting a large family and his sister Josephine, their carer, but had lost his wife. He had given up politics in 1887 to edit and part-own the Wellington *Evening Press* and was piling up libel actions over the next two years. Sir John Hall used his contacts to try to secure a position for Withers in other New Zealand banks, but was unsuccessful. Wakefield's sister Josephine, who had hitherto worked as a housekeeper in various Wakefield households and in the households of relatives, took the Wakefield children first to Wellington, then to England to live. All, including Aggie, admired her, for, as Aggie wrote to her aunt and uncle, 'Joe is so good, she has not said one word of blame to me – such charity does make one feel remorse & sorrow far more than harshness & unkindness would do.'[32]

Aggie's daughter, Aimée Mildred Withers, was born in September 1886. In July of that year, Will Hall, Aggie's solicitor cousin in Invercargill, wrote to John Hall with the news that there were complications relating to the divorce and remarriage which would result in her father taking Aggie to Australia to repeat the ceremony with Withers. Will said:

> It has occurred to me that a point in connection with Withers & Agnes may not have been satisfactorily settled. [...] It is this, that under the Divorce Act a marriage cannot take place between the parties to the suit until the expiration of the period fixed for appealing, i.e. three months after the decree was made absolute. As Agnes was I think married within that time, their marriage is consequently invalid, at least so far as the legitimacy of her children is concerned, though it might be sufficiently binding for some other purposes [...][33]

Withers and Aggie were therefore remarried in Australia by the Registrar of Marriages, West Hothom, a suburb of Melbourne, with her father George as witness along with the registrar clerk. George was also striving to find work for his new son-in-law in Australia but 'our efforts have so far been without avail'.[34]

After his divorce, Edward Wakefield lived in Wellington. He had lost considerable money and was still causing his father-in-law grief, as John Hall recorded in his diary:

> George much exercised by Wakefield's sudden return from Timaru, having lost a law suit & £400. He seems in inextricable difficulties, & G., altho' he may get some nominal security, will lose the £1,500 he has guaranteed. [...] Never saw George so haggard & unwell. My heart bleeds for him.[35]

George, initially reluctant to consent to his daughter's marriage to a man he instinctively disliked, had allowed himself to be persuaded by convention and the fear of public opprobrium to give in to Wakefield's persuasions of his heartbreak over the divorce. More galling was the knowledge that Wakefield had probably bought his share in the *Evening Press* with money George had loaned him. He had characteristically already libelled a public figure in the paper. George was a kind and loving man, whose energies had been diminished by illness. Life was looking grim.

For George, meeting Josephine and her little Wakefield charges, his grandchildren, in Wellington before he and Agnes left for England had been painful. '[Wakefield] [...] brought down Josephine and the two little girls, *Grace* and *Mildred*, from their perch on the hills [...] the dear little things looked so much grown and so really pretty. But dear John my heart bled when I looked at them and thought of their poor Mother. I was in fear they might mention her but they never did.'[36] He wrote to John, now in Sydney attending to his daughter Mary who was dying there of tuberculosis, 'In all I have done in this last sad year I have acted so far as I could see for the best, and as yet I cannot perceive as how I could have done better.'[37] He felt very demoralised about 'injuries inflicted on us by those we love best'[38] and was fighting hard not to become embittered.

Today, Edward and Aggie would have taken part in mediation before their divorce and would have shared custody of their children. In the 1880s, it was possible for George to feel he had done the honourable thing by giving evidence against his daughter to ensure that Withers, a man 'blackballed at his [...] club', would not gain influence over and custody of Aggie's children.

George and Agnes continued to write to Aggie. In a letter to her Uncle John from Hook Bush in July 1887 she said, 'It cannot be long now before we get our first letters from the dear travellers. I do long for them, when they come regularly, we shall not seem so far apart.' By early 1888 her husband, Edward Withers, she reported, had found temporary work as a clerk in a coal merchant's office. The last letters from her 'dear parents' had been from the coastal town of Eastbourne.

After the collapse of their daughter's marriage, her remarriage and the other dramatic events of 1886, George and Agnes Hall remained in England for the next four years. As George remarked, 'at present I shrink from the thought of taking up abode in N.Z., which is only fraught with, to me, painful memories of much suffering.'[39] They took lodgings in Warrior Square, St Leonard's-on-Sea, then St Helier, Jersey, venturing to London occasionally for medical advice. George's continuing digestive problems and other health issues prevented a long sea voyage back to New Zealand for the time being. Christmas in 1889 was spent alone in a Jersey boarding house, raising a glass to recall the happy extended family at other Hororata Christmas dinners of former years before 'time and death and sorrows had made gaps never to be healed'.[40]

Life was to improve for Aggie and Edward Withers. He found work as an accountant in Dunedin and by 1910 was manager for William and Strachan & Co, a Dunedin brewery.

Edward Wakefield after the divorce

By 1889, Wakefield had turned to writing full time as a career. Living in New York, he completed a book entitled *New Zealand After Fifty Years*, to launch at the Paris Exhibition – Exposition Universelle – held from May to October 1889. An important feature was the Colonial Exhibition, which competed for attention with the Eiffel Tower and Machinery Hall. Wakefield professed to be saving to support his children but he was actually fighting another libel action as a result of a discussion in his Wellington paper, the *Evening*

Press. He was still its co-owner with William Roydhouse. The libel in Stewart vs Roydhouse concerned a Dr Stewart's behaviour and whether he had committed manslaughter in allowing a patient to die. Damages were set at £2,000 (possibly over £120,000 today). The defendants wanted the trial to be in Dunedin not Wellington where Wakefield had been editor of the paper, or Christchurch where he was notorious as an MP, well-known and disliked.

Meanwhile, Josephine struggled to manage his children's welfare on her own meagre resources and their father's literary income. George and Agnes Hall moved between boarding houses in St Leonards, St Helier and Croydon, near George's sister Grace, who was mourning the loss of her son, John. They were able to visit their grandchildren and be watchful over Josephine's well-being.

George kept his brother John well informed of all the family news. He became obsessed with the financial provisions he had made to Wakefield and spent a great deal of his time and energy attempting to reclaim monies from his son-in-law. George's own financial situation was reliant on investments and somewhat precarious. Awaiting the arrival of Josephine and the children in England, he wrote to John from St Helier in April 1889:

> Josephine and our grandchildren [are] expecting to come to England [...] and Wakefield [is] coming to England by San Francisco. What does it all mean? Has he sold the paper? If so he ought to reimburse me in whole or part what I have paid him. [...] So far as Wakefield is concerned I think, all things considered, he could not take a more advisable step than that of leaving N.Z. I have no doubt he could do well as a journalist in London. [...] Agnes tells me it has long been Josephine's wish to break the children from all old associations. I cannot blame her

but it will be a hard task. [...] In my letter to Williams [George's solicitor in N.Z.] I said [...] I had no desire to put Wakefield to such extremity as might take away the power of supporting his family. But short of this I ought to expect him to re-imburse me to the greatest extent possible. He always looked to the sale of the paper [the *Evening Press*] as a means of doing so.[41]

9.8 *New Zealand After Fifty Years.*

Edward Wakefield's *New Zealand After Fifty Years* was a handsome book with a green cloth cover engraved in gold leaf, showing a New Zealand cabbage tree, a Māori carrying a long digging stick, a moa bird and a tent. It is well illustrated throughout with beautiful engravings and photographs, among them Captain James Cook, the kiwi, Hororata Terrace Station, Māori weapons, views of the Thames goldfields, Parliament Buildings and Government House, Wellington, Nelson College (a private school), and the rooms of a master's house in Christ's College, Canterbury. It was clearly more than an account of one Englishman's experience of the new colony at this international showing. With government sponsorship it was a recruitment tool for new settlers and a vehicle for New Zealand industry to promote itself in the world. Opposite the title page, which bears an engraving of Māori men dragging a canoe out to sea, is a picture of Edward's uncle, Edward Gibbon Wakefield, 'founder of New Zealand'. The title page shows it was published in New York, London, Melbourne and Paris (the French Consul in Wellington, Count Joffray d'Abbans, had a hand in the French edition). The *Timaru Herald* claimed that the French government intended to 'take a large number of copies' and that some of the material had been derived from the correspondence of early French missionaries. At the end of the Introduction is a beautiful map of New Zealand produced by the Government Survey Department. The book was considered a first-rate public relations tool for New Zealand, regardless of a blatant bias in favour of the Wakefield family and Edward's relatives, giving an up-to-date account of the history and development of the new colony. There is nothing in it to indicate that Edward Wakefield's personal life had been turbulent, that he was enduring a public libel trial with possibly terrifying financial consequences for his career and future, or that some of his relatives had been through the gravest trials of their lives (he was a witness in his friend Tom Hall's first poisoning trial, giving evidence about a key reference book on poisons he had seen in his possession, and Tom's best man at his wedding). Wakefield wrote:

It is the strongest wish of those who love it best, that New Zealand may never be flooded by a promiscuous immigration of the dregs of old countries; or attract such a greedy rush of capital as to make it a mere gambling hell of speculators and monopolists. But it is their firm belief also, founded on the data of the past and the present, and on all reasonable calculations of the future, that it is destined within the next half-century to be the most populous and prosperous of all the British colonies in the Southern Hemisphere.[42]

As described earlier, his son 'Chunky' had arrived in Timaru by steamer from Akaroa. Discussing the next generation of settlers, Wakefield plays this up a bit:

> [Young people] travel about so much, and see so many changes, and know so much of the world, that a journey has no terrors for them, but it is only a pleasure. The idea of prolonged separation is not at all oppressive, because they think nothing of coming or going a distance which would seem appalling to youngsters in their own class in old countries: and in any case they are always within a couple or three days' post of their parents. It is not thought any adventure, for quite little schoolboys to travel a hundred miles or more, in a coasting steamer; or a train or coach, with nobody in charge of them [...][43]

Sometimes Wakefield's earnest wish to convey only the best in New Zealand's new society to potential immigrants and readers overcomes his desire to tell the truth: 'There is [...] little parental discipline in the colony, because there is but little need for any. As to the prevailing liberty tending to run into licence, there are no evidences for that.'[44] This is a bit rich coming from a man whose wife had just committed adultery with his friend, and who he had recently divorced, whose friend Tom Hall had just been convicted of the attempted poisoning of his wife and whose business had collapsed through fraudulent practice; whose relatives by marriage, George Buceo Hall and young Jack Hall (the latter his employee on the *Timaru Herald*), had been exiled by their families for what seemed excessive behaviour. However, the book clearly had a promotional purpose to attract more settlers, tourists and business and the government was presumably happy with the outcome. It followed other similar books used to attract labour and settlers to New Zealand, perhaps most similar in format to Charles Hursthouse's *New Zealand, or Zealandia: the Britain of the South*, published in England in 1857 in two volumes, with exquisite watercolours which made a cob farmhouse in rural New Zealand look like an attractive estate in Devon, thus appealing to the desire for land unattainable in England to those whose status prevented such riches.

George and Agnes Hall read their former son-in-law's book in Jersey. They found it very good but 'rather too rosy in outlook' with 'nothing but praise for New Zealand and everybody in it',[45] though George conceded that the book was beautifully illustrated. He was increasingly worried for his daughter's children and their beleaguered Aunt Josephine. He fretted about the collapse of Wakefield's evening paper in Wellington and the remote likelihood of Wakefield's debt to him being repaid, and worried about the lack of attention their father paid to his children. He knew that his own contribution to the family's welfare was inadequate.

Wakefield had certainly conceived a brilliant book project. It had begun as a handbook of New Zealand, written while he held government office, but turned into a more popular book after a Cabinet split when his services were dispensed with. The Wellington-based monthly journal, *Typo*, claimed 50,000 copies were to be printed and described Edward Wakefield on 25 May 1889 as 'the ablest journalist our colony has produced' and 'one of our men of mark'. Wakefield had managed to break free of New Zealand with the project and for the first time was able to extend his writing career. He explained his plans to George in a letter written in March 1889 before he left New Zealand:

> I also have several other literary works, commissions, for writing and other matters in hand for America. In short

I appear so far as one can possibly foresee, to have now the best opportunity I have ever had for really trying what I can do on a large field, free from adverse conditions which have been almost overwhelming in N.Z.

I have made every provision against failure, and I have every confidence of success if only I retain my good health. I have made arrangements for the Evening Press being carried on in my absence for 6 months at all events, by the end of which time I shall know for certain whether I am to make a career at home or to return for a time to the colony. Roydhouse has agreed to pay me at £350 per annum in England from the paper for six months at least, or for as much longer as may be agreed. I have further made some arrangements for entering again literary work as soon as I reach London and have my book off my hands; so that at the worst I shall be doing better than I am here, with prospects of making a career which is totally debarred me here. I cannot enter into all the details here, but I wish to give you as clear a view of our plans as I can at this moment so as to catch the mail tomorrow. I cannot tell how long I shall be detained in America until I arrive there and interview the publishers. It may be only a week, it may be a month; but it will not be longer than I can help. At all events unless something unforeseen should happen, Josephine and the children will arrive in London on about the 30th May and Josephine will telegraph to you at Croydon from Plymouth so as to let you know of their whereabouts. I am sorry to say Josephine is far from well. […]

I expect to be able to return tomorrow night to Wellington, where of course I have a great deal to do. […] I dare say you will at first think these are bold steps, or perhaps rash steps to take, but I feel sure that when you learn all, you will entirely approve of them. They offer, in my firm conviction, the only way out of a sea of difficulties. [...] I have had a long talk with Wynn Williams [his solicitor, too], and told him all my plans, in which he concurs, I doing all in my power to meet his views. I cannot write more tonight. With united love to yourself and the Mother.

E.W.

[Note from George at end of this forwarded letter – to John:] For JH. Private: I only trust for the poor dear children's sake his sanguine hopes may be realised. We shall be very pleased to see them again. GWH.[46]

George and John were watching the developments over Wakefield's newspaper with interest in late 1889. George wrote to John on 15 November from Jersey advising him to 'step in at once' should the owners of the *Evening Press* be declared bankrupt or there was a 'transfer' of ownership. He had to consider Wakefield's children and he also had been given a 'lien over the paper' which 'out of consideration for the interests of his business only, we forebore to register'. Besides, 'anything we could save would be better for the children'.[47] With George's help, Josephine had started Eddie (Chunky was now 14) at a school in Sydenham.

In frustration at his distance from New Zealand and the time taken for news to arrive, George wrote with increasing resolve about Wakefield to John on 5 February 1890 from Jersey:

Virtually his interest [in the *Evening Press*] was *bought with my money and belongs to me*. I wished to do nothing that could interfere with his getting a living for his family

by successfully working the paper, but if it comes to selling
or winding it up, the case is *altered*.[48]

George did recover his £1,500 from Wakefield after the paper
was sold to a Mr R. S. Hawkins of the Wairarapa, in April 1890.
Wakefield instructed William Roydhouse, his co-owner, to pay
Wakefield's share of the proceeds into George's account. George and
Agnes immediately made plans to visit New Zealand and they did so
on the *Rimutaka* on 19 September 1890.

Wakefield never returned to politics after 1887. He spent some
time in America after the publication of his book, but returned to
London where he became New York representative for the British
and United States Agency in 1890. A letter from him to George
explained what this entailed:

My dear Pater

[…] I am employed in establishing an Agency in London
and New York for the investment of English capital in
America and the management of various businesses
between the two countries. So far, the people I am acting
with have only paid my expenses and given me £5 a week
for myself; but if I succeed in establishing the Agency
on a satisfactory footing, I am promised a permanent
[position] with a share in the concern which may be of
considerable value. […] I have got Sir Edward Stafford,
Sir Edward Thornton, and Lord George Campbell to join
me and to put some money into the business in order
to start the Agency under powerful auspices, and I shall
probably have to go backwards and forwards between
London and New York several times in order to complete

the organization. If I find I shall be likely to leave before you come to Town, I will run down to Jersey for two or three days.[49]

According to George, who Wakefield had visited in Jersey, his son-in-law had a sixth share of the company and had been made managing director with a salary of £850 a year. The agency was presumably the brainchild of Edward Stafford, a former New Zealand premier (1865–1869). Stafford had taken the lead and introduced Edward to Lord Campbell and Sir Edward Thornton, minister to the United States from 1867 to 1881. 'It is only for the children and Josephine's sake we can take an interest in what he does,'[50] George told John. Edward Wakefield's sister, Josephine, was practically the surrogate daughter of the childless Staffords, according to Philip Temple, the Wakefield family biographer. Edward Wakefield had been briefly Stafford's private secretary in 1866 and after Stafford's defeat in 1869, secretary and cabinet secretary to Premier William Fox. Wakefield's obituary in the *Otago Daily Times* of 9 October 1924 claims that the agency appeared to collapse in 1891 pending a financial crisis, whether internal or external is not clear.

In England, Wakefield did not achieve the notoriety or fame he had in New Zealand. He wrote a book, *Sir Edward William Stafford, G.C.M.G: A Memoir*, for private circulation, and a series of articles, 'Walks with Thackeray', about his friendship with the famous novelist as a young aspiring writer before coming to New Zealand. These were published in the *Spectator* in the last year of his life, 1924. He was also associated with the Royal Colonial Institute in London (now the Royal Commonwealth Society), a charity dedicated to education and research on Commonwealth issues. There is at least one talk by Wakefield on record from the Institute based on his in-depth knowledge of New Zealand politics and affairs. In old age and blind, he lived in the Carthusian Charterhouse almshouse in Clerkenwell, London, as a pensioner. This beautiful old almshouse, created in 1611 by a commoner, is famous for its associated school, one of the leading public schools in England. The accommodation, cloister and church have the atmosphere of an Oxford college. Wakefield's oldest son, Edward/Eddie (Chunky) in a loyal letter to Sir John's son Godfrey, described the Charterhouse as a fitting end for his father, 'who was always a worker for the British Overseas Dominions, and was capable of appreciating the literary, artistic and often deeply learned atmosphere of the Charterhouse.' For 'every one of the "brothers" must have accomplished some more than ordinary service for the Empire during his life, to become eligible [...] and many of them [...] were among the most prominent writers, painters, scholars, soldiers, naval men or pioneers the country has produced.'[51] Edward Wakefield died in the summer of 1924 while staying at the Richmond Club, Petersham. His funeral took place in Richmond.

Josephine predeceased Edward. With her household responsibilities looking after his children, she never married and Edward was buried beside her. She kept her intention to keep his children separated from their mother.

Aggie's mother, Agnes Emma Hall, visited Josephine in London in September 1902, seven years after George Hall's death. She wrote to John, 'Eddie [27] and Oliver [25] are lodging at present in the same house as their Aunt Josephine, 5 Smith Square, Westminster',[52] a street behind the Houses of Parliament and much sought-after by parliamentarians.

Years after these events, I met Aggie's great-granddaughter, Angela Kendall, who said her grandmother Queenie would never talk about the family to her. Angela, a Nightingale nurse who had worked at Charterhouse school, felt the events of 1886 and the fallout from the divorce of Aggie and Edward Wakefield were still influencing the generations who followed. Her husband, Simon, who had researched the Wakefield family, including Edward Gibbon Wakefield, Felix and their two brothers who went to India to escape the influence of EGW, was clear in his judgement:

> Clever the Wakefields may have been, but too often lacked wisdom and integrity in decision-making. They treated both women and money badly and were unreliable in their loyalties (if they had any). Their disjointed, often interrupted educations were largely incomplete and their dreams too often became their masters, as most lacked self-discipline to counter-balance their ambitious ideas. It is amazing that despite their obvious shortcomings they managed to achieve what they did.[53]

Notes and references

1. TWH to JH, 29 April 1886
2. In *Letters to Grace: Writing Home from Colonial New Zealand*, along with those of her mother, Aunt Rose and Aunt Sarah. Edited by Garner and Foster, 2011, Canterbury University Press.
3. Agnes Mildred (Aggie) to Grace Neall, 10 July 1868.
4. Aggie to Aunt Grace, 23 December 1868, from Addington.
5. While in prison, appalled by what he saw of chained prisoners and executions for sometimes minor offences, E. G. Wakefield produced two important studies on the treatment of the condemned criminal which led directly to the reform of criminal law. His book, *A Letter From Sydney with an Outline for a System of Colonisation*, was published in 1830.
6. GWH to JH, 11 June 1873, Leeston. 'Unexceptional people' seems harsh, but perhaps George was ignorant of the fact that Edward's uncle, Captain Arthur Wakefield, the New Zealand Company's agent for the settlement of Nelson, had planned and laid out the town before being killed by Māori at the Wairau Massacre in 1843 during a dispute over land ownership.
7. GWH to JH, 22 December 1873.
8. GWH to JH, 5 February 1874.
9. GWH to JH, 7 April 1874, Addington.

10. GWH to JH, 6 May 1874, Addington.

11. GWH to JH, 27 July 1874. Rose's husband, John, became the political champion, strategist and advisor to Kate Sheppard, leader of the women's-right-to-vote movement in the 1890s.

12. GWH to JH, 31 July 1874, Addington.

13. TH to JH 28 July 1874.

14. GWH to JH, 27 July 1874, Addington.

15. TH to JH, November 1874.

16. GWH to JH, 17 Dec 1874, Dunedin.

17. TH to GWH, 21 April 1876. This particular conversation may have had wider implications. See Chapter 8.

18. JH to John Neall 24 August 1876.

19. TWH to JH Timaru, 2 April 1882. Since Wakefield had been editor in 1874 and seemed capable of combining editorial duties with his political ones, the change of ownership of the paper must have necessitated his official reinstatement.

20. GWH to JH 24 May 1884.

21. GWH to JH 9 October 1884.

22. John Hall Diary,1884, Terrace Station Archive.

23. GWH to JH, 13 July 1883. Major Edward Withers (1804–1883) led a party of loyal Māori with the support of Chief Ihaka Whanga in an attack on Te Kooti. He was appointed Commander of the Hawkes Bay District in 1878. Source: The Family of Major Edward Withers, Ancestry.com.

24. Joshua Williams, later Sir Joshua Williams, was commemorated in a slim volume, *Portrait of a Judge: Sir Joshua Strange Williams*, written by the retired MP and one-time prime minister of New Zealand in 1926, W. Downie Stewart. It was first printed in 1945 by Whitcoulls, the firm I worked for in Christchurch as a desk editor and publicity officer, from 1979–1981. On leaving Whitcoulls to return to England with my husband and two children, I was presented with a copy of this 'Portrait' by our wise senior editor, Bob Gormack. Since I knew very little of the significance of Judge Joshua Strange Williams at the time (though I'm sure Bob did) or any significant history of my own family, I gave it a scan reading. It was only when I began to research this book that I discovered Judge Williams's importance in three family hearings: the trial of Tom Hall, the divorce of Aggie Wakefield and another case detailed in Chapter 11. What was more, the pencilled signature in the front of this second-hand copy was that of 'Cecil J. Tocker', my own maternal grandfather's. Was Cecil researching his future son-in-law's background before he consented to his daughter Helen marrying him? If so, Cecil, who became the Very Revd C. J. Tocker, Moderator of the Presbyterian Church in the year of my birth, must have decided that Tom Hall III, Richard's son, was an excellent choice, which he was, and my parents were married in 1943. It is unlikely Bob would have known the Tocker connection but he may have known the Hall connection. The book was part of a personal library disposed of after Cecil Tocker's death and picked up by Bob in a second-hand bookshop. Downie

Stewart describes the judge as a 'man of outstanding qualities of heart and mind', as 'humble in spirit', showing 'exquisite and gracious courtesy to young and old'. Young Tom was lucky to have such a man preside over his trial.

25. *Otago Daily Times*, 3 May 1886, Papers Past.

26. TWH to JH 22 May 1886.

27. GWH to JH, 18 June 1886.

28. Aggie Wakefield to JH and RH, 30 June 1886. This is a rare letter written to John and Rose Hall together for 'I have not time to write two letters'.

29. Agnes Emma Hall (Aggie's mother) to Grace Neall, 10 July 1863.

30. John Neall to JH, 26 December 1865, Hall papers, ATL.

31. GWH to EW 20 April 1883.

32. Aggie Wakefield to JH and RH, 30 June 1886.

33. WYH Hall to JH, 19 July 1887, Invercargill.

34. GWH to JH 17 January 1887.

35. GWH to JH, 31 April 1887.

36. ibid.

37. GWH to JH, 4 May 1887.

38. John Hall Diary, 22 December 1886.

39. GWH to JH, 3 February 1889, Green Street, Jersey.

40. ibid.

41. GWH to JH 3 April 1889.

42. Edward Wakefield, *New Zealand After Fifty Years*, Cassell & Company Limited, New York, London, Paris and Melbourne, 1889, p. 224.

43. ibid., pp. 52–3.

44. ibid.

45. GWH to JH, 20 February 1890.

46. Edward Wakefield's letter of 21 March 1889 to GWH enclosed in one from George W. Hall to John Hall.

47. GWH to JH, 15 November 1889.

48. GWH to JH, 5 February 1890.

49. Edward Wakefield to GWH, 26 April 1890.

50. GWH to JH, 13 June 1890, Jersey.

51. Edward H. St G. Wakefield to Godfrey Hall, 19 December 1924.

52. Agnes Emma Hall to JH, 11 September 1902

53. Simon Kendall to author, 24 September 2018.

IO

JOHN HALL, HIS CHARACTER, INTERESTS AND INFLUENCE

'Mr John Hall must be confessed by his colleagues, to be by a
long way their foremost man [...] He is a great strength to the
Canterbury Government [...] dear to memory, rising with a perky
action on his toe-tips, and sucking in inspiration for each sentence
with a noisy relish.'[1]

This warm pen portrait by the *Lyttelton Times* when John returned
to provincial politics in 1864 pinpoints his contribution to local
government, but also the fondness with which he was held by
those who worked with him. Because he did not court publicity,
as his biographer Jean Garner explains, he did not appear as such a
prominent figure in early histories of New Zealand. W. J. Gardner, in
his portrait in the *Dictionary of New Zealand Biography*, sees him as
'the leading politician in nineteenth-century New Zealand'. William
Gisborne, in his book *New Zealand Rulers and Statesmen from
1840 to 1897*, described him as 'one of the best public men in New
Zealand'. This was largely because of his long, 15-year dedication
to provincial politics (he was chair of the first (1854–1855) and
third (1870–1871) Canterbury Provincial Councils), his promotion

of the goal of self-government, regionally and nationally, and his contribution to democratic reform. At a national level, his posts included provincial secretary in 1855 and secretary of public works in 1864. He was premier from 1879 to 1882, during which time he restored the country's finances, and was the leading parliamentarian supporting and introducing women's suffrage in 1893. Because New Zealand was the first country in the world to give women the vote, this brought him international fame.

John, as uncle to the Timaru Hall boys and to Aggie Hall, was clearly closely enmeshed in the lives of his relatives who thought of him fondly as a generous benefactor, helpmate and mentor. His status in the colony evoked awe in Aggie who had expressed herself terrified of confronting him with what she knew he would consider a moral sin. The swiftness with which Thomas and George moved to exile George Buceo and Jack Hall from the colony took place against the backdrop of their brother's national reputation, too, though he at all times of crisis showed himself to be undeterred, unpanicked and only helpful.

The first Canterbury Provincial Council comprised men of high calibre, many the product of English public schools and universities. Though John Hall did not have a university education, his father's early influence, his European education and his innate gifts assisted his development. Among the group were James Edward Fitzgerald, the witty Irishman with wonderful gifts of oratory, who became the first superintendent of Canterbury province, and founder of the *Press* newspaper in Christchurch; Henry Tancred, a former officer in the Austrian army, who became the first chancellor of the University of New Zealand; William Rolleston, the last Superintendent, a Cambridge graduate and runholder, who managed to extract large endowments for education from landholders; William Sefton Moorhouse who was a leading spirit in the Lyttelton Tunnel enterprise, which connected port and city; and Henry Sewell, a constitutional lawyer, who became briefly the first premier of the country. Sewell, who comes across as rather condescending in his journals, described the young John Hall as a valuable administrator and Superintendent Fitzgerald's 'vizier'.

In later life, after succeeding Sir George Grey as premier, John Hall remembered his old friend Fitzgerald, now in decline with a huge family of 13 to support, by appointing him auditor-general and sending him off to Australia to report on the way Australia organised its public accounts and auditing process. This was in 1880 when public debt had to be reined in drastically, something John Hall managed to do. He also supported proportional representation, opposed federation with Australia and opposed free trade, which he thought would strangle the development of manufacturing in New Zealand – necessary to provide a wider economic base than agriculture. He streamlined government and increased efficiency by centralising all departments into Wellington. He introduced triennial parliaments, and transferred the management of the railways to an independent board of management to reduce the risk of political favours determining developments. As the 'High Priest' of the rural land-owning interest, he introduced important stock-protecting requirements, including against the dangerous condition, scab.

Public service supported by pastoralism

John was not a charismatic public speaker but more a moderate, seeking compromise and consensus. He was a very effective debater. Any speech of his was always supported by the appropriate facts and figures. Gisborne saw the great secret of his success as his industry and indomitable pluck. He never spared himself and, on some occasions, stood at his post in spite of serious illness. As a statesman he demonstrated moderation, judgement and common sense; ready to retrace his steps when he made a mistake and seldom at fault in what Gisborne called his 'dead reckoning', his judgement. His failings were slight – he was fussy over detail, occasionally petulant and narrow in some of his political views.

He was of average height, not imposing, but energetic and reliable. He collected and filed information and letters meticulously, kept a journal and managed his properties shrewdly and frugally. In 1891, according to W. J. Gardner, his Rakaia Terrace Station had improved in value to £94, 264. He networked continuously and was generous with his patronage to others, particularly his extended family. He did not believe in inherited power and wealth but in a meritocracy of effort and hard work which he exemplified himself. He was a politician for nearly 40 years and even when out of the country, was always actively researching information which would benefit New Zealand, particularly the wool or dairy industry. He was regarded as a leader in stock breeding and in 1892 spoke with three other New Zealanders at an Australasian stock conference on breeding for the new refrigerated economy.

He made regular visits to Britain – ten in his lifetime and usually to recuperate after excessively hard work – until ill health prevented his return after 1905. For 55 years he was a liveryman with the Leathersellers' guild in London, who commissioned his portrait by Henry Grant in 1903. It was lost when the hall in which it hung, along with other famous leathersellers, was fire-bombed in 1941.

John Hall could see the bigger picture, but also the smaller one. One telegram I found in his papers concerned a message from his brother Thomas thanking him for a potato-peeling machine he was sending to the Timaru Hospital, which Thomas was involved with. On his deathbed in 1907, he ensured all Christchurch children and those from Hororata could attend the International Exhibition by paying their entrance fee.

10.1 The old woolshed at Rakaia Terrace Station. Some 20,000 sheep were shorn there in the 1869–1870 season. John Hall was one of the first exporters of frozen meat to Britain.

In politics, John Hall was pragmatic and a conservative with a small 'c'. As a pastoralist, he belonged to a property-owning elite who had considerable economic and political power which many large landowners feared might be eroded and threatened by any extension of suffrage. His biographer, Jean Garner, thought it therefore somewhat ironic that John Hall was one of the founders of New Zealand democracy. It was his ministry that enacted residential manhood suffrage in 1879, granting the vote to all adult European males after 12 months' residence in New Zealand and six months in an electorate. Māori men had already been granted suffrage in 1867 in four special Māori seats. Universal suffrage was not introduced in Britain until after the First World War. Hall did this because not to have done so would have driven his political party, representing farming and business interests, to oblivion.[2] Likewise, he supported votes for women partially to counter the Liberal threat to his own party by boosting voting numbers, but in fact the Liberals won power and kept it for 20 more years.

Though John had not as much worldly experience as his brothers before leaving England, he was to eclipse their achievements completely in terms of his political career at provincial and national level in New Zealand. While his brother Thomas applied himself energetically to pastoral farming and local affairs and his brother George at one time represented Heathcote on the Canterbury Provincial Council and, like Thomas, was a Justice of the Peace in Timaru, neither achieved John's heights.

There were close ties between Thomas and John over the Timaru hospital and harbour developments in Timaru, but they did not always agree on local government issues. During the 1860s, when an economic depression was beginning to take hold, a row broke out over rating for the purpose of funding public works, particularly roads. Toll gates were discussed and dismissed because they were difficult to enforce in remote areas, particularly on runholders. John Hall suggested a sheep rate, but this was rejected by the Provincial Council, the majority of whom were runholders. John Hall represented Mount Cook District at the time and requested road boards limited their demands on the provincial treasury to what was immediately necessary. His brother Thomas with Richard Turnbull, a Timaru businessman, led the charge for separation of the southern districts from Christchurch. A precedent had been set by the New Provinces Act of 1858 which enabled the districts of Hawkes Bay and Marlborough to form separate provinces and keep local revenue for local projects. John, who was Secretary of Public Works, tried to satisfy the demands of South Canterbury by offering a separate board of control for public works, but this was met only with demands for a larger fixed share of the revenue so he withdrew the offer, apparently in some disgust.

The John Hall Papers in the Turnbull Library contain periodic requests for help from the public, such as any politician might receive. Among the most interesting of these was a letter from the novelist Anthony Trollope, at the time not as famous as he would become. He wrote on 19 February 1865 from Waltham Cross where he was working as a surveyor for the Post Office. Knowing John Hall's previous connection to it and his reputation as a pastoralist, he wrote that his son John, aged 18, was 'desirous of settling himself in New Zealand'. Trollope wished to place him with 'some large sheep farmer with whom he may learn the business'. I have not seen John

Hall's reply, but no doubt he reminded Trollope that his properties were managed by men other than himself, since he was now heavily involved in provincial and national affairs.

John Hall became a member of New Zealand's second parliament in 1856, representing Christchurch Country District, and commuting by sea to the Auckland Assembly from Rakaia Terrace Station. He was paid an honorarium of £1 a day as an out-of-town member and could not have sustained his involvement without his farming income. When William Fox became premier in April 1856, John was appointed to the executive council and became colonial secretary, working 16-hour days. But the Fox ministry only lasted three weeks and though Edward Stafford invited him to join his new ministry, John refused. When he resigned his seat to return to England in 1860 he had a reputation as an incorrigible opposition terrier, seen by Premier Stafford as one 'whose insatiable thirst for information would neither allow a Government to be idle, not the House to be uninstructed.'[3]

There is one episode in his life, not that well known, which highlights his willingness to throw himself into the centre of events, no matter how dangerous or difficult.

An adventure in the First Taranaki War

John Hall participated as a volunteer in the First Taranaki War at Waitara in March 1860 at a time when he was an opposition member of parliament. He relished his involvement and role in the course of the war as a 'courier' sent by the governor, Colonel Thomas Gore Browne, to Sydney to ask for military reinforcements for government troops. The letter below may have stimulated him to see for himself the events brewing in Taranaki. Its author was William Fox, leader of the 'Wellington Party' that favoured the provinces. Hall shared Fox's view that Provincial Councils should deal with issues of regional interest and he supported Fox rather than the Canterbury candidate, Henry Sewell, thus helping to bring down Sewell's ministry in April 1856. William Fox, who was to become premier in 1861, wrote to John:

> Sorry to hear of your intended departure at so early a date. [...] There is said to be a native war brewing at Taranaki, the troops & militia called out against the natives etc. I don't think it will come to much, as Wiremu Kingi the Rebel chief is unpopular & will meet with little support, unless from some of the Waikato who are too far off to join very zealously. It is a difficulty arising out of the Anti-land selling league, and directly involves the Government whose surveyors Kingi has stopped. Do you remember our encountering them (Stafford, Rich[ar]d & the little attorney) at the top of Mount Eden one Sunday?[4]

The war was over a disputed block of 600 acres of land at Waitara known as the Pekapeka block, near the mouth of the Waitara River in North Taranaki. Settlers had pressured Governor Gore Browne to acquire more land because they were worried over the future of the province – men of capital were leaving – and were keen that he support those Māori who wanted to sell. New Plymouth at the time was a skeletal settlement of a few wooden houses along the waterfront. The new land would allow the development of a town and port. The block was first offered to the New Zealand government by a minor chief, Pokikake Te Teira, but the offer was vetoed by the paramount chief of the same Te Atiawa tribe, Wiremu Kingi. Governor Gore Browne at first stressed he would not buy any land if there was dispute about its title, but he believed that Kingi, who had been living on the Kapiti Coast, had no customary rights. Since the signing of the Treaty of Waitangi 20 years earlier, some Māori were united in a Māori King Movement centred in the Waikato which opposed the sale of Māori land and the spread of British sovereignty. On 4 March, Governor Browne had ordered Colonel Charles Gold and the 65th regiment, the Taranaki Militia and the Taranaki Rifle Volunteers to occupy the block of land at Waitara in preparation for survey.

On the night of 15 March 1860, when John Hall left Lyttelton and began his diary account of the war at Waitara, Kingi and his men had built an L-shaped *pā* at Te Kohia at the south-west of the block in readiness to defend the land. The *pā* commanded the road access. Elderly Māori had removed the surveyor's boundary markers and government troops responded. Gold's troops of 500 men with two 24-pound howitzers forced Kingi to abandon the *pā*. No Māori were killed and the British retreated to the town, but Māori war parties attacked farms south of New Plymouth, killing six settlers. Māori reinforcements arrived from other tribes and a *pā* was built on a hill at Waireka south-west of New Plymouth and four kilometres from the Omata stockade on the road to the town, mentioned in the diary below.

On 15 March 1860, after seeing his brothers ('George and Tom [...] on board'), John Hall sailed in the *Airedale* from Lyttelton for New Plymouth. Before dawn he was woken by the signal gun for Sir Charles Clifford's station at Flaxbourne, near Blenheim, and Sir Charles came on board to talk with him. At Wellington he 'found orders to embark the detachment there and sail again in three hours'. By 17 March he went ashore at New Plymouth, where military preparations were in progress, and found that nearly all the settlers – especially in the direction of Wiremu Kingi's *pā* – had abandoned their farms and homesteads:

The settlers seem satisfied of the necessity of the extreme measures which have been adopted to cooperate most willingly with the authorities. Sent Maclean [Donald McLean, Native Secretary] to the Governor to say I should be happy to serve in any capacity in which I could be of any use. [...] After lunch started with a party for the direction of the Waitara, having heard that the 24 pounders had got into camp at 9 am this morning & that operations would be commenced forthwith against the new Pah covering about an acre of ground. This & another one apparently prepared *over night* between Thursday and Friday. [...] Outside the Pahs a deep fosse, with a light covering of brushwood.[5]

He noted that there was not a district better suited for Māori warfare with its 'hide & seek tactics'. The group he was riding with was overtaken by a mounted escort, calling as they passed, that firing had commenced at the Bell Block House. His group were moved back but took no notice of the signal. Captain Stewart arrived and gave them the 'pleasing intelligence' that they were cut off from the town by a body of 250 to 300 natives who had risen to the news of the actual commencement of hostilities. A council of war was of course held, but the intelligence was decided to be too improbable and unauthenticated to stop their progress. Accordingly, on they went, regardless of all precautions, until they came to the *pā* of the chief, Mahau.

The chief was understood to have made very friendly protestations but was not to be trusted. So, with the exception of the sailors, they kept close to their horses. Just before leaving Waitara, they were somewhat startled by 'a dense cloud of smoke on the road' between them and the Bell Block House. They could only attribute it to the firing of some deserted farm buildings by hostile natives, who they feared would probably intercept their return. However, there was nothing for it but to return the best way they could.

John's group returned without incident to the town which they found 'melancholy' and deserted. It was here that just before taking up his watch, 'I found to my intense mortification that my revolver would not act, the lock being out of order. Sat up from 12 to 3 & then called McLean, but finding he was not likely to keep a good watch, I kept on till 5 when daylight gave a [respite] to our fears.'

On Sunday 18 March, he was tired because of two sleepless nights and Waitara Pā had been evacuated. He never felt more strongly the appropriateness of the prayer for delivery from the perils of the night. He walked to Henui to get his revolver fixed but could not so 'laid in a supply of tomahawks as the only probable weapons'. On 21 March, because the weather was bad and boats were unable to go, his party rode to Omata, reaching the camp there at 2 am. On Thursday 22 March he commented that 'whatever beats the Maoris, it will not be good officering'. He had met Colonel Gold and two others and decided they had 'barely brains for one among three'. He then went through the 'Pah at the Beach' which had been destroyed above ground, though some of the trenches were still perfect, and returned to town by the beach, in one or two places 'at a hard gallop', arriving by 2 p.m. He dined with Governor Gore Brown in the evening. On Friday 23 March there was a great meeting of friendly natives at the town *pā*. It was arranged that John Hall would take the Governor's dispatches to Sydney and Melbourne and ask for reinforcement. On Saturday 24 March, he re-embarked on the *Airedale* for Auckland where he stayed at the Tancred's home.[6] He noted that on the following two days 'everybody in Auckland agog with news from the seat of war'. On Wednesday 28 March, he sailed on the *Lord Ashley* for Sydney with 40 male immigrants who were leaving from Auckland, their New Zealand immigration plan having been unsuccessful. He saw landfall on Wednesday 4 April at daybreak, 40 miles south of Sydney.

On Thursday, 5 April, at 10 a.m. John 'waited on Sir W. Denison [Governor of New South Wales] to give him any information he might require'. John was not pleased with Denison for 'he showed how even a clear man may speak nonsense when speaking of matters he does not understand. He said Land Purchases objected to even unjustly by Maoris ought to be dropped for a few years, when their numbers would have become insignificant & opposition futile: Pahs should be *built round* with a wooden enclosure & their occupants starved.' Denison's answer about reinforcements, however, John thought was satisfactory. 'All that could be spared from Sydney would be sent at once, & he would telegraph to Melbourne whence others would probably be despatched; altogether he supposed 500 men would be sent.'

The military operations in Taranaki finished a year later on 17 March 1861, according to James Belich in *Making Peoples*, with tribes from South Taranaki and the King Movement in the Waikato and further afield assisting. 'Thousands of imperial troops and millions of imperial money,' he writes, 'did succeed in conquering and confiscating around a million acres of Waikato land, in taking Ngaruawahia and Rangiaowhia, and in permanently weakening the power of the King Movement.' The Waitangi Tribunal was set up by an Act of Parliament in 1975 to provide a legal framework for claims for the return of Māori land to be heard. In 2014, 154 years after imperial forces first fired on Te Kohia Pā near Waitara, a Deed of Settlement was signed between Te Atiawa and the Crown.

John's involvement in this initial Taranaki war was brief. His duty undertaken in Australia, he filled in time exploring Sydney which he found 'most charmingly situated' and 'exquisitely beautiful'. He then continued to England via India and the Suez Canal. Sir George Grey was recalled to New Zealand in 1861 to replace Gore Browne as governor because of his better knowledge of native affairs. James Edward Fitzgerald, former superintendent of Canterbury Province and now the new editor of the Christchurch *Press*, thought Grey a more hopeful candidate for the job 'if he will perceive *the* work to be done is to amalgamate the Maori into the constitution, not to keep them distinct'. As James Belich explains in *The New Zealand Wars and the Victorian Interpretation of Racial Conflict*, 'The British were never happy about Maori control of the interior. They particularly objected to perceived Maori contempt for the government and its coercive power. Indeed, they commonly attributed the problems concerning land and law to this factor.'[7] The Māori King Movement for Māori confederation, organised from the Waikato, by the first Māori king, Potatau Te Wherowhero, was perceived as a direct threat to imperial sovereignty.

Given what was erupting in the North Island in terms of Māori-Pakeha relations, it seems significant that when John Hall left Christchurch for the North Island on this trip, having been resident magistrate in Christchurch, he was farewelled by 60 Māori, all leading men from Kaiapoi, Rapaki and Port Levy, who praised his kindness to the Māori people as a magistrate and asked him to tell the British government that European and Māori were living together in peace, 'like elder and younger brothers', that 'the Maori has surrendered his lands for the settlement of the Pakeha, and that the Pakeha has in turn enriched the Maori with Christianity and many other good things.'[8]

In his reply, John advised his well-wishers not to become involved in the North Island King movement, and not to send money to the Māori King, Potatau, but to keep it and tell him 'that you are going to build a church and support a teacher, and will give your money to that'. Queen Victoria was the queen of the Pakeha and the Māori, she appointed magistrates and made laws for both races and there was peace in the land. If there are two masters in a house there is confusion. They should concentrate not on Potatau but on increasing their own power by growing crops for themselves and selling the surplus to the Pakeha; in other words, be entrepreneurial and follow capitalist principles. He also advised them to educate their children in the learning of the Pakeha. A teacher had been appointed and would soon have a house. They must support him and send their children to be taught by him. He spoke about the division of land, requesting that in dividing their own land, Māori should give a share to the school and to the hospital and to the church, since these were things which are wanted by all Māori. 'If this is not done, there can be no school and no education for your children; and no hospital.' After his reply, he and the Māori elders ate together and in the early evening, according to the *Lyttelton Times*, the chiefs 'departed in a state of perfect contentment, and with many ardent expressions of farewell'. Since a newspaper reporter was present, John Hall had obviously expected this gathering to be reported widely. It is not clear what his mission to the North Island was intended to achieve. Perhaps he regarded himself as an emissary who might resolve the dispute, given his effective relationships with South Island Māori, honed during his period as a magistrate and sheriff.

Although united in their support of regional government, John and his friend William Fox were not of one mind in their approach to the Māori land question. He received a blast from William Fox over this issue. Fox, who was to experience four periods as premier, was a qualified lawyer and had a less sanguine view of the government's role in fighting the King movement in the First Taranaki War and so attacking what he perceived to be a well-meant attempt to establish self-government among the Māori. (Henry Sewell, briefly first premier of New Zealand in 1856, also supported this view. He saw the King Movement as the efforts of a people struggling for government and law, to effect for themselves what colonial government had failed to do for them.) Fox saw a chance for racial harmony overturned by Governor Gore Browne's bolstering British sovereignty at all costs.

John Hall had passed on a description of his military involvement in the Taranaki War to his friend Fox who wrote furiously from the Rangitikei, unimpressed with what he perceived as John's 'ludicrous description of military encounters'. He wrote on 30 April 1860 to say that in his view once the 'King movement' is attacked 'all south of Auckland [...] will fly to arms':

> Very large reinforcements might cow the natives but otherwise they are quite ripe for rebellion. [...] And notwithstanding that all this has been brought about by the wretched hole & corner, irresponsible administration of native affairs.[9]

He considered McLean had no policy and the 'natives are ten years older than they were in Grey's day, & fifty years sulkier & more dissatisfied'. Grey and McLean had treated them 'like spirited children'.[10]

Eight months later he and John were still discussing this important issue. Fox wrote:

> You are really wrong in the conclusion at which you & other colonists at home have arrived "that the war was inevitable & that the Govt had exhausted every means of conciliation". It is no use arguing the matter in a note, but I cannot help assuring you that you *are* wrong. There was no necessity for a war. It is a pure fiction to say that it was a question of

the Queen's supremacy. If it had been so, you would have seen the whole body of natives engaged in it long before this. Down to this time not more than 1500 of them have engaged in it. They no more wished for fighting than you did. The King movement agitation was a sagacious & well meant attempt to establish self-government among them, which instead of treating it with "neglect & indifference" as McLean advised, had [it] been turned by the Governor under Fenton's advice to useful ends, would have attached the natives to our laws & institutions. If the war had become inevitable it was Gov Browne's neglect & childish weakness in submitting to McLean, that made it so. But it never was so – & the British nation has no other basis on which to rest its quarrel than this judgement of a sub-commissioner of the Waste Lands department that he had effected a valid purchase which in the opinion of many much better qualified than he is, was altogether invalid.[11]

Donald McLean, referred to in Fox's letter, was the previous Governor Grey's chief land purchase commissioner with a working knowledge of the Māori language and earlier experience in New Plymouth as sub-protector. Some historians recently have concurred with the tenor of Fox's letter above, seeing it as unfortunate that Gore Browne was not better briefed by McLean in the likely consequences of his acceptance of Te Teira's offer to sell the Waitara block. Would war have been avoided if the Waitara block had not been sold or would it only have postponed confrontation?

Gentlemen's clubs and marriage

John put his early involvement in the First Taranaki War behind him and left Australia for London. On arrival, he was admitted as a colonial member to the Parthenon Club on the payment of ten guineas. This gentleman's club was located in the former house of the architect John Nash, at 16 Regent Street, and featured exceedingly comfortable accommodation with good cooking and wines. There he could meet

10. 2(a) John Hall and (b) Rose Dryden c.1861, at the time of their marriage in Holy Trinity Church, Hull.

with members of the English establishment and build influential contacts. His introduction was facilitated by Fox, his qualifications sufficient as a member of Governor Gore Brown's executive council and someone who had enjoyed a large share of public esteem. As his biographer Jean Garner says, by the time he left New Zealand in March 1860, John Hall had proven to himself that he was right to have emigrated and that his confidence in his powers was justified. He had left Britain a competent but frustrated civil servant and returned the possessor of extensive property and a politician who had risen to the rank of minister of the crown. Drawing on his experience in the London club scene, he was a founding member of The Canterbury Club in 1872. which attracted mainly importers, bankers, lawyers and accountants and was said to have the best dining and hospitality in the city.

This first return to England enabled John to visit his ailing father and step-mother, his sister Grace, and to reacquaint himself with and court Rose Dryden, the sister of Agnes Hall, George's wife. The Dryden sisters were raised in Cottingham, near Hull, and the families had known each other since childhood. On 3 April 1861, like his parents before him, John and Rose were married in Holy Trinity church, adjacent to Hull Trinity House. They arrived in New Zealand in September 1861 and John resumed political life when Fox became premier in 1863. He was able to introduce the Waste Lands Bill which secured major benefits for big runholders like himself and his brothers, a ten-year extension to land leases and a land tax which favoured those, like him, who leased more than 5,000 acres.[12] Although not prepossessing in stature – John was known by the press and others as 'Little Johnny' – he was highly respected as a trustworthy administrator and spokesman. W. H. Scotter, the historian, remarked of his influence by 1875: 'it was said that he had become not only the "mouthpiece" of the squatters' interests, but altogether the most influential man in the affairs of the province. The resilient, voluble Hall rather than the sensitive Rolleston [Superintendent] spoke for the Canterbury property owners from this time.'[12]

Rose and John lost their first child, Godfrey, who died prematurely in 1862, the year of his birth. '[He] grieved so much more than most men would for the loss of so young a child except sometimes when he came to cheer me when I was made to go to lie down,' Rose told Grace. 'He never ceased to watch our little treasure from the time it was taken ill until it was taken from us.' The following year, when John's political career took off – he had been made mayor of Christchurch and also elevated to the Upper House in parliament – Rose gave birth to their first daughter, Mildred. By 1867, John's increasing status put more demand on their social life.

In December, Rose was 'astonished to find some new ministerial arrangements were likely to necessitate a residence in Wellington at least during the Session and a consequent giving of dinner parties'. She asked her sister-in-law Grace to send from Hull curtain fabric, carpets, damask and sheeting for servant bedrooms and other articles which could not be found locally. She requested two dozen dinner napkins, two dozen wine glasses, glass dishes for sweets and 12 jelly glasses, four dinner decanters, six long damask table cloths and 24 tumblers. 'Papa offered me the whole dinner service when I married,' she wrote, 'but I thought I should never need such things in N.Z. Now if we are to have all the bother of dinner parties I should like to do the thing well.'

Socialising for Rose did not come naturally. '[It] is always an effort to me to come out of my shell. Like Papa, I am very much a stay at home,' she wrote to Grace early in John's political career.

An experiment with humble bees

John took an interest in the science behind farming in New Zealand. In 1873, on another trip back to England with Rose and their children, he volunteered for an assignment which could benefit pastureland in New Zealand. This story was told to me by William Miller whose forebear, Thomas Nottidge, had come to England to act as an agent for the Canterbury Acclimatisation Society, established in 1864.

At the time, clover, a staple pasture crop, did not seed adequately because the New Zealand honey bees were not able to pollinate it effectively. Their tongues were not long enough, a discovery made by Charles Darwin in his *Origin of Species* (1859). Red clover consequently had to be sown each year from imported English seed. Dr Frank Buckland, associated with the South Kensington Museum in London, forerunner of the Science Museum, came up with the idea of introducing to New Zealand the longer-tongued, humble or bumble bee, which was able to pollinate clover. John Hall was courier who took the consignment on his return voyage in 1876. The journal *Nature* (14 October 1875) announced that the courier would be 'a member of the New Zealand Counsel [Executive], who is provided with every necessary for their welfare during the voyage. They are expected to arrive [...] midsummer in the Antipodes.' The drop in temperature by the time the *Orari* reached the southern seas was a killer. John Hall had asked the ship's captain

10.3 (a) Lounge chair advertisement; (b) Literary stand advertisement sent by George W. Hall for John Hall to purchase in England, 1874.

to hang the box of humble bees from the ceiling of the ship's saloon to keep it at an appropriate temperature. The bees were in nests and humming when the ship passed through the tropics, but as temperatures fell their humming stopped. On the 84th day, the majority had become mildewed and died despite John taking them into his cabin at night during the cold weather and regulating the temperature to 60 degrees Fahrenheit with an oil lamp. Their tray was saturated with honey water. Some were still humming until two days before arrival in New Zealand. He used this failed experiment to advise Thomas Nottidge in July 1883 to send out hibernating female humble bees next time.[13]

Every trip back to England necessitated complicated visits to the Army and Navy Stores and bookshops to complete the requests from his brother George, who also drew on John to send him books. One such was the most up-to-date atlas, for instance, and various personal items to support George's lifestyle, such as a Meerschaum pipe with 'stems 15 inches in length and not too slender or they warp with the heat'. Additional items for George were the remarkably modern-looking lounge chair and the literary stand illustrated here, so he could recline and still read in his poor health. They were dutifully shipped out to New Zealand in crates.

John Hall and Parihaka, November 1881

John Hall was premier during the Māori passive resistance at the village of Parihaka in the Taranaki area of the North Island in which two Māori prophets, Te Whiti o Rongomai and Tohu Kakahi organised passive resistance to European occupation of confiscated land in the area. The background to these events, preceding his term of office as premier from 1879 to 1882, occurred during the George Grey Ministry when an influx of European settlers in Taranaki heightened a demand for land. In this second war, government surveying began on land to be offered for sale that had previously been confiscated from the Māori during earlier wars. The two prophets organised their followers to plough and fence the land to which they felt they still had rights and to resist all attempts to survey it.

John's actions stemmed from the results of a royal commission he set up to investigate land grievances in Taranaki. It was led by his friend Sir William Fox who was against the government purchase of land at Waitara. Te Whiti would not cooperate with the commission or let his people read the report, which ultimately allocated 25,000 acres to the people of Parihaka as well as a further 714 acres for cultivation, fishing and burial grounds. He thought the land was held directly from God and not in the gift of government to confiscate or create reserves, even if this would ensure peace. Māori sovereignty had been ceded by the Treaty of Waitangi, he thought. Te Whiti was quoted by the United Press Association announcing his decision to fight to defend his idea of Māori sovereignty. John Hall's decision to force Te Whiti to surrender he justified on humanitarian grounds, 'We are anxious to make such a display of force as will convince these poor infatuated people of the utter hopelessness of resistance and so avert a collision,' he wrote to his friend Francis Dillon Bell on 3 November 1881.

The Parihaka village was self-sufficient in food crops. The Hall government, in response to settler fears of renewed armed conflict, tried to close down Parihaka, which by now had a population of 2,000 people, by organising a military assault of 1,589 troops and 644 armed constabulary at dawn on 5 November 1881. Te Whiti and Tohu were arrested and jailed, and 1,600 people were dispersed across Taranaki. Those 600 remaining were issued with passes to control their movements, supporters were sent home and their whares at Parihaka taken down.

In justification of the decision to send in the troops, John Hall wrote to William Pember Reeves, agent-general to the government in London, after Reeves published a description of the Parihaka invasion in his book *The Long White Cloud*: 'If you had been at my elbow you would have been compelled to approve. No set of men were ever more anxious to make every concession [...] which could be done without sacrificing the authority of the Gov[ernmen]t.'[14]

Te Whiti counselled his people to passively resist the 120 armed constabulary who initially approached Parihaka. This they did with girls skipping on the approach, children singing and women proffering baked bread. John Hall evaded the difficulty of trying the two Māori leaders for sedition by asking Parliament 'for authority to assign the Prophet "residence" for a limited term in some part of the Colony where he will be harmless'.[15] Te Whiti and Tofu were assigned a warder and toured the South Island. Overcome by fatigue and overwork, John Hall resigned in April 1882 despite having won another election in December 1881. He was knighted in the Queen's Birthday Honours in 1882.

10.4 (a) Sir John in the year of his knighthood, 1882 and (b) Rose, Lady Hall.

Visitor's to John Hall's Terrace Station homestead at Hororata today will notice the Māori carvings affixed to the front-facing verandah. These were acquired for Sir John by Gilbert Mair (1843–1923), who was one of the officers participating in the raid on Parihaka and famous for training and leading a guerilla unit of 100 Te Arawa men in the final campaigns against Te Kooti in 1870–1872 before he found sanctuary in the King Country. The slabs originally formed the top sides of a canoe of the Ngati Pikiao tribe, which, refitted, had conveyed Prince Alfred, second son of Queen Victoria and the Duke of Edinburgh, across Rotoiti and Rotorua Lakes in 1869, on the first royal visit to New Zealand. Later they formed part of a tomb of a young chief, Hemana Taranui and belonged to Te Pokiha Taranui, the principal chief of the Bay of

Plenty who had led Te Arawa troops in support of the government against the King Movement and against the rebel Hauhau, Te Kooti and his supporters. He had at first refused 'most indignantly' to sell them to Mair, a collector of Māori artefacts. As Mair told John Hall, 'Lately, however, he became very angry with the son of the deceased chief for taking a wife from another tribe and by way of offering him a slight, sold the tombstone, or rather the tomb, to a European [...]'[16] Mair sold them to Sir John in 1889.

To have carvings fronting his house from a now controversial period of his premiership, previously owned by a Māori chief who had led government forces against the King Movement, was a continual reminder of this episode in John Hall's life, perhaps signifying to him that he had carried out to his fullest ability the law as it was then and the 'mastery – by peaceful means if possible, but still the mastery – over the Natives [...] they must be content to be governed by the same

10.5 (a) Hororata homestead now called Terrace Station as it was in 1889 and (b) as it is today with verandah showing Māori carvings supplied by Mair.

laws as their European fellow citizens are.'[17] Māori-Pakeha ownership of early artefacts is often blurred, particularly when gifting has occurred. In this case, documentation says they were sold by Māori to a Pakeha who sold them on to Sir John.

Supporter of the vote for women

John Hall's political thinking about women's position in society, their economic dependence on men and their relative inequality was most likely to have been influenced from his time as a magistrate in Canterbury, dealing with the effects of dissolute husbands or impoverished women. He became a hero of the women's suffrage campaign, supplying strategic advice which helped ensure success for its advocates. In 1889, he advised Kate Sheppard, the leader of the New Zealand suffrage movement and a member of the Women's Christian Temperance Union, on the value of the mass petition as a political instrument of persuasion. He had historical knowledge of its use as a political instrument; in Hull through Wilberforce's anti-slavery movement and in London when he served as a constable in the Chartist uprisings which also used the petition as a political tool. Sheppard at first rejected the idea and only took it up after his efforts to advance women's suffrage in the House had been defeated in 1890.

In the 1880s, social reformers saw alcohol as the cause of economic and social instability. It led, they thought, to poverty, ill health, neglect and abuse of children and immorality. These ills were particularly prevalent in rural and industrial areas and ports where itinerant labour congregated. Sir John had supported the first petition for women's suffrage to Parliament brought by the Women's Temperance Union in 1891. He worked with Sheppard when she presented her third, and this time successful, petition to the House, leading the parliamentary fight to have legislation passed. Sixty-five per cent of New Zealand women over the age of 21 voted in the first election after the Electoral Act of 1893 was passed.[18] His views were pro-women rather than pro-temperance and he was not shackled by class bias in promoting his beliefs. The value of women's suffrage and the interests of conservative government and the family are summed up in his letter to George Bernard Shaw in 1892:

> Experience, wherever Women's Suffrage has been tried, shows that Woman's influence is exercised on the side of law and order; and I have been unable to hear of any place in which this concession when once granted has been regretted. It will no doubt increase the influence of the "family" which is conservatism of the best kind, unconnected in any way with wealth or social position.[19]

John Hall thought it was unfair that intelligent, law-abiding adult women were placed on the same level as children, lunatics and criminals in being excluded from voting. He also thought it absurd that men could vote whether or not they were drunk, had deserted their wives or been in prison. Women who had maintained their families throughout these adverse circumstances could not vote. He was not alone among parliamentarians and premiers in supporting the vote for women. Julius Vogel had written a feminist

10.6 Cartoon showing John Hall with Sheppard in the palm of his hand.

novel comparing the liberation of women to the emancipation of the Jews; Harry Atkinson supported women's suffrage; Robert Stout was married to a feminist, Anna Paterson Logan Stout, and in the final push, in the General Assembly, where only men had seats, he was supported by Premier John Balance and Alfred Saunders, MP for Selwyn and a former superintendent of Nelson Province.

Sheppard was hugely bolstered by John Hall's continued political support as the letter below shows. After a debate on the suffrage issue in late 1900 within the Anglican church ruling body, another conservative bastion of power, she expressed her passionate gratitude:

> My feelings really got the better of my judgement more than once yesterday during the debate at the Synod. Each time that I saw you enter the Library I felt like rising & waving a handkerchief to greet you, but the thought that I might be looked on as one of the 'wild' women who were in favour of your motion, restrained me, and I refrained for the general good.
>
> Again, during the hearing of some of the weak-kneed, illogical remarks set forth, I could scarcely refrain from indulging in expressions of scorn, but luckily managed to set... myself (on every task!) and keep these under [control], not withstanding the boiling cauldrons that were seething within me. I was disappointed that so few, comparatively, spoke in favour of the motion, and even those who did support you did not dwell enough on the broad principle of allowing all members equal opportunities *irrespective of sex*. You and only you struck that chord.
>
> But don't you consider it a triumph to be beaten only by *one*? I do, and so I congratulate & thank you with all my heart.[20]

In his political persona, John Hall was very much on the side of women, but in his personal life he was conventional in his behaviour towards his wife, Rose. Her primary task was to be a supportive wife and mother to his children. He was in this a typical Victorian patriarch, as were his brothers. In letters to their sister Grace, often the men referred to their wives affectionately as 'Mrs Tom', 'Mrs George' and 'Mrs John', as often as Sarah, Agnes or Rose. Their wives wrote to Grace about domestic matters, leaving comment on local and national issues to the men.

Rose adored her husband and was sometimes scolded by him for her idolatry. After him, God was her master, clearly expressed at moments of crisis. When their first child Godfrey died in 1862, after only 13 days of life, Rose clearly saw his death as having some higher purpose which only God knew. John concurred with this view. 'We both feel so convinced of our need for chastisement that we can but thankfully say God has withheld a heavier trial and only laid that upon us which He will enable us to bear,' Rose wrote to Grace in February that year. John felt guilt after Rose died in May 1900, following an earlier stroke, reflecting that he had perhaps not appreciated her enough in life, and left money in his will for a church to be built at Hororata in her memory, St John's.

A year after her marriage to John, when Rose had barely had time to adjust to life in the new colony, she complained to Grace, 'Fancy, we have not seen [John] now for more than 5 months! How should you like that, you fortunate wife blessed with the constant companionship of an indulgent husband.' She also complained to her sister Agnes that her husband's long absences away on political business had placed an almost intolerable strain on her at times as she dealt alone with family illnesses, overwork, recruitment and loss of servants, and isolation at Rakaia Terrace Station, Hororata. When John Hall was about to leave for a parliamentary session in

Wellington lasting for three months in July 1865, she wrote to Grace, 'My dear husband will be absent which insensibly depresses one and produces a weak and faithless foreboding of evil.' Perhaps aware of the strain on his wife, John was back for a few days in early August, 'delighted to see his wee bairns again'.

Four years later, after giving birth to her fifth child, her exhaustion and depression were only too apparent, not surprisingly:

One gets very tired sometimes both in body and mind and longs for rest. Were it not for the hope and wish to see our darlings grow up I should not care how soon the end came.[21]

10.7 The huge paper petition for women's suffrage, which included the signatures of 31,872 women, one in four from all social classes in the colony. Sir John Hall unrolled it dramatically on the floor of the House when the issue was debated. It was the beginning of the long struggle for women's rights in New Zealand.

In the public sphere, his loyal advocacy of the vote for women ensured John Hall's was the only male name on the Kate Sheppard memorial erected recently in New Zealand to commemorate the women's suffrage battle. Whatever his reputation had been over the decision to invade the pacifist village of Parihaka, it was redeemed almost entirely with his championing of women's right to vote. His fans today go well beyond New Zealand. The city of Hull has recently commemorated this achievement with a plaque to be placed in Brook Street, his childhood home. Robb Robinson, a Hull maritime scholar, said to me, 'William Wilberforce put Hull on the map for his work in advocating the abolition of slavery and freeing 10 per cent of the world's population. We should have a statue in Hull for John Hall who freed 50 per cent of the world's population.'

In 1893, when the Electoral Act gave the vote to women in New Zealand, Sir John was not to know that the life of his nephew Richard Hall and an affair with his housekeeper Caroline Matthews would demonstrate that despite this new freedom, there was a long way to go before women would have better support for the problems of dissolute husbands and impoverished families.

Notes and references

1. *Lyttelton Times*, 21 April 1864.
2. Jean Garner, *By His Own Merits: Sir John Hall – Pioneer, Pastoralist & Premier*, Dryden Press, 1995, p. 301.
3. New Zealand Parliamentary Debates 1858–60, p. 47.
4. William Fox to JH, 1 March 1860.
5. John Hall diary, 1860. Donald McLean was Chief Land Purchase Commissioner in the new Land Purchase Department who was in favour of rapid land purchases from Māori to facilitate European settlement.
6. Henry J. Tancred was to become the chancellor of the newly formed University of New Zealand. In early Canterbury he had been chief justice and head of the police. John Hall became a Justice of the Peace in 1854 and Commissioner of Police and Sheriff for Lyttelton in 1856, in effect, chief magistrate, despite having no legal training.
7. James Belich, *The New Zealand Wars and the Victorian Interpretation of Racial Conflict*, Penguin Books, 1998, p. 79.
8. *Lyttelton Times*, 14 March 1860. Walter Buller's report on the population of Canterbury Māori at the time gave a total of approximately 299, living at Pigeon Bay, Port Levy, Akaroa, Kaiapoi and Rapaki. Buller was present at this farewell gathering as interpreter, along with Mr Justice Gresson. I am uncertain of which school John Hall referred to in his address. There had been a Native School at Kaiapoi which had closed in November 1852. An attempt to re-open it by Superintendent James Edward Fitzgerald had not been successful when an application for the necessary grant was turned down by the general (central) government.
9. William Fox to JH, 30 April 1860.

10. ibid., 24 May 1860.

11. William Fox to JH, 31 December 1861, MS 1784, correspondence 1861, John Hall Papers ATL.

12. W.H. Scotter, (ed. W.J. Gardner), *A History of Canterbury, Vol. 3, 1876-1950*, Christchurch Centennial Historical and Literary Committee, 1965, Whitcombe & Tombs Limited, p. 29.

13. Sir John's letter to Nottidge dated 17 July 1883, is in the Essex Record Office, Chelmsford, ref. D/DQu addl (accession number A13745, bundle 3).

14. JH to William Pember Reeves, 18 August 1899, MS X923, p. 78, John Hall Papers, ATL.

15. Hazel Riseborough, *Days of Darkness: Taranaki 1878-1884*, 1994, Allen & Unwin, p. 177.

16. Gilbert Mair to Sir John Hall, 19 September 1889, John Hall Papers, TSA.

17. John Hall, *Speeches delivered out of Parliament by the Hon. Sir John Hall, K.C.M.G., Prime Minister of New Zealand from October 8th, 1879, to April 21st, 1882*, Christchurch 1911, pp. 29 and 25.

18. Dr Jean Garner, 'Sir John Hall and Women's Suffrage', in *Historical News*, October 1993, No 67, p. 9.

19. JH to George Bernard Shaw, 16 November 1892, MS 916, John Hall Papers, ATL.

20. Kate Sheppard to Sir John Hall, 24 October 1900, John Hall Papers, ATL.

21. Rose Hall to Grace Neall, 6 July 1869.

11

RICHARD AND CAROLINE AND A POLITICAL CONSPIRACY

'Dick brought his wife and two children to see me, children nice. Wife better than expected.'[1]

'Afternoon to Dick's house to see wife & children & have tea. Wife does not improve on closer acquaintance. Dick seems intent.[2]

When Sir John Hall visited his nephew Richard ['Dick'] Hall and his wife Caroline in February of 1905, it was probably the first social call he had paid them since their marriage on 2 October 1901 after the death of Caroline's first husband, the solicitor Richard Matthews. Richard and Caroline, though together for a decade before she was introduced to the

11.1 Caroline's daughter Mabel Matthews, and the Hall children, c.1901.

former premier, were now respectable, living in Richard's house, Dalrymple Road, Appleby, Invercargill, with their four, previously ex-nuptial children. Tui, George, Sidney and Tom were baptised in All Saint's in Invercargill, two weeks after their parents' wedding in the same church and were now socially acceptable.

My father, little Tom, remembered sitting on his great-uncle's knee on this 1905 visit. Sir John gave the children a half-sovereign for their money boxes. Richard's 'intent'-ness may have been worry that his wife and children would not pass muster with his uncle, and judging from his comments, Caroline barely did. Her reputation had been besmirched publicly with Richard's ten years before as a result of events of a political and a personal nature.

Caroline Matthews had borne seven children to her first husband between July 1881 and August 1892 before he deserted her. She had obtained a separation order from Matthews in 1893 on the grounds of cruelty. He was known as a man who preferred to recite biblical texts to his children rather than put food in their mouths. Matthews had represented bankrupts and debtors in the debtors' court during the difficult decades of the 1870s and 1880s, when New Zealand was experiencing a period of economic recession. He maintained that the police had spoiled his chances of work and obtaining credit by pursuing him to obtain maintenance money to support his family. What money he had paid towards his family's needs was administered through Richard Hall's legal practice.

Divorce in Victorian New Zealand for a woman was almost impossible, the woman having to prove extreme cruelty, or extreme sexual behaviour. For a man, his wife's neglect of household duties was a sufficient reason and, as was demonstrated in Aggie Wakefield's story (Chapter 9), adultery was sufficient for her to lose access to her children. In Caroline's case, she appeared to be the only earner in the family after her husband deserted. By the year of her second marriage, some of Caroline's older children, Ethel and Harold, for instance, were probably working since they were now 19 and 17, but her younger children Guy (15), Clarence (13), Eric (10) and Reg (9) were young enough to need care. The two families lived together in Richard Hall's home in Invercargill, the older Matthews offspring at one dinner table, the little Halls at another. When not keeping house and home, Caroline sometimes sang at local gatherings and had a fine voice. The photograph 11.2 (a) shows her daringly exposing her neck at a time when women were strictly covered up, indicating the image was probably a love token for her husband-to-be.

11.2 (a) Caroline with neckband and (b) Richard W. Hall.

On his holiday in the south in the summer of 1905, Sir John, now widowed, with Richard, Caroline and their eldest son George, took a day trip to Stewart Island on the ferry from Campbelltown (now Bluff), the small seaport at the bottom of the South Island, south of Invercargill. The island's beautiful bays and inlets and bush-covered slopes were a natural attraction. Richard's father Thomas had died in December 1895 and Uncle John had been a co-executor of his estate with

Richard and Will Hall. Sir John's curiosity about the woman who had captured his nephew's heart and been the centre of so much newspaper coverage would have been high.

During his visit to England in 1897, on a Sunday in October, Sir John had driven across London, through Regent's Park and Camden Town, along Seven Sisters Road to Stamford Hill to see Sarah Hall's sister, Mrs Chippingdale. He found her confined to a room with rheumatism. She seemed 'very glad to talk over Sarah' and also Sarah's son Will and his children but 'no mention of the bad ones' (Tom, George Buceo, and young John (Jack); the eldest in gaol, the next exiled and killed in the first South African Boer war, the last exiled to North America). What he didn't know on that visit was that his equilibrium was about to be shattered by another family crisis when a letter from his station manager arrived with an enclosed newspaper clipping, informing him that Richard had been charged with obtaining a 'noxious thing to cause abortion'. Another nephew was about to be added to the list of 'bad ones'. His mistake was to have become a person of interest to a powerful politician bent on dragging him into the public eye to avenge his own humiliation over a court case Richard had prosecuted.

As a boy, Richard had been plagued by a weak chest. His ill health had kept him from attending school with his brothers at the Pigeon Bay Academy on Banks Peninsula, until he joined them at the age of eight. His mother was worried about sending him away to school because she felt he would not get the care he needed, and this proved correct. After a year he was returned home ill and was enrolled instead at Oamaru Grammar School, near Timaru where his parents resided, when the principal teacher from his former school transferred there. By the age of 16 he appeared to have overcome his former frailty, as John Hall described to Grace's husband, John Neall, in England:

Richard is going up to the [Rakaia Terrace] Station with me tomorrow, in charge of a pony which is being sent as a present from his father to his cousins. He seems a very nice lad, and has just left a large school, where he came out as head boy and had a watch as a prize for his good conduct. I saw him yesterday catch the pony in the paddock, jump on him without saddle or bridle and ride him at a canter and gallop several times around the paddock. Ask Johnny [Neall's son] what he thinks of that![3]

Richard seemed to have had a strong character as well as physique, the more remarkable given his shaky start. In 1883, when working as a clerk in the Queenstown branch of the Bank of New Zealand, an incident caused him to be transferred to the North Dunedin branch. As his father described to John Hall, '[…] an influential customer came into the bank, drunk, and not only took liberties with Dick as Bank Clerk, but also personally and the result was as well as I remember he got an inkstand at his head and turned out of the premises. No doubt served him right but being an influential client it had to be smoothed over.'[4] What had provoked the incident? An intimacy with the client's wife, apparently, who had no doubt reported to her husband that 27-year-old Richard Hall was a good listener, since Thomas thought it 'a most outrageous thing for a married woman to confide her complaints against her husband to another man, especially a single one'. Perhaps the handsome young bank clerk was not as innocent as he appeared and had indulged the client's wife in an unsuitable way. Despite this incident, his father, ever vigilant over his sons' advancement, told John now in England after resigning his premiership on the grounds of ill-health, that he 'would wish your interest on [Dick's] behalf that he might not be overlooked in the line of promotion by weightier interest when you are away'.[5] John promoted his brothers' and nephews' interests where he could. His patronage seemed endlessly bountiful, though Thomas had impressed on Richard that 'his position must rely on his own endeavours principally and almost solely'.

In 1884, John and Rose Hall returned from England where they had been living for a year with their two daughters while their son Wilfred was at Oxford and son Godfrey at Radley, an Oxfordshire boarding school. John recorded a visit at Hororata in December in his diary:

> Indoors nearly all day writing for English mail. About 3 p.m. young man came in dripping wet, whom I did not recognize, but soon saw to be Dick. Looks thin and dark about the eyes. Seems to be doing pretty well at law learning. Sent Bryan [groom] to Dunsandel for young Tom, who arrived about 8.30, not so wet as I had expected. Read some of Diary to them.[6]

His nephews returned a month later and John remarked that 'Young Dick is much improved: more subdued and less impudent than formerly. Seems to realize he has to make his way in the world. Tom as pleasant a companion as ever.'[7] Richard, 28, was articled to his brother Will in June 1884 and passed his first law exam in November that year. He and Will formed a legal partnership, Hall Bros, Solicitors, in Invercargill.

In 1895, Richard had engaged the capacious, womanly, Caroline Matthews as a housekeeper in Invercargill. Her seven children had been frequently without food and she without means since her husband had deserted the family in 1893 after the birth of her youngest child the year before.

Richard was now 39, still unmarried. He had probably suffered from the opprobrium that had haunted his family after the trial of his brother Tom in 1886. He did not care much for public opinion, but his chances of marrying well were not optimal. In the first year of her employment with Richard, Caroline became pregnant to him. She could not afford another child and on his advice sought medical help in Campbelltown (Bluff) out of gossip's way, a safe place to see a doctor about her condition. She stayed in a boarding house run by a Mrs Gorman, who questioned her reasons for coming. Discovering Caroline was seeing a doctor and assuming she was seeking an abortion, she threatened to inform the police. Abortion was illegal. Caroline, in response to aggressive questioning, begged Mrs Gorman, for the sake of her existing Matthews children, to say nothing. She threatened to drown herself if the landlady were to hand her over to the police. Mrs Gorman, as reported in the press, replied that the children would be better off without her. Abortion, though common at the time (shown by the frequency with which women were admitted to hospital with blood poisoning, or septicaemia), was technically a crime, though lightly policed. There were few families who had not been in this predicament themselves and it was very hard to get a jury to convict.[8]

The locals and indeed the whole of the New Zealand population had recently been appalled and enthralled by the case of Minnie Dean, a Southland woman, who had been in the business of taking in and caring for unwanted babies for money, most born out of wedlock. At her trial, some children were found to have died from illness but 14 were unaccounted for according to her own record. In one case she had allegedly hurled her charge from a train window. A conductor on the train had noticed her arriving with a babe-in-arms and a hat-box but later saw her alight from the train without the baby. She was arrested and charged with murder. Minnie Dean's execution in Invercargill took place in August of 1895, the year that Caroline was seeking medical help at Campbelltown, Invercargill's port town.

Abortion, and/or the abandonment of unwanted children was a hot topic at the time which contributed to the way Caroline's plight was reported by the press when her story came to light in 1897.

Richard was worried Mrs Gorman would gossip about Caroline's visit to her boarding house. Though his father Thomas had died in December 1895, his mother Sarah was still alive and he did not wish his relatives to know of his relationship with Caroline or scandal to taint his business activities. He and Caroline were living out of wedlock and she was not yet divorced from Matthews. Caroline had experienced a previous miscarriage and had been told by doctors on that occasion that a further pregnancy would endanger her health. Two years after Caroline's visit to Campbelltown, in June 1897, Richard and Caroline were suddenly arrested and charged by the police.

The Invercargill and national press erupted in a lather of lurid sensationalism. The story was telegraphed by the Press Association to the metropolitan daily newspapers as well as the smaller regional papers with the headline, 'An Invercargill Sensation', and careful emphasis on the word 'poison' in the body of the story, which carried a reminder of the Tom Hall scandal almost a decade before but also reflected the Offences Against the Person Act of 1866. This stated that any person who tried to abort a foetus by using 'any poison or other noxious thing' could be given a life sentence:

> A sensation was caused here yesterday by the arrest of Richard Williamson Hall, solicitor, on a charge of procuring a medical man, Dr Torrance, of Campbelltown, to administer and cause to be taken, by one Caroline Matthews, the wife of another solicitor, certain poison or noxious things, with intent to procure miscarriage. The offence is alleged to have been committed as far back as

October 1895. Mrs Matthews, who has been living apart
from her husband for several years, was also charged with
unlawfully permitting the poison to be administered to
her. Through counsel, when brought before the Court,
she desired to state that Hall had nothing to do with the
matter of which he is accused. Both were remanded for a
week on bail. Hall in £1000, and Mrs Matthews in £600.[9]

The case was heard behind closed doors but widely reported. These
dramatic newspaper descriptions suggested a possible police interest in
exposing Richard Hall. One newspaper suggested he was trying to get
the police who held the evidence about the supposed abortion out of
Invercargill because of potential damage to his law partnership. The case
was extensively reported in the *Otago Witness* of 28 June 1897.

Dr James Torrance, Caroline's doctor, maintained throughout
in his evidence that he had only ever administered drugs for what
he thought was a natural miscarriage. He said that the one drug he
had given Caroline was a sedative. He was a good man doing his best
not to collude in the efforts to put Richard and Caroline in jail and
to downplay the efficacy of the drugs administered since he was also
under scrutiny. His explanations were somewhat gnomic. The two
pills he had given her would not procure an abortion. But if nature
were about to procure an abortion, then it was the proper thing to
give. His reputation, too, was on the line.

Richard, in evidence, said Caroline's health was poor and he
had recommended a fortnight in Campbelltown in Mrs Gorman's
lodgings. Mrs Gorman in her evidence maintained Caroline had seen
Dr Torrance late in the day, walking to his rooms in the dark. She had
taken it upon herself to lock Caroline in her room and tried to refuse
admittance to Dr Torrance when he returned with a sedative, though
she later took it to the patient. She said that the room Caroline

occupied had been set up for a confinement. She had told the doctor she would get Hall into trouble and into gaol. She had later visited Hall in his office and threatened to go to the police. He had offered her £100 to keep quiet, but later withdrew this offer, telling her that her threats to inform the police were blackmail.

Caroline had told Mrs Gorman that monies she received from her husband in maintenance for her family came through Hall Bros. Richard Hall, she said, had given her work and had been very kind to her. She had worked for him since her husband had left her. Richard, in his evidence, said he intended to marry Caroline if she could divorce.

Immediately after the 'Invercargill sensation' story was published, Richard had a defence ready. It was headlined in the Christchurch *Press*, telegraphed from Invercargill to Christchurch by the Press Association:

ALLEGED POLITICAL CONSPIRACY
It is stated on the best authority, that the defence of R.W. Hall, solicitor, charged with in 1895 the administration of a noxious thing with intent, will be an allegation that the charge is the outcome of a political conspiracy, and that strong evidence in support of that contention will be forthcoming.[10]

This political conspiracy defence concerned the J.[Joseph] G. Ward case and a petition directing the liquidator of the assets of J. G. Ward to institute a prosecution against Ward and John Fisher. The Ward case was a high profile one. Ward (later Sir Joseph Ward, a cabinet minister in the Seddon government, and twice prime minister of New Zealand), was at the time of Caroline's unwanted pregnancy, MP for Awarua, near Invercargill, and managing director of J. G. Ward

Farmers' Association of which he held the majority shares. John Fisher was the manager of the Association which became insolvent and left Ward liable to be declared a bankrupt. Richard Hall, solicitor, had acted for the shareholders. In a biography of Judge Joshua Strange Williams, the eminent supreme court judge who had presided over the Ward case, journalist Downie Stewart noted:

> The evidence showed that the balance-sheet [of J.G. Ward Farmers' Assoc.] had been falsified, and that the bankers of the Association had been fraudulently misled. They had been induced to discount drafts on London for £30,000 on warrants purporting to represent oats, which had turned out to have no existence. [...] Mr Ward was absent from New Zealand when this fraud was committed, and although he signed the balance-sheet on his return, he stated he did not and could not give the business any large personal control – that he accepted the facts as put before him and depended on others who were responsible to him. But in addition to managing the Association, Mr Ward had been trading on his own account, and was indebted to the Association to the extent of £55,000. He was in fact hopelessly insolvent. [...] Two of Mr Ward's friends made an offer to the liquidators of the Association to buy it on condition that they were allowed to take over Mr Ward's debts too.[11]

Judge Williams refused to allow this offer, which he viewed as an offer of 'hush' money. He held that in ordinary circumstances the Association would go into liquidation and Ward go bankrupt: 'I look at the case from its commercial aspect only, and on Mr Ward in his business relations. That Mr Ward is a Member of Parliament and holds political office is, from the point of view I have considered the case, irrelevant.'[12] Ward's bank, the Colonial Bank of New Zealand, was also indebted by £90,000 of which £55,000 was Ward's. He had hoped to induce the Colonial to amalgamate with the Bank of New Zealand to disguise this fact. Sir Robert Stout, a fellow member of the House, had introduced a Guaranteed Banks Amalgamation Prohibition to prevent this happening. Ward was Colonial Treasurer at the time and was forced to resign his parliamentary seat over his dishonest practices. Undeterred, he stood in the resulting by-election three weeks later and was astonishingly returned again as the Member for Awarua.

Richard's letter to his cousin Dryden, Sir John's son, explained his view of the mess he and Caroline were in. At the time it was written, Sir John and Rose, Lady Hall, were still out of the country.

Invercargill, New Zealand

24 June 1897

You have of course seen the a/c of this hideous scandal – & both Will and myself think it best I should write you a line [...] to let Uncle know our views of the matter.

First of all then – so far as I am concerned the thing is an abominable conspiracy & nothing else & this we anticipate being able to sheet home. That a lot of mud will be thrown & stick too there can be no doubt – but as to the last paragraph of the newspaper notice – it has nothing to do with me – but is an outside affair altogether – Solomon is going to act for me & I hope to see him shortly.

Probably the matter will not be started for a month or 6 weeks.

Believe me when I say that I can't describe my regret at the sorrow it must cause to all my relatives.

Yours affectionately

RW Hall[13]

Dryden wrote to his father on 6 July 1897, enclosing Richard's letter and explaining that the 'abominable conspiracy' was 'presumably on the part of J. G. Ward & others against whom Dick's firm was acting in the recent litigation', and saying he thought the charge looked 'ridiculously weak', taking into consideration that 'it relates to something done two years ago that almost the only persons whose evidence could substantiate the charge are the very persons who have been the principals in the matter' but nevertheless thought the scandal was 'most humiliating' for the family. The matter was *sub judice* [still under judicial consideration], so the papers were silent on the matter. Dryden's sister Mildred, in particular, was very cut up about it. She wrote to her father too on 4 July, remarking, 'I cannot help feeling that there must have been something not right in Dick's conduct to his enemies [for them] to imagine they had any chance of success in their making such an accusation against him.' She added that the papers were sure to make much of it if it was political and felt that something was sure to come up about the other dreadful Tom Hall case. John Hall recorded discreetly in his diary on 3 August, 'Sad news re Dick at Invercargill.' He had heard of the arrest through his estate manager, John Fountaine, and Rose was anxious to return home. He asked Dryden in a letter on 4 August to 'keep us informed as promptly as you can of how the matter goes [...] There seems no end to our family troubles.'

Will Hall, Dick's brother and partner in their legal practice, told Mildred and Dryden how he saw Richard's position:

[…] down here it is universally regarded as a political blow aimed at us for the part we have taken in connection with the Ward Assocn & sympathy has been shown to us from all quarters. Dick as well as the woman [Caroline] asserts his absolute innocence & goes about his work daily with absolute unconcern as if nothing has happened affecting himself: in fact I think it hit me worse than himself. All we can do is fight the thing out to the end.[14]

A detail that was never mentioned in the court reports or in letters from Richard or Will was that Ward's mother, Mrs Hannah Ward, a widow, owned the Club Hotel at Campbelltown at the time,[15] and may have known of Caroline Hall's presence in the town. The arrest of Richard and Caroline occurred almost exactly a year after Ward, as a bankrupt, was forced to resign his ministerial position. He had openly avowed in his long and colourful resignation speech in the House on 11 June 1896 to avenge himself on those members of the 'political conspiracy' who were concerned to ruin him privately and hound him out of public life. He had avowed that 'I have a right to ask that my accusers should be put under the same ordeal as I have been put'.

Ward's speech occupied 40 columns of *Hansard*, the New Zealand parliamentary record, and listed in detail the sins – mostly financial and political – of those who had brought him down. As the historian, Tony Simpson, remarked, 'Ward neglected only to mention the person who was the principal author of his misfortune – himself.'[16] As he harangued the House and his enemies, *Hansard* gives the impression that his colleagues sat in enthralled silence except for the occasional brief injection of 'Untrue' or 'No!' Among his cited enemies was, tellingly, 'the brother of a murderer' [clearly Richard W. Hall, solicitor for the shareholders], among others.

Ward then openly expressed his intention to avenge himself on these enemies, in words which sounded more like those of a mafia boss than a member of the House, saying, 'I am on the job, and I intend to be on the job about the private affairs of some of these men who have been going about living on the shareholders of the Bank of New Zealand – these men who have been prepared to turn myself and wife and children out on the streets – who call themselves honourable men.' His other targets were heavyweights in the House, such as Sir Robert Stout, the senior Member for Wellington City, and Mr Duthie, the Member for Wellington Suburbs (said to be conspiring against him with other members of the business community) – he accused both of dubious business dealings; Mr Tolhurst, manager of the Union Bank of Australia, Mr G. G. Stead, who controlled articles appearing in the Christchurch *Press,* and the editor of the *Evening Post*, the significant newspaper in Wellington, seat of government. He was incensed that comments had been made about his case in the *Post* and the *Otago Daily Times* (the hearing was in Dunedin) while it was *sub judice*. He had also been 'attacked' and 'persecuted' and 'pursued' by men outside the House as well and again named, 'in Invercargill, Mr. Hall, nephew of Sir John Hall, another solicitor, actively at work – so far as I was concerned – and who professes to represent people who have never had sixpence of interest in anything that I am connected with, and to not one of whom I owe a penny a piece.' Richard Hall certainly answered to Ward's description as defender of the remaining shareholders of Ward's insolvent company and qualified as one of his arch enemies. Since Ward had been on the high seas between England and New Zealand when the case came to court, his manager had to deal with it alone and the solicitor defending the shareholders had had a working advantage in serving subpoenas and submitting other evidence.

Ward claimed that in 'a large town in the colony', before the Judge gave his decision, 'there was a secret meeting of bitter political opponents [...] These men met, and were acting in conjunction with men at three other large towns, for the purpose of seeing what was to be done if the Judge gave his decision in my favour.' They apparently sent a telegram asking him to resign his position as minister and if he did all opposition to him would be withdrawn. If Ward subsequently was true to his claim to 'fight' these perceived enemies, 'and to die fighting if necessary' and 'have the opportunity yet of [...] having their private doings exposed', these avowals of revenge, made in the House, point to Ward being possibly covertly involved in the resurrecting of the alleged abortion issue affecting Richard and Caroline and their subsequent arrest by the police in Invercargill in the year following his resignation. The action accords exactly with his threats of attacking his enemies in their private lives. By that time, Ward's resurrection had been accomplished and he was once more MP for Awarua, south of Invercargill, with power and influence in the region.

11.3 Sir Joseph Ward with his private secretary, James Hislop (centre) and others, *c*.1901 courtesy of Joy Hall, (née Hislop).

John Hall, an old friend of Judge Williams from earlier days in provincial government and the setting up of Canterbury College in Christchurch, took a dim view of Joseph Ward, whose extravagance offended Hall's Yorkshire prudence and thrift. A diary entry on 12 February 1897, made on a visit to Richard's mother Sarah after her husband's death, relates: 'To Invercargill. J.G. Ward next compartment of corridor *reserved for him.*' And after dealing with his brother's estate with his nephews Will and Richard, and going on a jaunt with Sarah to Bluff, he took a train to Dunedin and again saw, 'Hon. J.G. [Ward]. Whole compartment reserved for himself.' Presumably Mr Ward was travelling at the taxpayer's expense. John, who in office had closely supervised the country's financial recovery from a debt crisis in the late 1870s by careful and moderate borrowing, could never have approved of this indulgence. Nevertheless, in the year of his death, even John Hall requested Prime Minister Ward's aid in securing the release of his nephew Tom from gaol (see Epilogue). There is little in his diary recordings of this period to show he was influenced by the events that so affected his nephew Richard.

The 1880s and 1890s, were a time of hardship with bankruptcies occurring frequently every week, as we saw in Richard Matthews' legal career. Ward's bankruptcy was highly significant because he was also treasurer in the Liberal government and thought to be the most likely successor to the residing prime minister, Richard Seddon. Following his return to parliament and having repaid his debts to those who had honoured them, he was again colonial treasurer and did succeed Seddon as prime minister when he died in 1906.

On the day of the trial there was considerable sympathy for Caroline in the courtroom when she gave her evidence. The description of what happened is revealing in terms of the lengths to which Ward and his associates were prepared to go to bring down the Invercargill solicitor involved in his public humiliation, unless the details following were simply coincidental. As the newspaper court reports disclosed, Caroline's handbag, lost on the railway and containing a private letter to a woman friend in Australia outlining her dilemma, had been found (by whom, we don't know) and handed to police who had sold it to a woman at the Bluff (we don't know who). The letters had been shown to others and given to the police. They appeared as evidence in the case. The jury, by now well informed about the details and reasons for Ward's resignation, and well aware of the part that Richard Hall had played in the J. G. Ward case, behaved fairly. The behaviour of the original complainant, the boarding house proprietress, Mrs Gorman, who had informed on Caroline, appeared in the newspaper accounts to be malicious and venal, though she had a legitimate grievance about use of her rooms. Richard Hall's defence, that he consulted Dr Torrance to attend Mrs Matthews in the event of a natural miscarriage, was agreed by the jury and Dr Torrance could not account for the miscarriage on any other supposition than that of natural premature birth. The supreme court was occupied all day on 22 September in hearing the case. After retiring for half an hour, the jury returned a verdict of not guilty; the defence was upheld.

As a result of the publicity and scandal, Richard and Will Hall's legal practice was dissolved at the end of March 1898 (Caroline was then five months' pregnant with Richard's second child), much to the consternation of their mother, and an advertisement in the *Southland Times* announced 'R.W. Hall is happy to see clients at my new office in the Colonial Bank Buildings'. Will asked Uncle John for money to buy Richard out of their partnership, to which John Hall replied that he would give the money on the 'condition that [Will] makes a binding agreement not to intrude upon his [Richard's] wife and son'.[17] John Hall was executor with Will and Richard for their father's estate. Will told Mildred when the case was first disclosed in the press, that 'But for the children I would leave the colony but having built up a very good business here it seems wrong for their sakes to throw it away.' Poor Will, the only son of Thomas W. Hall to escape scandal, was forced to periodically entertain this idea of escape. 'It almost makes one think after all we have gone through, that our branch of the family is laboring under some curse,' he told Mildred.

Will joined the firm of Hall, Stout and Lillicrap as a senior partner in 1901; his partner was the brother of Sir Robert Stout, one of Ward's stated enemies in the House, and prime minister during the years 1884–1887. He was also the judge in Tom Hall's first trial. John Frederick Lillicrap, Will's other new legal partner, was described in the *Cyclopedia of New Zealand* as one of the most promising members of the profession. Richard continued practising alone. He still described himself as a solicitor in Invercargill in 1905–1906[18] but his professional life had been blighted by the public disclosure of his private life and the lost partnership with Will Hall. In December 1908, Richard left Invercargill for Ohakune, a little over a month after Sir Joseph Ward, now prime minister, had declared open the Main Trunk Line railway between Auckland and Wellington. Perhaps declining business opportunities for Richard had prompted the decision to go north, or the fact that Caroline's daughter Mabel, the family's former nursemaid, was now married and living at Ohakune and might be an additional carer for his son Tom (her husband was quartermaster in the army at nearby Waiouru), who accompanied him. Family rumour has it that he and Caroline were having problems in their marriage at the time. His other children apparently remained with Caroline in Invercargill where her mother also lived. Little Tom, my father, attended the primary school at Ohakune until December 1914 when he became a telegraph boy with the Ohakune Post Office.

Ohakune was growing as a farming and milling town with its own town council and presented possibilities for work. The school roll was 64 by 1907 and the town had most of the essentials, from smithy to school and post office, butcher and baker. It still lacked sealed roads, though, and after rain its citizens were often ankle-deep in mud. Richard set himself up as a solicitor with Mr A. W. Gould in a room in the Club Hotel,[19] but this new beginning turned sour. After three months he was charged with having stolen the sum of £17.1s.3d., the property

11.4 Caroline with her sons by Richard Hall, *c*.1907.

of a man called William Cootes of Raetihi who Richard had represented in a court case and who still owed him for his services. By 14 April 1910 he had been struck off the roll of solicitors of the supreme court of New Zealand for making use of £17 given to him by a client in payment of the balance of a judgement (Richard had not yet been reimbursed by the client for witness statements and subpoenas he had paid for but this did not excuse his lapse). He and friends had refunded the £17 but his misconduct had consequences. He was given leave to apply for reinstatement after two years, and meanwhile could work as a clerk for another solicitor.[20] The immensely complex court report entailed much to-ing and fro-ing to obtain payment, multiple cheques, one of which was lost, and what looked like careless bookkeeping rather than intentional malpractice. I do not think Richard returned to legal practice. He probably thought the odds were stacked against him. By 1919 he was reconciled with Caroline and living in Taihape in the North Island. At 63 he was earning a living there as a 'sawmill hand',[21] a sad decline for a formerly competent solicitor. He and Caroline eventually moved to Wellington to be near some of her by now adult children, including my father, who contributed to his parent's support until he married in his early forties.

Caroline's family

Richard's wife Caroline had first married Richard W. Matthews, solicitor, in September 1880 at the age of 18, when Matthews was 41. He had overseen her mother Jane's probate issues after her first husband, George Hunt, had drowned in the New River Heads whilst crossing with a wedding party to Ruapuke Island.[22]

Caroline's mother had inherited some property from George Hunt, who had owned the original sawmill in Invercargill. She then married Caroline's father, who cited himself in her marriage notice as 'Humphrey Peters McCrystall, Esq. M. D.[23] He was certainly Humphrey Peters but he was not in fact Dr John McCrystal, the name he gave to the resident magistrate in Invercargill when he presented his medical qualifications to become one of the town's first three doctors. John McCrystal was a Royal Navy surgeon and a Fellow of the Royal College of Surgeons of Ireland and had obtained his qualification a quarter century before Humphrey Peters' birth.[24] His identity had been stolen, perhaps from the newly introduced British Medical Register, first published in 1858, the year before Peters/McCrystal arrived in Riverton. In the various extant accounts of Humphrey Peters his assumed name is spelt differently almost every time. I use 'McCrystal' for consistency.

McCrystal set up a bush section in Dee Street, Invercargill, alongside two other doctors, Martin and Monckton. He practised as a surgeon in the whaling station of Riverton, the more populous centre of the 1850s, where he was one of very few white settlers among a Māori population. Robert Vulpy

11.5 Humphrey Peters/Dr McCrystal.

Fulton, M.D. Edinburgh, recorded in *Medical Practice in Otago and Southland in the Early Days*, that:

> To Riverton in 1859 came John M'Cristal from India, where he had served as an army surgeon during the Mutiny. He was young, apparently under 30, good-looking, tall, and straight as a dart. [...] There was no opening for a medical man; no one was ever ill, and there were only occasional accidents.[25]

According to Fulton, when his medical knowledge was not required, McCrystal busied himself splitting posts and rails required for fencing materials in the bush slopes of the hills at the back of Riverton. One day he was called on to amputate the leg of a cooper, Owen McShane (known as Cooper), who had burnt his foot while drunk and sleeping near an open fire. Cooper had contracted lockjaw after unsuccessful treatment by Dr Martin, Invercargill's other resident doctor. Some young men went up the bush to McCrystal's camp and fetched him down to see the man:

> The doctor had neither instruments nor chloroform – as I have stated, he was not practising his profession but was engaged in bush work. However, he went out to Paulin's butcher shop at the back of the public house, got a butcher's knife and a meat saw, and with these he amputated the leg. Mr Hunt asserts that this was true; he was present all the time. Three men [...] helped to lift Cooper from his bed to the table, and he himself held the leg while Dr M'Cristal took it off below the knee. Cooper bore the operation without flinching, and made a good recovery. A ship's carpenter who was knocking about

Riverton made him a wooden stump, and he lived fully for 20 years.[26]

McCrystal also performed a mastectomy on a woman when he was recovering from a drugged state. He was addicted to morphine, perhaps taken originally to dull pain received from a wound or maybe a legacy of his days in India. The locals of Riverton valued his services despite his addiction. Fulton recounts details of a Māori woman suffering from breast cancer, who was due to be operated on by him:

> The husband went up into the bush to seek him, and found him lying in his tent in a semi-conscious condition from some drug which he was in the habit of taking. The husband [...] got the doctor on his back and carried him through the bush to the patient's bedside. He seems to have had the sense enough to take what was required for the operations, and also something to square himself up. He was allowed a little time to come round, and then took off the woman's breast. The operation was successful and she lived for many years.[27]

An intervention by McCrystal when a measles epidemic hit the Māori community of Riverton probably saved many lives. He locked the tribe's chief, who had the illness, in a Captain Howell's house, thus saving all those who might have contracted measles from him. The chief recovered without complications.

Humphrey Peters/McCrystal, whose mother had died when he was 13, enlisted in the army in 1848 at the age of 18, ranked as situation gunner, 2nd Troop Horse Brigade Artillery, Bombay Presidency.[28] Before that he had apparently been an apothecary in the town of Arundel, Sussex, in England. He had arrived in India on the *Dartmouth* in 1849 and was discharged from the army in 1852, before the Mutiny began.[29] According to his granddaughter, Tui Hall (Richard's eldest child, my aunt), he had indeed practised surgery, having 'walked' Guys Hospital, London, where he had learnt his skills. At the time, students at Guys were required to serve an apprenticeship of five to seven years and then 'walk the hospital' as a surgeon's dresser or physician's pupil for six to 12 months while also attending courses on anatomy, surgery, midwifery, medicine and chemistry.[30] Tui told me Peters/McCrystal had served in the Indian Mutiny[31] but fled to New Zealand after apparently killing a man in a duel over a red-haired woman (Tui had inherited the woman's Indian silk shawl). There are several inconsistencies about this story because the dates simply don't add up. It is more likely that young Humphrey Peters had been an apprentice to an apothecary in the town of Arundel because he was only 19 on arrival in India. Since he was discharged from the army in 1852 'unfit for service', the duel story may be true. Perhaps he did his Guys' apprenticeship in the seven years before his arrival in Riverton. It is unlikely he re-enlisted to serve in the Mutiny, which took place during the years 1857–1858, because a comprehensive search of British Army records by a professional researcher in military subjects in the UK, conducted under Peters' own birth name, Humphrey Peters, and his assumed name, John McCrystal, produced no record of service in the Indian Mutiny nor any record of service as a surgeon or assistant surgeon in either the British Army or the Indian Army.[32] Whatever McCrystal told Dr Fulton about his credentials, they appear to have been embellished somewhat, which makes Fulton's recollection of the amputation and mastectomy even more hair-raising unless he had done a surgical apprenticeship. An amputation, mastectomy and control of infection do imply at least some medical knowledge. In the *Southland New & Foveaux Straits Herald* of 13 July 1861 he also advertised himself as 'J. McCristol, surgeon and accoucher', so he presumably had experience of delivering babies too.

Peters/McCrystal's addiction to morphine, which he no doubt found easy to access having established his credentials as a doctor on arrival in New Zealand, led to an overdose of the substance from which he died in 1873. Whether the morphine was an antidote for physical or mental pain we do not know. The *Southland News* opined that his living so long was a puzzle to those who knew that for the last 15 years he had been in the habit of taking drugs in quantities that would be considered fabulous. He held the reputation of being a successful surgeon, and when free of the influence of his favourite medicine, said the paper, was a welcome guest in many social circles.[33]

Notes and references

1. John Hall diary, 18 February 1905. Richard by then had four children.

2. John Hall diary, 21 February 1905. John also visited his niece Aggie Withers at this time, he recorded, finding her well. 'Mrs Dick', Caroline Hall, was staying with Aggie's family on his visit. 'Girls in good spirits,' he wrote.

3. JH to JSN, 15 April 1872. Johnnie was John and Grace Neall's oldest son.

4. TWH to JH, 13 January 1883.

3. Russell Tuffery genealogy.

4. *Southland Times*, 4 October 1880.

5. TWH to JH, 19 January 1883.

6. John Hall diary, 31 December 1884.

7. ibid., January 1885.

8. Sandra Coney, 'Abortion from the 1880s to the 1940s', in *Standing in the Sunshine: A History of New Zealand Women Since They Won the Vote*, Penguin Books, NZ Ltd, 1993, p. 73.

9. *Feilding Star*, 24 June 1897.

10. *Press*, 25 June 1897.

11. W. Downie Steward, *Portrait of a Judge: Sir Joshua Strange Williams*, Whitcombe & Tombs 1946, pp 60–61. Ward was appointed postmaster general by prime minister John Ballance in 1891 and later became treasurer after Ballance's death. In this role, to be declared 'hopelessly insolvent' by Judge Williams and

be forced to file for bankruptcy in 1897 led to him resigning his parliamentary seat. Popular, he regained it in the resulting bi-election. John Hall opined to a colleague, Hankey, in a letter written on 19 February 1895: 'About Mr Ward, a few words in confidence may be useful. It is many years since he was a Post Office messenger; of course the fact that he has worked himself to his present position shows that he is clever – he is also very presentable & plausible. But safe men here speak of him as a "plunger", and as a person whose statements on public or private affairs it is not safe to accept or to act upon without confirmation.'

12. *Portrait of a Judge*, p. 63.

13. RWH to Dryden Hall, 24 June 1879.

14. WYH Hall to Mildred Hall, John Hall's eldest daughter, 1 July 1897.

15. *Te Ara, The Encyclopedia of New Zealand*, biography of Joseph George Ward, read online 15 February 2015.

16. Tony Simpson, *Shame and Disgrace: A History of Lost Scandals in New Zealand*, Penguin Books, 1992, p. 97. Ward's speech appeared in New Zealand Parliamentary Debates, Third Session of the Twelfth Parliament, period 11 June to 7 July 1896, pp 18–38.

17. WYH to JH, date unclear, MS X921. Richard and Caroline's firstborn was Tui in July 1897; their second-born was George Onslow, a son born on 4 October 1898. Clearly, Tui did not count in terms of inheritance, even at that young age. That Caroline had named her first son by Richard, George Onslow, is interesting. Family anecdote has it that her father, Humphrey Peters – apothecary, surgeon, and sometime bush-fencer – was descended from the Second Earl of Onslow, who may have fathered his mother Caroline (born 1805). She was descended from the Gratwickes of Ham. Tui's middle name was Gratwicke.

18. NZ Electoral Rolls 1853–1981, Electoral Year 1905–1906, No. 2233: 'Richard Williamson Hall, Dalyrymple Road, Appleby, Solicitor'.

19. Merrilyn George, *Ohakune: Opening to a New World*, 1990, Kapai Enterprises Ltd., 1990, p. 000.

20. The *Evening Post*, 14 April 1910, *Papers Past*.

21. NZ Electoral Rolls, 1853–1981, Electoral Roll 1919, Region Manawatu-Wanganui, District Rangitikei Supplementary Roll, No. 8295.

22. Russell Tuffery genealogy, Ancestry.com (Australia).

23. *Southland Times*, 4 October 1880.

24. Archivist, Trinity College Dublin, to MT.

25. Robert Vulpy Fulton, M.D. Edinburgh, *Medical Practice in Otago and Southland in the Early Days*, pp. 115–16.

26. ibid., p. 115.

27. ibid., p. 116.

28. Bombay Soldiers Records, 1840-1840 (L-Z), India Office record, London, L/MIL/12/112, from Russell Tuffery.

29. India Office Record, reference L/MIL/12/13, from Russell Tuffery.

30. Guy's Hospital School (1755) Online Records, Ref. code GB 0100G, read on 16 March 2016.

31. The Indian Mutiny (1857–8) was an unsuccessful rebellion by Sepoys against British rule in India over the issue of the introduction of the Enfield Rifle. To load cartridges into the rifle soldiers had to bite off the cartridge ends which, it was rumoured, had been lubricated with lard from pigs and cows. Oral contact with the cartridge ends was therefore an insult to Muslims and Hindus.

32. Dr S. C. Blank, commissioned by Russell Tuffery, was able to verify Humphrey Peters' service in the Indian (Bombay) Army – Peters enlisted in the artillery corps on 13 December 1848 as a former apothecary – but he did not receive the medal issued to all soldiers who served in the Indian Mutiny, and did not receive a pension for service with the Indian (Bombay) Army (ref. L/MIL/12/112, India Office). Blank concluded, 'I am disappointed in that I was unable to substantiate all of the "legend" of HP/JC but at least we are now closer to the truth and unable to consider some of the "legend" as possible speculation.'

33. *Southland News* 13 August 1873.

EPILOGUE

As in all family dramas, people ask, 'But what happened next?' The following paragraphs, I hope, tie up a few loose ends. Though the sub-title of *Sailors, Settlers and Sinners* formally ends the book in 1907, the year of Sir John Hall's death and the end of Tom Hall's imprisonment, I have extended the time span briefly here.

Tom Hall's release

By April 1901, Tom Hall had served 16 years of his life sentence in Mount Eden Gaol. He had sought to give as little trouble as possible and during the first ten years had 'worked very hard often far above my strength – fully expecting both things would be taken into consideration but no, as it turns out; it would have been better for me to have loafed instead'.[2] He had played the organ at the prisoners' services, but his asthma and bad health had forced him to give that up, along with a flower garden he had tended. Hard labour had taken its toll. He had seemingly been a model prisoner. Another unwell prisoner, Fred Lough, possibly a school teacher, had attested publicly in a newspaper that Tom had contributed to his recovery, saving his own rations to give to him in order that he have more food. He, like Tom, was in the prison hospital, sleeping in an adjoining room.

He drew the doctor's attention to my state, and got medicines, administering them as directed [...] he did not even shirk the disagreeable parts of a nurse's duties; for when wracked during the night with cough, he shared with me the mixture he used himself for relief. He enlisted the sympathies of the prison cook, who smuggled small palatable dainties to the hospital, and kept life in my thankless body.[3]

Tom now craved release. He felt as time went on he could see himself dying in prison. He was 53. He wrote to Sir John: 'My father is dead, my mother is dead, Kitty is cutting the last link – and after 15 years imprisonment I am still in prison with an undefined sentence. Like the prisoners in the Bastille, the longer I am confined, the worse does my position seem to become.'[4]

Tom's health had deteriorated. In March 1898, his brother Will reported that Tom had suffered 'an attack of angina pectoris' which suggested something seriously wrong with his heart. 'He perhaps rightly attributes it to the

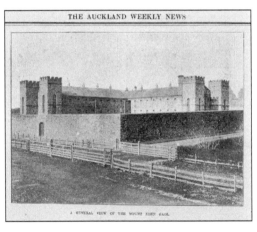

THE AUCKLAND WEEKLY NEWS

A GENERAL VIEW OF THE MOUNT EDEN GAOL.

E1 Mt Eden Gaol, Auckland.

long continued strain of asthma'[5] wrote Will. He thought Tom was likely to live longer in gaol where he had rest and medical attention than outside. Nevertheless, Richard went up to Auckland to get a second medical opinion and the minister of justice agreed to Tom being examined by another medical man. No change in Tom's situation resulted.

Will and Richard in the following years would do all they could to get their brother released. As far as Will was concerned, this was only on the condition that 'he leaves NZ & never returns'.[6] He was keen that the family should also impose the condition that Tom not join his wife and child again. Will thought this would be simple enough to impose, but difficult to enforce. Richard had offered Tom a home, should he be released. Tom was very grateful to him but refused on the grounds that:

> you have all suffered enough through me – and under no circumstances would I remain in the Colony. On my own account I could never hope to escape recognition – and how could I face people. [...] Since my health has weakened my very life depends on getting to a warmer climate – if released.[7]

Though he had been free from asthma for two years thanks to a drug the hospital doctor had administered, he thought his position was worse than that of other prisoners.

> Through my difficulty in breathing I cannot like most men get the benefit of the quietness and repose of a cell when the day's work is done. I have to live in the crowded gaol hospital where one's nights are always more or less disturbed and not once in a month do I get up in the morning refreshed.[8]

Tom had seen an opportunity in April 1901 for remission of his sentence at the forthcoming coronation of King Edward VII; it was customary on such occasions to show clemency to long-serving prisoners. For Tom it was, *'the one chance'* he could ever hope to have, and he wrote to Uncle John to ask for his help: 'All other Colonies I believe liberated or mitigated sentences at the beginning of the Colony when the Commonwealth was inaugurated. New Zealand proposes to do something soon.'[9]

Sir John, who had hitherto kept strictly to the ethical code of not using his powerful public position to intervene to help his nephew, now began to correspond with Kitty about a possible divorce from Thomas. She replied that 'it was natural for Tom to wish to be free, poor fellow'. Since his mother had died, 'he is so cut off from everyone now.'[10] Sir John informed Tom of his and Kitty's plan in the letter below, which was first read and approved by Kitty before posting:

London, 18 June 1901

My dear Tom

I have received through Kitty your letter of 12 April. You will doubtless know before this reaches you that she is proceeding to New Zealand to take proceedings for obtaining a divorce. I must say, with every will to be considerate to you, that I think this is a justifiable & desirable step, and I hope you will so look upon it. It is surely reasonable and just that your wife & son should be absolutely protected against any attempt on your part to return to the marriage and *absence of this protection would greatly militate against any remission of your sentence.*

This being done, and security being given that you would remain *out of N. Zealand* I should be very glad, for your father & mother's sake as well as yours, that your punishment should be ended. If I could help I would do so – but I cannot [Thomas W. Hall had died in 1895 and Sarah Hall in 1899]. Any interference by me would certainly do harm, and in my absence from New Zealand I cannot call on assistance from others – but I will write to your brothers.

I do not know of any probability of an early remission of sentences generally, and it is very improbable that anything of the kind will take place before the King's coronation, which is not expected to take place before June 1902. If my life is spared I shall be in New Zealand before then, and as I told you in Auckland shall be ready to help you [financially] to make a start in life somewhere out of New Zealand.

Do not think me unkind in writing as I have done [...] to your wife and son, especially [as] the latter has dictated my words [...]

Goodbye, dear Tom. I hope to be spared to see you released, but for the case that I should not, I have provided for you in my will, for some assistance being given to you.

Your affectionate Uncle

John Hall

Sir John then wrote to Will to rally Tom's brothers:

For your father and mother's sake I hope that you or one of you will sometimes write to him. His crime has been a great one, & his character not too wise, but I hope that his flesh & blood should not leave him without a chance of making a living himself. I would agree to the [release] of sufficient money from your father's legacy to enable him to go to Australia & give him a start there. I would also give him some myself. Please let Dick know what I have written.[11]

In his reply, Tom said he felt deeply that at Sir John's age and with the work he had done and the name he had made, he should not be worried about his affairs, but he also felt that his own position and the affection his uncle had for him must plead for him. He could not thank Sir John sufficiently for providing for him.[12]

Tom was ready to concede to a divorce. '[Kitty's] letters and kindness to me all these years – I can never forget – and so long as she does not marry again – I am only too glad she should obtain a divorce – if it is for Nigel's benefit, and will make her happier.'[13] He did not want her to remarry, he said, because if she had further children with a new husband, Nigel's position would be made worse.

Kitty, leaving the 15-year-old Nigel in England in a boarding school in Tonbridge, came to Auckland and in August 1901 sought help from her brother's lawyer over the divorce. In her letter to Tom requesting the divorce, Kitty said that what had prevented the request earlier was consideration for his mother. She applied for the divorce to the Auckland court since 'I am not well known so my appearance at court would not be noticed as it would in ChCh. […] You have been so good to me that I like to save you all any disagreeableness […]'[14]

The case was to be heard in Auckland in December 1901 and Tom requested it be heard in chambers to avoid publicity that might harm his possibility of release. The divorce was granted. Tom never saw Kitty or his son again.

Tom was not released during the coronation amnesty. Sir John wrote to Tom in December 1902 enclosing two books, the only letter he received at the time. His uncle's kindness released memories of a happier past. In his reply he wrote:

> As you can imagine, your letter brought back a flood of Xmas recollections. How many Xmases I have spent at Hororata. I cannot remember – but everything about the place seemed to stand out before me with all of you, as one has so often seen you, from the party riding and driving to Church on Xmas morning, with perhaps a ride about the Run in the afternoon. Then after tea a stroll about the garden until dark, then some bright music and singing. Ah! It comes back all too vividly. [15]

Kitty had by now informed Nigel for the first time of his father's history. He made no response, she told Sir John.

Attempts by Kitty in Auckland to rally support for Tom's release among her family and friends were unsuccessful. She wrote an anxious letter to Sir John in November 1906 to say her brother 'does not think our help would alter the decision & shirks any responsibility for obtaining Tom's release, as he is not sure Tom may not give Nigel & me further care or trouble.' She continued: 'I am writing to you, as I feel that no one cares much what becomes of Tom, but you & me. I feel for poor Tom in his hopeless despair & wish to help him. But still rather quake for what the future might bring if he was released. My feelings are so mixed between pity & fear.'[16]

Sir John and Tom's brother Will began again to see if they could get Tom's sentence commuted. Sir John had written to the solicitor who had defended Tom in his first trial, Perry (of Perry Perry & Kinnerney, Timaru) to see what level of public support there would be for such a move. Will summed up the local feeling, 'It seems that Timaru people are not likely to hello, except perhaps a few of those who were friends in time past.'[17] It was Kinnerney's view that any attempt, however judiciously made, to obtain support locally would not only do harm by arousing antagonism, though he was anxious to do anything he could in the direction indicated.

Nevertheless, Tom petitioned for release in mid-1906. His petition had to be considered by the prime minister, Sir Joseph Ward, and the cabinet. It was refused, with no reasons given. While the minister of justice, James McGowan, was in favour, one cabinet minister, William Hall-Jones (previously William Jones, no relation) was not. Hall-Jones (Liberal prime minister 1906) had said that he would do everything in his power to prevent Tom's release.

By 1907 Sir John was ill and near to death. He had accepted the mayoralty of Christchurch so as to officiate during the Exhibition year of 1906, but was unable to do so through illness and was being nursed by his daughter Mildred at her house in the Cashmere Hills. One of the last things he did was to petition the current prime minister, Sir Joseph Ward, again, on behalf of Tom, using his declining health to apply pressure, as Tom's letter to Sir John of 18 December 1906 makes clear: 'I am very grateful to you for seeing Sir Joseph Ward and for your efforts on my behalf. It was the first day of hope – and cheered me greatly.'[18] This letter shows that though the cabinet decision was negative, the prison governor

E2 Handwritten letter excerpt from Tom Hall to Sir John Hall, 18 Dec 1906.

and other dignitaries were very much in favour of his release after a 20-year incarceration.

A telegram Sir John received from Ward on 17 January 1907 stated: 'The matter referred to is receiving attention. I will send you a confidential message regarding it from here 17 Jan [19]07.'[19] On the 28 January 1907 another telegram arrived, saying: 'Hope your health is better. For your confidential information the matter has been referred to the Judge for his views. If favourable likely success.'[20]

Tom was released in late 1907. Sir John had died in June the same year, thereby absolving the government from any implication that they had been influenced by a former premier in their decision. Both his father and Sir John Hall had provided for Tom and, as predicted and arranged, Tom left New Zealand for Australia. He lived on the Queensland coast as 'Paul Newstead', finding a woman companion who only ever knew him under his new name, and work as a commercial photographer. He received assistance from trust monies left for him by his father and uncle. Kitty continued to provide him with an annuity even after their divorce, sent via her sister in New Zealand. Tom died in 1929 aged 81.

Jack in exile

Disgraced young Jack Hall, who had been unceremoniously dispatched from New Zealand in 1886, disappeared from the family correspondence until 1898, three years after his father's death and 12 years after his exile began. His wife and children had rejoined him soon after he arrived in the USA. He sent a pencilled letter in response to one from Will, co-executor of his father's will, which gave details of their father's estate of which he would also be a benefactor. It is so sincere that it is difficult to imagine his original misdemeanour could have been extremely serious. The 'resolution of partnership' he mentions is the dissolution of their law practice by Will and Richard after the publicity that followed Richard's public outing over his wife-to-be's 'miscarriage'.

Portland, Oregon, 21 May 1898

Dear Will

I have not written you for many a day, though a few lines from you would at any time be welcome. Put all these mercenary matters on one side, Will, & write as brother to brother now & again. Dick wrote a while ago & sent me a Statement of Accounts of the Estate but not what revenue was coming in – I almost hate the name of the thing [...] What I want to write about is only as regards our Mother. I had a letter from her 'via' Vancouver today, so heartbroken she says little, but you know what it means to read between the lines. She thinks your resolution of partnership is for the best but dear Will, do try & see that her declining years are made as easy for her as possible. Dick, I understand, is living with her now, & she has got a new companion. Why don't you let me know once in a while the real state of her health. Let the estate go hang, but there should surely be enough to keep her in comfort. You know I have not the foggiest idea of what the incoming or outgoing LSD of it is.

Things are looking better for me now as I have a job. The chance to take charge of the work on the fortifications at Narrowstone Park at the entrance to Rupert Sound (Port Townsend) about 200 miles from here & about 40 from Vancouver Island, or else put in the Government Locks on the Gambill River about forty miles from here. I have also a good deal of work ahead in Portland [...] When you get this write me a brotherly letter & tell me how things are going with you. I am going to write Mother tonight again, though I posted one already in the early part of the week via 'Frisco. I never write to anyone in New Zealand though I keep posted up in all your political movements. Things have changed very much since I left. Our children I am very proud of, Will, & you may be [of] your nephews. I do not say they are without sin, but they are without vile. Milly is away just now. Ted is head clerk to Kellaher & Co, wholesale merchants but joined the naval brigade last night & woke up this morning to find he had been ordered to Manila in the Philippine Islands. Lizzie is in a great state about it. Of course as he is under age we can stop him going [...] George is 6 feet high & joined also but in the Engineers. He & Fred the 'baby' can do just about anything almost with machinery either electrical or steam. [...] Tell Jack Frederick when you see him that Edward Hall & George Hall, Timaru boys, have enlisted in the naval brigade for the Philippine Islands. They both passed high in school honours. – I suppose you will write to Uncle John now & again. When you do again, mention some of these facts to him, so that he may see some of his relations in this part of the world are keeping up the Viking republic.

Well, dear Will, scratch me off a line now & again, if it is only a blank page with your autograph on it. The Mother gives but dismal accounts of Tom's health, but I suppose it is hoping against hope with him – so far as a happy release is concerned. Goodbye – write as you would have written twenty years ago.

Your affectionate brother

J. Hall[21]

Jack's pride in his two sons is touching and his irritation with Will, though humorously expressed, obvious. Will was the most vocal of the brothers in the continued exile of Jack from New Zealand.

Aggie's children by Wakefield and Withers

Josephine Wakefield was a dutiful and caring surrogate mother to her four Wakefield nieces and nephews. The oldest son, Edward or 'Chunky', fought in the Boer War with the Somerset and Wiltshire Yeomanry and later served in the South African Constabulary. By 1924 he was living in New York, married with no children and working as manager of the touring department of the Automobile Club of America. He joined the Canadian airforce in 1917 but was honourably discharged a year later with rheumatic fever. He married Annie Webster-Wedderburn in 1903 and they moved to Staten Island, New York in 1913 and later back to England. He died before the Second World War and is buried in the parish churchyard of the Sussex village of Thakeham. Oliver Wakefield, Edward and Aggie's third son (Gerald died at birth), became a house master at the Viticultural Station at Rutherglen in Victoria, Australia. After losing his mother early, his life experience fitted him perfectly for the role. He wrote to John Hall in 1906 to say that he was looking after 'wards of state & mostly orphans' who were sent to him to train in viticulture or agriculture and to be 'otherwise fitted mentally & physically for the battle of life'. He was glad his two sisters Queenie (Grace Josephine), and Mildred were now married, Queenie to Dr Tom Bragg, an Edinburgh- and Glasgow-trained surgeon, who was in charge of the English hospital, 'the Orthington [...] at Wei Chen in Northern China' where Queenie was 'devoted to her missionary work'. Mildred had married an Anglican vicar, Fred d'Arblay Burney and, according to Oliver, they were 'thoroughly happy in their beautiful home at Harworth Vicarage', in Nottinghamshire.[22]

Oliver became a banker with Drummonds Bank in Trafalgar Square, London. He never married and was a 2nd Lieutenant in the Household Battalion of the Brigade of Guards in the First World War. He died on 12 October 1917, aged 40, 72 days into the 100-day battle at Passchendaele. Killed by a shell, his body was never found but his name is carved on the great wall at Tynecot, the largest Commonwealth war cemetery in the world. His commanding officer wrote, 'his men were devoted to him; through all this bad weather he kept them all going.'[23]

The ongoing distress from being torn from their mother after her divorce is apparent in a touching letter Aggie's youngest daughter Mildred wrote to John Hall's son Godfrey in 1920. Mildred had not seen Aggie, living in New Zealand, since their parting:

> The news of my mother's death reached me through Queenie – I should like you to know something of what she has always been to me. From the day I last saw her, when I was about four years' old, I believe no day has passed that she has not been in my thoughts. The beautiful memory of her has literally lived with me – yet I have not spoken of her, and never knew she would wish me to be in touch outwardly, as I believe we always were in thought. To have known of her lasting love [...] would have broken what was nothing less than a life-sorrow from that day onwards. My own love for her only deepened as I grew up – and no one knew that I ever thought of her. But I want you to know, because I know how you all cared for her.[24]

Aggie and her second husband Edward Withers had an enduring marriage and four children but their lives were not without pain.

Though Aimée, their first-born in 1886, lived until 1956, Ethel born in 1888 with spina bifida was wheelchair-bound. Peter, born in 1891, died in infancy. Irene, born in 1891, married an Australian, Harold Pearce, and died aged 21 in Hong Kong of dengue fever in 1912 after the birth of their daughter Mollie. Edward died in 1914, Aggie in 1919.

The senior Halls and their wives
In the mid-1890s George and Agnes were living in Christchurch after returning from England. Thomas and Sarah were living near their sons in Invercargill. The brothers died almost in synchrony at the end of 1895, before the news of Richard and Caroline Hall's unfortunate problems hit the headlines. First George suffered a stroke on Christmas Day, and on the same day John Hall received two telegrams from Richard, 'Father sinking/Father passed away.' John took the early morning train the next day with his son Godfrey, and at Timaru was met by his nephews, Will and Richard Hall. After seeing Thomas's solicitor, he attended his funeral. He found Sarah very frail and weak but she survived another four years, dying of Bright's disease in October 1899. Her social life, apart from a few close friends, must have become very restricted after Tom Hall's trial and incarceration, and the shock of enduring the publicity surrounding her youngest son, Richard, in June 1897 over his lover's 'miscarriage' and the J. G. Ward case, weakened her further. She continued to write to Tom in Mount Eden Gaol and to Jack in Oregon but died on 28 October 1898, aged 82, after a fond visit from Sir John Hall who was keen to pay his last respects and ensure her sons Will and Richard would manage her affairs. After his stroke, George died in February 1896 and was buried at Hororata. His wife Agnes lived another 21 years, dying in November 1917, aged 91.

E3 Sir John Hall on the verandah of Terrace Station, Hororata, wearing a mourning band for his older brother, Thomas, c.January 1896.

Sir John Hall

John continued to visit Aggie and her new family whenever he went south to Timaru, His strong sense of duty made him one of the most faithful observers and supporters of the extended family throughout his life – as is his great-granddaughter, Kate Foster, today, as keeper of the family archive at Hororata. In 1905, two years before his death, he was busy settling his nephew Will's daughter, Cecil, into a Parisian finishing school. Cecil's mother Ruth had died young in 1887, and the family were concerned that she learn suitably feminising skills to enhance her marriage prospects – the French language, art and music. John had lost his wife Rose in May 1900, after an earlier stroke, and he was lonely in the Hororata homestead, which seemed big and empty with his children married and elsewhere, his friends and political colleagues 'with whom I have laboured [...] now passed away'.[25] Leaving a desolate house, he welcomed the chance to help Cecil and spend time with his daughter Mildred, then living in Britain, to visit old haunts in Hull and to take final leave of his sister Grace.[26]

Will Henry Hall

Will, who Sir John described as 'the most taciturn man' he had ever met, maybe had quite a lot to be taciturn about as he witnessed and sometimes involved himself in the more turbulent lives of his brothers

Tom, George Buceo, Jack and Richard. Widowed in 1887, the year after Tom Hall's two trials, when his wife Ruth died of peritonitis, he brought up his two sons and daughter alone. Perhaps his capacity for empathy and emotional engagement with others had been severely tested. After Ruth's death, he added his mother's maiden name to his own, becoming Mr W. Y. H. Hall, the Y standing for 'Young'. When Richard Hall went north to Ohakune, Will continued practising law alone in Invercargill, but joined Hall, Stout and Lillicrap in 1901. He went to England in 1906 and visited his daughter Cecil in her finishing school in Paris. During the First World War he worked in France establishing canteens for the forces, returning to New Zealand in 1918 to take up law again. When he died in 1926, aged 72, his obituary stated that he was the 'most widely read man in Invercargill'. Strangely, similar words were said of his Uncle George in his obituary. Will was one of the founders of the Southland Frozen Meat Company and later its legal advisor.

A child of Richard and Caroline

My father Tom, named after his grandfather, Thomas W. Hall, was the youngest in the family and apparently the favourite of his mother. When Richard W. Hall left for Ohakune on Christmas Day 1908 after a rift with Caroline, he took Tom, nearly eight, with him. It was just over a month since Sir Joseph Ward had opened the Main Trunk Line rail connection between Auckland and Wellington. The town was unpaved and primitive. Tom was enrolled at Ohakune School from February 1909 where he remained until he was 14, on at least one occasion enjoying a group jaunt up Mount Ruapehu with his popular teacher, Joe Blyth, to see the crater. The boys and Blyth took supplies in on horseback, stayed in a mountain hut and used potato sacks to make a thrilling descent down the snowy slopes of the mountain. For sixpence Tom could attend the cinema in the town hall and see silent movies, though electricity in the town was not available until 1914 and a piped water supply and mains sewerage much later. Water came through the school roof, there was over-crowding, and on hot days lessons were often conducted in the shade of nearby bush.[27] He had to leave school before he matriculated so he could earn money for the family. He subsequently put considerable time and effort into the education he had earlier missed, studying at night school while holding down a permanent job. He 'sweated blood', he told his children, to pass his matriculation alone, studying mathematics, chemistry and physics without any formal assistance. He was in his mid-thirties before he achieved his Bachelor of Science degree, while also working full time in the post office, first as a telegraph boy, then a morse code operator and finally a telegraph engineer.

He married Helen Tocker (1918–2009), the daughter of the Revd Cecil and Elizabeth Tocker in 1943 when he was 42 (introduced to her by her mother, his bridge partner) and they moved to Palmerston North where he eventually became District

E4 **My father in his Victoria University of Wellington Bachelor of Science graduation gown.**

Telegraph Engineer. I discovered recently that during the Second World War he was a captain in the home guard, useful for his knowledge of morse code and internal communications should the Japanese stage a successful invasion and disrupt these. Tom's legacy of having to leave school early provoked a determination that the same would not happen to his children. He ensured all six had a university education and they became in order of age, high school teacher and civil servant; agricultural scientist; civil engineer; journalist and academic publishing editor; investigative television journalist/film director/film producer; and nurse. Perhaps his uncle's incarceration and his father's foreshortened career had instilled a belief in ethical behaviour as an absolute standard. You always told the truth. You behaved towards others as you hoped to be treated yourself. He also told the story of a boy he once knew (obviously himself) who had been asked to wait in a particular place while his father did an errand. He waited for hours and darkness fell but the father never returned. The moral was: never tell a child something you do not intend to honour. There were times, had it not been for Mabel, his half-sister, who also lived in Ohakune, that he might have gone without food. Living in Ohakune without his mother was a precarious existence compared to the days in Invercargill when Richard and Will shared a thriving legal practice and Richard's children were installed in Invercargill South School.

In my Introduction, I quoted from T.S. Eliot's poem, *Burnt Norton*, which begins with the idea that time present and time past are both present in time future, that your ancestral history comes with you into your present life and into your future. It is generally believed that Eliot derived these ideas from the philosopher Bergson, popular among his contemporaries. But this idea was not new. Some Pacific cultures believe that you walk forward by walking backward into your past. Similarly, when you enter a Māori meeting house in New Zealand you are believed to be walking through the body of your ancestors.

The concept of temporal flux and continuity also appears in Virginia Woolf's essay, 'A Sketch from the Past'. Hers was a more psychological approach, reflecting the new preoccupation of her time. Woolf wrote of her obsession with her recently dead mother, Julia, who before she was exorcised in Woolf's ground-breaking novel, *To The Lighthouse*, was a continual 'invisible presence' as

Woolf went about her 'day's doings'. Her essay's subject was the writing of biography where other 'invisible presences' were present too, the 'consciousness of other groups impinging upon ourselves; public opinion; what other people say and think', tugging the subject of biography this way and that. If we can't analyse these invisible presences, she wrote, we know very little of the subject of memoir. 'I see myself as a fish in a stream; deflected; held in place; but cannot describe the stream', she wrote.

After focusing on some of the strongest stories in one family's history, I hope I have provided enough context to understand the stream in which my ancestors swam. They too were subject to 'invisible presences' whether in the form of other people or social pressures. George Hall, the intrepid escapee from imprisonment in France, struggled against the countermanding influence of Aunt Mildred over his children, until three of them broke free with their emigration plan. Christian values also determined the Hall brothers' approach to ethical and moral problems. John, a leading politician and pastoralist, demonstrated this in his relationship to his relatives, the staff on his stations, the perpetrators in his magistrate's court, his constituents and their children. He succeeded with Māori in the South Island who praised his fairness to them in the magistrate's court, but is thought now by some to have mishandled the Parihaka affair through a determination not to compromise British sovereignty and to avoid another war. Thomas was balanced and civic-minded in his public engagement in the church, harbour and hospital boards as well as his local newspaper, and generous in his good will towards his dependants. George's civic sense emerged in his work as a JP and for a short time, as an MP. Their sister Grace, enmeshed in a web of Victorian religious values and duties, was an essential part of the family story as guardian of George and Agnes's daughter Aggie during her schooling in England and in maintaining a strong link with her brothers and their families through her letters, parcels and essential supplies from the department stores of Hull and London.

As her brothers made their way in the new society they maintained strong ties to each other, essential in a new unpredictable world. In turn, their example exerted a strong influence on the next generation. Thomas's sons, Tom, George, Jack, Will and Richard, were caught in a web of patronage and favours, enjoying privileged positions in the new colony, but at the same time often reacting against the pressures that these entailed, pressures of family position, inheritance, and environment.

Strong-minded Aggie, removed from her mother at a young age to be educated far away in a different country, formed a replacement relationship with her Aunt Grace who she then had to leave, and married first a man who proved unreliable and mostly absent. She was, too, like four of her Hall cousins, a casualty.

My father's silence about his parents' respective families and his past was a denial of the 'invisible presences'. The recollection of painful family events and the decline of his father Richard's career was too disturbing, too shameful, and might have been harmful for us to know. It was a testament to our trust in him that we never questioned this absence of detail until much later in our own lives. But silence has a way of speaking. *Sailors, Settlers and Sinners*, is an attempt to fill that silence.

Note and references

1. JH to WYH, 24 June 1901.
2. TH to JH, Xmas 1902.
3. Frank Lough, 'Can a Murderer Atone? A Revelation from Auckland Gaol', first published in the *Auckland Herald*, then on 5 March 1903 in the *Timaru Herald*, Papers Past.
4. TH to JH, 12 Oct 1901.
5. WYH to JH 4 March 1898.
6. WYH to JH 10 March 1898.

7. TH to JH 12 Oct 1901.

8. ibid.

9. TH to JH 12 April 1901.

10. Kitty Hall to JH 25 May 1901.

11. JH to WYH, 24 June 1901.

12. TH to JH, 12 October 1901.

13. ibid.

14. Kitty Hall to JH, 4 September 1901.

15. TH to JH, Xmas 1902.

16. Kitty Hall to JH, 12 November 1906.

17. WYH to JH, 8 November 1906.

18. TH to JH, 18 December 1906.

19. Sir Joseph Ward to Sir John Hall, telegram, 17 January 1907.

20. ibid., telegram, 28 January 1907.

21. Young John (Jack) Hall to WYH, 21 May 1898. Jack's sons, if they did enlist, were to sail as reinforcements to the Philippines where Admiral George Dewey in April 1898 had destroyed the Spanish Fleet. The US Congress had declared war on Spain demanding its withdrawal from the nearby island of Spanish-run Cuba whose sugar production was in direct competition with American sugar-producing companies. It also needed a strategic foothold in Asiatic waters and the Philippines situation offered an opportunity.

22. Oliver Wakefield to JH, 12 November 1906.

23. Simon Kendall to author, 14 July 2018. Simon is married to Angela Josephine (née Bragg), who is Aggie Wakefield's great-granddaughter and daughter of Queenie (Grace Josephine) Wakefield. Both mother and daughter commemorate Edward's sister Josephine, Queenie's surrogate mother, in their middle names.

24. Mildred Burney (née Wakefield) to Godfrey Hall, 17 October 1920, courtesy of Hugh and Jane Burney.

25. JH to his English friend, William Bell, 11 August 1900.

26. JH to his son Wilfred, 15 December 1903.

27. Merrilyn George, *Opening to a New World*, Kapai Enterprises Ltd., 1990, p. 275.

TIMELINES IN ORDER OF AGE

George Hall (1782–1865)

1782: Born the eleventh child of John and Eleanor Hall. Baptised in Holy Trinity Church, Hull, 6 February.

1787: At school in Sproatley, north-east of Hull.

1795: January. To sea as a cabin boy aged 13 on the transport ship *Neptune* during the French Revolution. Goes in the cutter with artillery captain, Wilson, to attend councils of war with French army under General Hoche.

On same vessel to Gibraltar to meet Sir John Jervis's fleet; sees the *Victory* (Nelson's ship); witnesses the sinking of HMS *Courageux* and the loss of 550 lives.

Returns to Hull on the *Frankfort* with Master Jackson.

1804: Aged 22 is captured by a French privateer from a British ship, the *Enterprize*, which he commands. Begins six years of captivity in France, first at Verdun then at Auxonne.

1810: 28 Feb meets a Hungarian officer in charge of a detachment of returning Austrian prisoners. Disguised as an Austrian soldier and with his friend Captain Anderson, escapes with the detachment. Are discovered and must reveal their names. Taken to the military prison at Strasbourg and having tricked officials into issuing them medical certificates they are transported by cart back to Auxonne.

1810: Begins his successful second escape on 20 November 1810. Arrives in England at 1.15 a.m. on first day of 1811.

1811: Arranges for the release of French prisoner Edward Torris.

1812–13: Becomes a Younger Brother of Hull Trinity House, then a Steward.

1812: (October)–1814 (January), assignment on the *Lord Wellington* to Malta via St Petersburg and London.

1817: 21 October, marries Grace Williamson of Hull at Hull's Holy Trinity Church. Lives at 54 Prospect Street, Hull.

1819: 4 March, registers his ship *Grace* in Hull.

1819: May–November, to Riga and Archangel in *Grace*.

1820: July–November, to St Petersburg in *Grace*. On 7 December, made an Assistant of Hull Trinity House.

1821: March–May, to Hamburg in *Grace*; July–November, to Limerick, Ireland.

1822: January–December, to Santa Fé, North America in *Grace*; follows the opening of the American prairies to traders the previous year.

1823–4: *Grace* commanded by R. Cresswell to Gibraltar.

1826: *Grace* commanded by Captain Wilkinson to Rio de Janeiro.

1827: On 29 May, two months before his wife's death, promoted to Elder Brother of Hull Trinity House. August, *Grace* commanded by George Hall, arrives in Bahia en route to Rio de Janeiro, Brazil. Moves from Prospect Street to Brook Street, Hull.

1828–9: Warden of Hull Trinity House.

1830: 26 July–14 September, *Grace* to Riga.

1831: 24 February–24 June, *Grace* to Leghorn (Livorno), Italy; 2 September–6 December, *Grace* to Cadiz.

1832: 27 April–15 August, *Grace* to Leith, Hamburg and Hull.

1833: 3 June–6 November *Grace* to the Charente, France.

1834: 1 April–20 June, *Grace* to the Charente, France; Thomas B. Smith commander on this trip; 6 August–20 December, Memel to Oporto, Master B. Smith commanding *Grace*.

1835–6: Warden of Hull Trinity House. 1836, opening of Junction Dock, Hull; George authorises building a lighthouse at Paull, East Riding of Yorkshire on the north bank of the Humber Estuary. It remains there still.

1837: Mid-June, visits John in school in St Gall, Switzerland.

1839: Expedition to Hamburg–Berlin–Dresden–Prague–Vienna–Treblitz–Dresden–Leipzig–Magdeburg–Brunswick–Hanover–Hamburg–Hull.

First publication of George Hall's *Journal of Two Escapes from French Prison During the War with Napoleon* (publisher John Mozley Stark). Includes at the end, 'Autobiography of a Little Sailor Boy'.

1841–2: Warden of Hull Trinity House.

1844: Buys Rose Cottage, Elloughton, as a second home.

1847–8: Warden of Hull Trinity House. 28 November 1848, marries Mary Ann Packman at St James's Church, Holloway, in London; struggles with his children over their mother's legacy.

1852–3: Warden of Hull Trinity House. Farewells first John, then George, then Thomas as they emigrate to New Zealand.

1860: Re-publishes *Journal of Two Escapes from French Prison During the War with Napoleon*; reprint by Truslove & Hanson Ltd, London. Omits 'Autobiography ...' but includes facsimile of letter of thanks to him from French prisoner Edward Torris.

1865: His wife Mary Ann dies on 15 February. He dies 29 August.

Buried in Sculcoates Sacristy by his daughter Grace.

George Williamson Hall (1818–1896)

1818: Born Kingston upon Hull, 5 August.

1827: Mother, Grace Williamson Hall, dies June.

1828: At school in Germany.

1834: *Aurora* (179 tons) London–Mediterranean, apprentice aged 15.

1835: *Toronto* (350 tons), Hull–North America, 'bound apprentice for 3 years'.

1836: *Marys* (310 tons), Hull-Baltic/St Petersburg, boy or deckhand (2 trips that year: July–Sept. and Oct.–Dec.).

1837: *Andromache* (346 tons), Hull–St Petersburg, Black Sea, 28 March, seaman, aged 18; includes Constantinople and Odessa, returns 9 December.

1838: *Houghton* (274 tons), April–July, Hull–Baltic, second mate.

1839: *Princess Victoria* (372 tons), London–Calcutta, mate.

1840: *John Marsh* (363 tons), Liverpool–East Indies, mate.

1841: *Lerwick* (363 tons), Liverpool–East Indies, mate.

1842: *Aurindohander* (220 tons), Calcutta–East Indies, mate.

1843: *Lady Nugent* (535 tons), London–East Indies, mate.

1844: *Sam Boddington* (523 tons), London–Bombay–Cape of Good Hope-Calcutta, second mate.

1844: *Mary Miller* (290 tons), Hull–South America, master.

1845: *Mary Miller*, February, Hull–Valparaiso–Talcahuano (included Copiapo), master.

Mary Miller, November, Hull to Valparaiso, Chile and port or ports on west coast of America, returning to Swansea, Wales, master.

1846: *Mary Miller*, April, Hull–Gothenburg–Valparaiso, master.

1847: *Mary Miller*, January, Valparaiso–Iquique (salt-petre port), South America–Dominica–Valparaiso–London.

1848: *Mary Miller*, January, Hull–Valparaiso via Beirut–Alexandria–Buenos Aires.

1850: December, at Port of Scarborough, issued with Master's Certificate of Service by Register General of Seaman by order of the Board of Trade (no 40968).

1850: 10 April marries Agnes Emma Dryden, daughter of William and Jane Dryden at St Stephens, Hull. They honeymoon at Chepstow.

1851: Daughter Agnes Mildred Hall ('Aggie') born.

1852: 26 March, brother John (unmarried) emigrates to Lyttelton, New Zealand on *Samarang* with a Canterbury Association ticket; arrives 31 July.

1 November George, Agnes Emma and their daughter Agnes Mildred leave London on the *Royal Albert* for New Zealand.

1853: George and family arrive at the port of Dunedin. He farms at Windwhistle with Thomas and John, living on the Rakaia Terrace Station for a short time.

1854: February, George takes over Run 97, which he calls 'Ashburton Forks Station', from William B. Tosswill. Later known as 'Ringwood' it comprises 6,000 acres in the forks between the north and south branches of the Ashburton River. It pastures 3,900 sheep on 8,500 acres by 1859. He and Agnes live there until 1863.

1857: With Edward Steriker, licenses Run 252, Sawdon. Taken over by Steriker solely in 1861.

1858: May, George with Edward Steriker, takes up Balmoral Station of 60,000 acres in the Mackenzie Country, extending from the Tasman to the Fork River with Irishman Creek at its southern boundary and the Jollie River at its northern boundary. Worked solo by George from 1862. Taken over by John Hall late 1866.

1861: February, in the General Election 1860–1861 George represents Heathcote on the Canterbury Provincial Council but resigns in 1862. His successor is William Sefton Moorhouse. A bad snowstorm in July leads to loss of sheep on Ashburton Forks station.

1862: Daughter Aggie begins eight years of schooling in England.

1863: Sells Ashburton Forks to Charles H. Greenstreet and retreats with Agnes to John Hall's Selwyn Station, adjacent to Rakaia Terrace Station, which he works for a year. He and Agnes move to Timaru until 1867. George serves as a Justice of the Peace in Timaru.

1868: February–September, George and Agnes live in 'Fendal Town', near Christchurch for the winter. In October move to 'the Nutshell' on Lincoln Road, Addington, Christchurch, to receive Aggie who returns from school in England.

1869: April, sells Balmoral Station to Alfred Cox.

1874: Daughter Aggie marries Edward Wakefield on 15 July.

1886: Agnes Mildred divorces Wakefield and marries Edward Withers on 12 August at the Weslyan Church, Christchurch. George gives evidence against his daughter to ensure Wakefield retains custody of the children.

October, George supervises the care of his nephew John Neall, who is dying of tuberculosis in Christchurch, nursed by a Mrs Hawkes. John dies on 17 October.

December – George attempts unsuccessfully to recoup money loaned to Edward Wakefield who plans on making his sister Josephine his children's carer and taking them to England where he will join them.

1887: January, George goes to Melbourne with Aggie to remarry her to Withers under Australian law after notification by Will Hall of a legal flaw in the first marriage to Withers.

March, George and Agnes sail to England via Rio de Janeiro in time for Queen Victoria's Jubilee.

1889: In lodgings with Agnes at St Helier, Jersey, until September 1890.

1890: September, with money recouped from Wakefield, George and Agnes return to New Zealand with Agnes on the *Rimutaka*; buy house and live in Papanui, Christchurch.

1895: November, George has a slight stroke and another, more severe, on 25 December which leaves him paralysed.

1896: 27 February, George, 78, dies at his rented 38 Park Terrace house, Christchurch. Funeral and burial at St John's churchyard, Hororata.

1917: Wife Agnes dies 2 December aged 91.

Thomas Williamson Hall (1819–1895)

1819: 18 November, born Kingston upon Hull, twin to his sister Ann Williamson Hall.

1826: His twin Ann dies on 1 June, aged 6.

1827: Mother Grace Williamson Hall dies in June, aged 39. Her sister Mildred takes an interest in the children's upbringing.

1832: At school at Saintes, Bordeaux, France. On 9 and 11 May, visited by his father.

1835: Apprenticeship begins possibly on the *Diana*, between Hull and Kronstadt.

1836: June, on board *Dauntless*, possibly sailing to St Petersburg.

1837: *Welton* (265 tons), Hull – St Petersburg, seaman.

1838: *Shamrock*, Hull – Hamburg, seaman.

1839: *Daniel Wheeler*, to Malta and Odessa, second mate.

1842: *New Express* (506 tons), London – River Plate, Argentina, first mate.

1843: *Andromeda*, July '43 to Feb.'44, London–Buenos Aires, Argentina, first mate.

1845: 3 May marries Sarah Young at St John's Church, Wapping, London's dockland. Master of the *Persian* 1845–6.

1846–7: *Andromeda*, Feb. '46 to Jan. '47, London–Honduras–Falmouth, master. Abandoned in the Bay of Biscay on final return. Rescued by the *Bangalore* from Madras.

1848: January, birth of first son, Thomas, Kingston upon Hull.

1849: Certificated by the Board of Trade as a master in the foreign trade.

1849: Purchases ship *Dauntless* (218 tons) from Tamar River shipyard, Launceston, Van Diemen's Land, 150 miles to the south of the Australian mainland.

1850: July, *Dauntless*, Cork–Cadiz–Montevideo–Buenos Aires, with Sarah and son Tom, master and owner. Birth of George Buceo at Buceo, Montevideo, River Plate, 4 October. George is baptised at St Michael's, Liverpool, on return.

1851: December, writes from Antwerp to John Hall re farming prospects in Argentina.

1852: January, writes from Cadiz to John Hall approving New Zealand as an emigration destination. Writes again in July warning that Argentina as an emigration destination is problematic.

10 September, son John (Jack) Hall born. Baptised at St George in the East, Wapping, 3 November.

1852: 16 December, Thomas and Sarah and their three sons – Tom, George, Jack – leave England for New Zealand on the *Mohammed Shah*. The ship catches fire near Australia and is abandoned. After rescue by the ship *Ellen* they are landed at Hobart.

1852: November, John Hall acquires Runs 112/113 for George and Thomas Hall south of the Rakaia River (Highbank, 45,000 acres). Licence cancelled when Rakaia Terrace Station on the north bank becomes available.

1853: 23 July arrives Lyttelton with family. Part owns licence with brothers George and John to Run 20, Rakaia Terrace Station, transferred from Mark Stoddart in May. Is near Windwhistle on the north bank of the Rakaia River. George and Agnes Hall had arrived April.

1854: Sells his share of Run 20 (Rakaia Terrace Station) to brother John, as does George, and moves to Kaiapoi.

11 July, birth of fourth son, William ('Will', 'Willie').

15 September 1854, Will is baptised by Mr Raven at Kaiapoi prior to a church being built. Thomas leases Rural Section 320 at Kaiapoi (50 acres of agricultural land).

1855: 1 January, Thomas W. and George W. Hall with William Beswick are on the committee for building St Bartholomew's church at Kaiapoi.

1856: 9 December, birth of fifth and youngest son, Richard Williamson Hall, at Elloughton Station (Blackford), near foot of Mt Hutt, Canterbury.

1857: Richard baptised at St John's, Kaiapoi, 16 August. Thomas acquires licence to Runs 291 and 329 July (Blackford) officially. Family living at Blackford, south of the Rakaia, grazing 4,000 sheep.

Secures pasturing rights to Braemar (approx 20,000 acres), Mackenzie Country, and stocks with shorthorn cattle

1858: Acquires licensed Runs 273 and 379, The Mistake, at Lake Tekapo (10,000 acres); Run 274, Braemar, East Stream on the Balmoral Plateau (10,000 acres); Run 275, The Wolds, west of Lake Tekapo near Mary Range (10,000 acres); Run 235 in Dec.1858 – Lake Pukaki (10,000 acres).

1859: Thomas and George sell Highbank, also Blackford. Thomas and family living in Timaru. Leaves high country station management for smaller-scale cropping and grazing on the outskirts of Timaru and builds Elloughton Grange there. Becomes a warden of St Mary's church near this time.

1862: Thomas is Commissioner for Timaru and Waitaki North for the Canterbury Provincial Council.

Serves on South Canterbury Board of Education.

Suffers a financial crisis, blaming William Ostler, manager of the Wold's station for stock losses – 1,000 ewes are snowed in and starve to death. Scab appears in the flock making it illegal to put rams out so Thomas cannot stock his runs as required by the terms of his licence.

1863: May, William Ostler accuses Thomas of stalling on the transfer of his share of the run and threatens him with a lawsuit.

Thomas made Warden of the Canterbury Marine Board of the Port of Timaru.

1864: William Ostler ceases to manage Thomas's Wolds Station.

1866: May, London share market crash.

1867–8: Sells Braemar to Alfred Cox for £1,000; sells The Wolds and The Mistake plus 7,000 sheep to A. B. Smith & Saunders (son Tom is main negotiator); co-owns Glenmore Station with John Hall.

March 1868, young Tom Hall becomes manager of John Hall's station, Castle Hall, throughout a hard winter of severe snowstorms. Huge stock losses. Son John begins job in the Wellington Telegraph Office.

1869: July. Son Jack takes charge of the telegraph office at Wanganui in the midst of a Māori insurrection.

1873: Son Jack works in the Napier Telegraph Office.

1874: Son George Buceo exiled from New Zealand after running out on debt.

Son Jack marries Elizabeth Ann Withers, daughter of Major Edward Withers.

Son Tom made accountant of the National Bank of New Zealand, Timaru.

1876: Replaces Mr G. Cliff (a mayor of Timaru) as a member of the first Timaru Hospital Board under Canterbury Provincial Government control.

1877: A member of the first Timaru Harbour Board. Continues on the Board until 1883.

1880: 29 December, son George Buceo, killed at Standerton, Transvaal, in the First Boer War, on saving his detachment from a Boer ambush.

1881: July, stables at his homestead Elloughton Grange on fire. Three valuable horses burnt. Premises uninsured.

August, Thomas sells Elloughton Grange, home and land in Timaru (1,010 acres) to William Grant.

1883: January. Youngest son Richard (Dick) moves to the North Dunedin Bank of New Zealand from Timaru after the Peston Affair (he threw an inkpot at a client who insulted him).

Thomas buys Dr Hammond's house on Le Cren Terrace in Timaru with stables and a good outlook over the sea.

June, Will is looking for a legal partner because of bad eyesight and joins forces with a Mr Hammersley who is in debt. Saved by intervention of Thomas and Will's brother Tom. Instead Will gets an English barrister to join him.

Long Depression 1883–1895 begins.

1884: May, Thomas made Chairman of the Board of the *Timaru Herald*.

June, son Richard leaves the Bank of New Zealand and is articled to his brother Will. In November he passes his first examination in law.

Son Jack works as a sub-editor on the *Timaru Herald*.

1885: Son Tom marries Kate Emily Espie, step-daughter of Captain Cain, Timaru.

1886: 12 August, young Tom arrested for attempted murder of his wife by poisoning.

1886: 11 October, son Tom's trial begins, Christchurch. Sir Robert Stout, Attorney General, presents the prosecution case. Tom is convicted and on 19 October receives a life sentence.

October, son Jack gets into trouble of an uncertain kind – likely to concern money or women.

Late October, nephew John Neall (sister Grace Neall's son) dies of tuberculosis in Christchurch. He is buried at Hororata. Station hands are pall-bearers.

November, son Jack is exiled to North America for bad behaviour. His younger brother Richard escorts him out of the country.

1887: 31 January, the second trial of young Tom begins for attempted murder of his father-in-law, Captain Cain.

April, Tom and Sarah move out of Timaru to lodgings near Invercargill.

September, Thomas resigns as a director of the Timaru Milling Company.

A letter to John Hall dated 18 February 1888 reports 'I have to be at the annual Milling Co. meeting this morning & expect it will be a stormy one. We left last year £3400 to credit in Profit & Loss Account & now it is £1500 to debt & no dividends paid. I fear that the amount invested in shares are almost valueless unless matters are very differently managed in future than they have been since I went out.'

22 September letter GWH to JH recounts that Tom's son Jack has work, presumably in California.

1887: 28 November, Thomas's daughter-in-law, Ruth Hall, Will's wife, dies of peritonitis in Invercargill.

1895: 15 October (on or about), Caroline Matthews, his son Richard's lover, in Campbelltown (Bluff), is seen by Dr James Torrance in relation to her pregnancy.

Christmas Day (or Boxing Day according to his will), Thomas dies at Invercargill.

1897: 28 June, son Richard charged with the administration of a noxious substance to Caroline Matthews, his lover, in order to procure an abortion. Both he and Caroline are arrested. Richard and Caroline's case is heard and both are acquitted. His defence is that the charge is the outcome of a political conspiracy to smear him for defending shareholders in the J. G. Ward Farmers Association case. Ward is bankrupted.

1898: 31 March, Will and Richard's legal practice (Hall Bros) is dissolved in Invercargill. Richard continues to practice law in Invercargill. Will Hall joins Stout & Lillicrap as senior partner.

1899: October, Thomas's wife Sarah dies of Bright's disease in Invercargill.

1901: 2 October, son Richard (45) marries Caroline Matthews at Invercargill after the death of her first husband. The four children of their liaison are baptised two weeks later in Invercargill.

1907: Son Tom Hall released from gaol. With £800 in trust to him from his father's bequest, additional money from John Hall and an annual allowance of £60 from his ex-wife Kitty, he sets up life in Queensland as Paul Newstead. He dies in August 1929.

John Hall, KCMG[1] (1824–1907)

1824: Born 18 December, to George and Grace Hall, in Hull.

At school in Hull until the age of 10.

1835: Attends Herr Tobler's German-speaking school at St Gall, Switzerland.

1837: At school in Paris.

1839: Boards with Herr de Dobbeler, manager of an insurance company in Hamburg.

1840: Returns to England and is employed in a London merchant's office.

1843: Appointed to Secretary's Department in the London General Post Office and in due course becomes private secretary to the departmental head.

1845: His reports on Lieutenant Waghorn's proposal on the overland mail route bringing mail from India via Trieste and through Germany to replace existing routes from Marseilles causes the plan for an alternative route to be dropped as impracticable. Is passed over for promotion to the job of chief postmaster at Brighton, on a salary of £600 because Queen Victoria promoted her own candidate. He leaves the service.

1848: In London, acts as a special constable attached to the Clerkenwell Police Court during the Chartist Riots.

1851: Travels while engaged as assistant to post office inspector; also holidays in Cumberland and Westmoreland, Channel Islands, Cornwall and France.

1852: 26 March, sails from London on the *Samarang* for Lyttelton, New Zealand, with two dogs and two servants. He is 27. Arrives at Lyttelton on 31 July 1852. During the trip he edits the ship's passenger journal.

4 August–20 November makes a tour of the North (Middle Island), particularly the Wairarapa and Hawkes Bay to reconnoitre best place for settlement.

Buys Stoddart's run and stock and settles on the North bank of the Rakaia River, Canterbury. This was Rakaia Terrace Station, named by M. P. Stoddart and Run 20 in the Province's records of runholders. After 1867 it included also Run 17. The present 'Terrace Station' refers to the remnants of the original station, of which 28,000– 30,000 acres were sold at John Hall's death in 1907.

1853: Elected on 10 September to represent Christchurch Country District in the Provincial Council Elections. The NZ Constitution Act had been passed in June 1852 which divided NZ into six provinces each with an elected superintendent.

1854: From 11 May is appointed Justice of the Peace for Canterbury. From October 1854 to May 1855 is provincial secretary under James Edward Fitzgerald, Canterbury's first superintendent.

1855: On 20 December becomes elected member in House of Representatives (the second parliament) for Christchurch Country District. In this year the Provincial Council had taken over the management of assisted immigration since the Canterbury Association was disbanded. An agent in England was appointed and a decade later 6,000 new settlers had arrived.

1856: Made colonial secretary in the Fox Ministry.

1856: On 28 October offered job as resident magistrate at Lyttelton, a position combining the offices of commissioner of police and sheriff. He transfers to a similar position in Christchurch where he remains until his trip to England in 1860. Secures rooms in Auckland near the General Assembly.

1858: Attends April to August Session in the General Assembly, Auckland; 21 September–January 1859 in Canterbury. In opposition.

1860: March – personally involved as a participant in the Māori War at Waitara, New Plymouth. By 23 March had agreed to act as courier to take government dispatches to Sydney and Melbourne asking for military reinforcements. From Australia embarks for England on 22 April via Suez and Cairo.

1861: In England. In April, marries Rose Dryden, daughter of solicitor William Dryden of Park House in Cottingham, near Hull. Rose is sister to his brother George's wife, Agnes Emma Dryden, both now settled in Canterbury, New Zealand.

1862: Returns to Canterbury. Christchurch is made a municipal district and John becomes chairman of the Christchurch Municipal Council. Street lighting introduced.

1863: Appointed first mayor of Christchurch but resigns in June to give more time to public duties (accepts the same role briefly in 1907). Is called to the Legislative Council in July. In December returns to the Canterbury Provincial Council.

1864: From March, acts as provincial secretary under Bealey until March 1866.

1865: Member of the Canterbury Provincial Government survey party contracted to lay a road to the west coast goldfields via Browning's Pass.

1866: Resigns his seat in the Legislative Council and by May is member for Rakaia in the Provincial Council. Wins Heathcote seat. Buys Joseph Beswick's run east of Fork Stream in Mackenzie Country plus 4,000 sheep to bail Beswick out of financial difficulties. Renames it Castle Hall station. Made postmaster general in Edward Stafford's ministry. Has to reside in Wellington.

1867: Makes journey to start west coast and other roads with Australian contractors. October attends Ocean Postal Communications Conference, Melbourne, representing the New Zealand government.

1868: Chairman of the Westland County Council.

1869: In February, after Stafford's defeat, resigns as postmaster general and electric telegraph commissioner but remains a member of Stafford's cabinet.

1872: Joins Fox-Vogel Ministry to guide government business through the Legislative Council as its leader.

1872: John and George sell their Mackenzie runs.

1872–3: Colonial secretary under Waterhouse. Retires for health reasons.

Returns to England early 1873 for relaxation primarily.

1875–6: In England and travels to Europe with Rose. In London. Returns to New Zealand in January 1876, carrying bumble bees at the request of the Canterbury Acclimatisation Society to help fertilise red clover. In Canterbury and Wellington.

1876: Declines Julius Vogel's offer to join his ministry because disagreed partially with Vogel's policies. In government without portfolio in Atkinson Ministry.

1877: In Canterbury and Wellington 1 Jan to 26 July. Member of the first Lyttelton Harbour Board which met this year.

1878: In Canterbury 5 January to 5 May.

1879: Premier 1879–82. Premier Fox persuades Hall to resign from Legislative Council and lead the Opposition in the House of Representatives. In October, Grey Ministry defeated and Governor Sir Hercules Robinson requests Hall to form a Ministry 10 October 1879. Hall also takes ministries of colonial secretary, post and telegraphs, customs. His majority is small and a want of confidence is tabled. Hall suspends government business for three weeks to persuade four Auckland members to cross the floor to support his government.

Helps to lower the national debt by cautious management of the economy.

1881: Sanctions the invasion of rebel Māori leader Te Whiti's settlement at Parihaka in November having converted to the views of his native minister, Bryce, and authorises the arrest of Te Whiti and Tohu. Te Whiti is held in gaol without trial. Sets up a commission to investigate native grievances.

1882–3: Hall wins small majority in election but in April resigns as premier on the grounds of illness. Returns to England on ship *Lady Jocelyn*. Is created KCMG on the Queen's Birthday Honours List, 1882.

1884: Visits Dresden, has a portrait painted and travels in Europe. Returns to New Zealand via America.

1885: By ship *Tongariro* to Rio de Janeiro with Rose; visits Argentina and returns to Rio. Goes to London on steamship *Rimutaka*.

1886: Visits Paris with Rose and daughters Mildred and Mary; returns to New Zealand on ship *Kaikoura* where he learns of the alleged crime of his nephew, Tom Hall.

1887: In Canterbury. Travels to Tasmania and Australia with daughter Mary. On 19 July discovers Mary has tuberculosis. In Canterbury, Wellington and Australia with Mary seeking a cure. Campaigns and wins the Selwyn seat in Canterbury on a platform of encouraging new manufacturing industries to diversify the economy and reduce Canterbury's high unemployment.

1888: On 2 March, death of his daughter Mary of tuberculosis at Rakaia Terrace Station. She was earlier nursed by her mother and sister Mildred near Sydney in the warmer, drier climate.

May–Sept at Wellington (Session); wife Rose and daughter Mildred to England. Mildred has a problem with her leg which needs treatment. Follows Rose to England with son Godfrey on ship *Kaikoura*. Spends time in Eastbourne, England. Godfrey, too, needs medical attention for a leg problem.

1889: Supports the first Representation Bill in favour of proportional representation. Keen to increase the voice of the rural sector in parliament and government wins a quota of 28 per cent in rural electorates, increased from 18 per cent (the 'country quota').

1890: Represents New Zealand with Captain William Russell, Colonial Secretary, at a meeting in Australia to discuss federating the six self-governing British colonies of Queensland, Victoria, Tasmania, South Australia, Western Australia, New Zealand and Fiji. New Zealand reluctant to become a member of the federation because would lose trading tariffs, a large part of its revenue, and also did not want its key politicians to be away from home in another parliament which it feared would dominate.

1893: Retires from political life after steering Electoral Bill giving the vote to women through the House. New Zealand is the first independent country to enable women's suffrage.

1894–6: To England on *Armond Belric* via Australia. Returns to New Zealand on *Ionic*. In Canterbury and Wellington.

1897: Visits England during Jubilee Year.

1900: Rose Hall's death 12 May.

1901: In March by *Britannia* to England. By December begins return to New Zealand on *Tamba Maru* via Hong Kong.

1903: On 6 February to England on ship *Ruapehu*.

1904: On 1 January returns to New Zealand on ship *Turakina*.

1906: Made mayor of Christchurch on 2 May for exhibition year. Pays entrance fee for Christchurch children to attend the exhibition as well as those from Hororata. Extremely ill.

1907: Dies at Park Terrace house, Christchurch, on 25 June. Buried beside his wife Rose in St John's churchyard cemetery, Hororata.

Reference

Compiled with inclusions also from W. J. Gardner's bibliographical essay from the *Dictionary of New Zealand Biography*,1990; Jean Garner's *By His Own Merits*, 1995; Bernard John Foster's essay on John Hall in the *Encyclopedia of New Zealand*, April 2013; Kate Foster's index of the John Hall Diaries, 2014.

SELECT BIBLIOGRAPHY

Abell, F., *Prisoners of War in Britain 1756 to 1815*, Ulan Press, 2012.

Ackland, L.G.D., *The Early Canterbury Runs*, 4th edn, Whitcoulls Publishers, 1975.

Allen, T., *A New & Complete History of the County of York*, vol. 10, I. T. Hinton, 1828.

Alpers, O.T.J., *Cheerful Yesterdays*, London: John Murray, 1928; reprint Christchurch, N.Z.: Capper Press Ltd., 1984.

Bellamy, J. M., *The Trade & Shipping of Nineteenth-Century Hull*, East Yorkshire Local History Society, 1971.

Belich, James, *The New Zealand Wars and the Victorian Interpretation of Racial Conflict*, Penguin Books, 1998.

Belich, James, *Making Peoples: A History of the New Zealanders from Polynesian Settlement to the end of the Nineteenth Century*, Allen Lane, the Penguin Press, 1996.

Brett-James, A. (ed.), *Escape From the French: Captain Hewson's Narrative 1803–1809*, London: Hodder & Stoughton, 1981.

Brooks, Van Wyck, *The World of Washington Irving*, E.P. Dutton & Company Inc., 1944.

Chapman, S. D., 'The International Houses: The Continental Contribution to British Commerce, 1800–1860' in *The Journal of European Economic History*, Rome: UniCredit, ISSN 0391-5115, vol. 6, 1977, 1, pp. 5–48.

Coney, S., *Standing in the Sunshine: A History of New Zealand Women Since they Won the Vote*, Penguin Books NZ Ltd, 1993.

De Monvel, R. B., *Eminent English Men and Women in Paris*, trans. G. Henning, London: David Nutt, 1912.

Dobson, A.D., *Reminiscences*, Whitcombe & Tomves Ltd, 1930.

Drower, G., *Heligoland: The Story of the German Bight and the Island that Britain Forgot*, London: The History Press, 2002.

Druet, J., *Hen Frigates: Wives of Merchant Captains Under Sail*, Souvenir Press, 1998.

Eldred-Grigg, *A Southern Gentry: New Zealanders Who Inherited the Earth*, A.H. & A.W. Reed, 1980.

Eldred-Grigg, *Sex and Drugs in Colonial New Zealand 1840-1915*, A.H & A.W. Reed Ltd., 1984.

Fraser, L. and McCarthy, A. (eds), *Far From Home: The English in New Zealand*, Otago University Press, 2012.

Fulton, R. V., *Medical Practice in Otago and Southland in the Early Days*, Dunedin: Otago Daily Times and Witness Newspapers Co. Ltd, 1922.

Gardner, W. J. (ed.), *A History of Canterbury*, vols I–III, Canterbury Centennial Historical and Literary Committee, Christchurch: Whitcombe & Tombs, 1971.

Garner, J., *By His Own Merits: Sir John Hall – Pioneer, Pastoralist and Premier*, Dryden Press, 1995.

Garner, J. and Foster, K. (eds), *Letters to Grace: Writing Home from Colonial New Zealand*, Canterbury University Press, 2011.

George, Merrilyn, *Ohakune, Opening to a New World: A District History*, Kapai Enterprises Ltd., 1990.

Gillespie, O. A., *South Canterbury: A Record of Settlement*, the South Canterbury Centennial History Committee, 2nd edn, 1971.

Gisborne, William, *New Zealand Rulers and Statesmen from 1840 to 1897*, Sampson Low, Marston & Co., London 1897.

Graham, P., *Vile Crimes*, Canterbury University Press, 2007.

Greenwood, J., *Greenwood's Picture of Hull*, London: Simpkin & Marshall, 1835.

Hall, G. 'Autobiography of a Little Sailor Boy' in *Stories of Two Generations*, Canterbury, New Zealand: Dryden Press, 1998.

Hall, G., *Journal of My Two Escapes from French Prisons during the War with Napoleon*, 2nd edn, London: Truslove & Hanson Ltd, 1860.

Hassall, C. E., *The Port of Timaru*, Timaru Harbour Board, 1955.

Irving, W., *Astoria*, vol. 1, Knickerbocker Edn, New York: G.P. Puttnam & Son, 1868.

Jackson, G., *Hull in the Eighteenth Century: A Study in Economic and Social History*, Oxford University Press, 1972.

King, M., *The Penguin History of New Zealand*, Penguin Books, 2003.

McIntyre, W., and Gardner, J., *Speeches and Documents on New Zealand History*, Oxford at the Clarendon Press, 1971.

McIntyre, W. David, *The Journal of Henry Sewell 1853-7*, vols I & II, Whitcoulls Publishers, 1980.

McKenzie, J. C., *A History of the Timaru Hospital*, Christchurch: Pegasus Press, 1974.

Morris, D. and Cozens, K., *Wapping 1600–1800: A Social History of an Early Modern Maritime Suburb*, East London Historical Society, 2009.

Oddy, J. Jepson, *European Commerce Showing New and Secure Channels of Trade with the Continent of Europe*, W. J. and J. Richardson, 1805.

Pinney, R., *Early South Canterbury Runs*, Wellington: A.H. & A.W. Reed, 1971.

Raikes, T., *A Visit to St Petersburg in the Winter of 1829–30*, London: 1838.

Riseborough, H., *Days of Darkness: Taranaki 1878–1884*, Allen & Unwin New Zealand in association with Port Nicholson Press, 1989.

Robinson, R., *Far Horizons: From Hull to the Ends of the Earth*, 2nd edn, University of Hull, PFH Productions, 2014.

Rodgers, N. A. M., *The Wooden World*, Fontana Press, 1988.

Simper, R., *North East Sail*, David & Charles, 1975.

Simpson, Tony, *Shame & Disgrace: A History of Lost Scandals in New Zealand*, Penguin Books, 1992.

Simpson, Tony, *The Immigrants: The Great Migration from Britain to New Zealand, 1830–1890*.

Stewart, W. Downie, *Portrait of a Judge: Sir Joshua Strange Williams*, Christchurch: Whitcombe & Tombs, 1946.

Storey, A., *Trinity House of Kingston upon Hull*, vols 1 and 2, Hull Trinity House, first printed by Albert Gent Ltd, Grimsby. Reprinted 1989 by Smith Settle, Otley, West Yorkshire.

Temple, P., *A Sort of Conscience: The Wakefields*, Auckland University Press, 2002.

Vance, W., *High Endeavour: Story of the Mackenzie Country*, 2nd edn, published by the author, printed by the *Timaru Herald*, New Zealand, 1965.

Villiers, A., *Square-Rigged Ships: An Introduction*, London: National Maritime Museum, 2009.

Vuillamy, C. E., *The Onslow Family 1528-1874*, London: Chapman & Hall, 1953.

Wakefield, E., *New Zealand After Fifty Years*, Cassell & Company, 1889.

Wilson, H., *My First Eighty Years*, Paul's Book Arcade, Hamilton, 1959.

Woodman, R., *Britannia's Realm: A History of the British Merchant Navy*, vol. 2, London: The History Press, 2009.

ABBREVIATIONS TO REFERENCES/RELATIONSHIPS

Aggie   Agnes (Aggie) Mildred Hall, 1851–1919, daughter of GWH and Agnes Emma; wife of Edward Wakefield (1), Edward Withers (2); mother of Edward (Chunky), Gerald, Oliver, Grace, Mildred (1) and Aimée, Ethel, Irene, Peter (2).

Agnes   Agnes Emma Hall (née Dryden), 1826–1917, wife to GWH.

BT   Board of Trade, U.K.

EW   Edward Wakefield, 1845–1924, nephew of Edward Gibbon Wakefield, first husband of Aggie Hall.

GH   George Hall, 1782–1865, father to GWH, TWH, JH, Grace.

GN   Grace Neall (née Hall), 1826–1920, sister to GWH, TWH, JH.

Grace   Grace Hall (née Williamson), 1787–1827, wife to GH.

GWH   George Williamson Hall, 1818–1896, son of GH and Grace.

JH   John Hall (Sir John),1824–1907, son of GH and Grace, father of Mildred, Wilfred, John Dryden, Mary, Godfrey.

JSN   John Sugden Neall, 1813–1881, husband of young Grace.

MF   Mildred Fowler (née Williamson), 1792–1861, sister to Grace Hall; aunt to GWH, TWH, JH and young Grace; wife of William Bean Fowler.

PRO   Public Record Office, U.K.

Rose   Rose Hall (née Dryden; Lady Hall), 1828–1900, wife of JH, sister of Agnes Emma Hall.

RWH   Richard Williamson Hall (Dick), 1856-1932, son of Thomas W. and Sarah Hall.

SH   Sarah Hall (née Young), 1816–1899, wife of TWH, mother of Tom, George Buceo, John (Jack), William, Richard (Dick).

TH   Tom Hall, 1848-1929, son of Thomas W. and Sarah Hall

TNA   National Archive, U.K.

TWH   Thomas Williamson Hall, 1819–1895, son of GH and Grace, father of Tom, George Buceo, John, William, Richard.

WYH   William (Will, Willie) Young Henry Hall, 1854–1926, son of TWH and Sarah; husband of Ruth (née Edwards).

INDEX

Aggie 207, 225n.2-5, n.7-8; her
son John Neall 228-229, **247**-248,
258n. 21, 259 n.36, 260-261,
272, 281, 301n.2, n.4, 303n.29,
321-322, 331-332, 334n.21, 338,
359n.3, 376, 380, 385, 391-392,
398, 401
Neall, John (son of Grace and John S.
Neall); 228-229, 241, **247**, 258, 281
Neall, John Sugden; 7, 159, 173-176,
178-179, 181, 190, 199-200, 260,
286, 302n.18, 303n.30, 338, 387,
391, 401
Nedwill, Dr Courtney; 241, 258n.11
New Express; 21, 134-**136**, 146n.14-
147n.16
New Zealand Wars; 316, 333n.7
Newgate Prison; 263
Newton, Revd John, Bishop of
Lincoln; 84, 115
New Zealand After Fifty Years; 292,
see Wakefield, Edward
Nienstedten; 128
North Sea; 30, 39, 56, 68n.37, 104-
105, 130-131

Odessa; 106-**109**; 124n.17, 132, 191,
385, 388
Ohakune; 19, 353, 360n.19, 377,
379, 398
Ostend; 51-52
Ostler, William; 210, 234, 389-390

Pacific Ocean; 149
Packman, Mary Ann (second wife of
George Hall); 7, 94-**95**, 153, 384
Paine, Thomas; 37
Parihaka; 324-326, 332, 380, 395
Paris; 41, 43, 68n.20, 73, 75, 290, 293,
303n.42, 377, 392, 395
parole d'honneur; 47
paternalism; 88, 250

patronage; 22, 88, 157, 215, 250, 252,
307, 340, 381
Peters, Humphrey (a.k.a. Dr John
McCrystal); 7, **355**-361n.32, 402
Pigeon Bay Academy; 203, 338
plague; 101, 107, **109**
Post Office; 88, 97, 109, 154, 161,
309, 353, 360, 378, 392-393
Pretoria, South Africa; 216-217, **220**,
224-225
Princess Victoria; 109-112, 124n.27,
385
privateer; 29, 37, 40, 52, 383

Raikes, Thomas; 103, 124n.10
Rakaia Terrace Station; 23, 175, 180,
185, 275, 307-**308**, 310, 331, 386,
389, 393, 395
Reeves, William Pember; 325, 334n.14
Riga; 33, 61, 129, 132, 384
Rio de Janeiro; 62, 66, 96, 141, 384,
387, 395
Rio de la Plata (River Plate); 134, 145,
160, 165, 227, 388
River Hull; **96**, 127
Riverton; 355-358
Rose Cottage, Elloughton, Yorkshire;
95-96, 384
Royal Albert; 164, 177, 260, 386
Royal Commission into Shipwrecks
(1873); 142
Royal Navy; 40, 355
Roydhouse, William; 291, 298
Russia; 33, 38-39, 57-58, 61, 68n.42,
106-107, 130, 151

Saintes (France); 73, 79, 128, 388
Samarang; 163, 167n.7, 169, 171,
173, 200n.1, 386, 393
Samuel Boddington; 112, 395
Santa Fé; **64-65**, 384
Scarborough; 13, 71, 77, 82, 88, 100,

46998275R00244

Printed in Poland
by Amazon Fulfillment
Poland Sp. z o.o., Wrocław